# Dying Testimonies of Saved and Unsaved

*All 236 Accounts of Christians and Sinners on their Deathbeds*

By Solomon B. Shaw

PANTIANOS
CLASSICS

Published by Pantianos Classics

ISBN-13: 978-1974692903

First published in 1898

# Contents

*Introduction* .................................................................... iv
Part One - Testimonies 1 to 60 ............................... 7
Part Two - Testimonies 61 to 120 ...................... 77
Part Three – Testimonies 121 to 236 ............. 132

# Introduction

The influence of human testimony and experience has had much to do with the destiny of mankind in all ages of the world.

Multitudes have gone to heaven by giving heed to the testimonies and example of the righteous; and on the other side multitudes have gone into eternity to suffer the torments of hell forever, because they were led astray by the influence and example of the wicked. Yet God has declared that the time will come when every knee shall bow and every tongue shall confess Christ as the Savior of the world and even here God has influenced both the children of God and the children of the devil to witness to their moral condition in health, in sickness in prosperity, in adversity, and at death. Not only have millions upon millions of God's children witnessed in life and death of Jesus' power to save. but most infidels, skeptics and sinners of every grade are constrained to acknowledge the truth of the Christian religion before they die. And surly, if the testimony of mankind is ever to be taken as the truth, it must be when in the presence of death, for most men are honest while dying.

Death is a transition from one degree of spiritual life or death to another. The saved are translated from life to life more abundant, while to the unsaved death is only the entrance upon the second death of eternal separation from God. In the Bible, death is called a sleep, a departure, a translation, etc. Multitudes, while dying, see and hear things that are not seen or heard by others.

Our book reveals the awful contrast between the dying testimonies of the saved and the unsaved. It reveals the inexpressible happiness and joy of the righteous about to be translated from their home on earth to the paradise of God. On the other hand it reveals the awful remorse of conscience and the untold mental agony of souls facing death and the judgment, unprepared.

We have not described the last hours on earth of Bible characters, as everybody has access to the Holy Scriptures and can read for themselves. We have given the last words of many noted skeptics, infidels and atheists, and also of many noted and devoted saints. Some infidel writers have died unconscious, without leaving any dying testimony. The same is true of many of the most noted and devoted Christians. Many great and good men have died unconscious, but they have left their lives to testify of their preparation for heaven. We have omitted the names of the unsaved for the sake of their living friends and kindred, except in the case of noted infidels, and we think that their last testimony should be given in order to as far as possible counteract their ungodly influence.

For over a year we have had the publication of this book upon our mind and heart, and have given much time and thought to the securing of proper material, and have been greatly blessed of God in its preparation. We have endeavored to use nothing that is not well authenticated, and to make the book entirely unsectarian; having used the testimonies of God's children as we have seen able to secure them, without regard to denominational preferences.

Much of the material for this volume has been written expressly for this work by us and our friends. We have advertised in various religious papers, and have in this way received many experiences. Through the kindness of Dr. L. B. Balliett, of Allentown, Pa., we received manuscript that he had designed for a similar work, from which we have selected a number of excellent articles. We have secured and read the biographies of many noted and devoted saints of all denominations, and have carefully quoted their last words. Foxe's Book of Martyrs has also been of great value; also a book entitled The Power of religion; another, The Contrast Between Infidelity and Christianity. We have also received valuable information from the various encyclopedias. We have also been helped by a book of dying testimonies of preachers of the Gospel, entitled From Life to Life, and many other similar books.

We have prepared the manuscript for this book in the midst of many cares, but have done the best we could, with God's help, to make a book that will be used of God in the salvation of many souls.

Our Heavenly Father has done everything that divine wisdom, love and mercy can possible do for the salvation of mankind. "For God so loved the world that He gave His only begotten Son, that whosoever believeth on Him should not perish, but have everlasting life."

He has sacrificed His holy patriarchs, prophets and apostles, and-has influenced a multitude of other saints to suffer and die at the hands of wicked sinners; and who can describe the persecution and torture inflicted upon God's children by the enemies of Christ; and all of these sufferings have been endured for the sake of rescuing suffering humanity.

The Word of God tells us that without controversy great is the mystery of Godliness. We live in a world of mystery! We are a mystery to ourselves! All creation is a mystery! Life, death and sin are great mysteries! The best of us know but little, but the way of salvation is so plain that a wayfaring man, even a fool, need not go astray. The most important thing for mankind to know in this world is the way of life and salvation, and this blessed knowledge is not received by tradition; it is not to be found out by tradition; it is not to be found in the school of science or philosophy. Salvation is of the Lord, and a revelation from heaven.

The testimonies of the righteous at the hour of death, and the awful mental agony of the lost as they bewail their lost condition, has caused us to cry out to God in prayer, whole nights at a time, for the salvation of souls and a revival among the professed people of God. O Lord, revive Thy work, should be the earnest prayer of all Christians night and day.

We pray that this work may be greatly used of God in the salvation of a multitude of precious souls, and that Christian workers may be filled with the fullness of God, ready to meet Him when He calls. We are,

*Your Brother Saved By Grace,*

*S. B. Shaw*

# Part One - Testimonies 1 to 60

### 001 -- TRIUMPHANT DEATH OF IGNATIUS

Ignatius, one of the ancient fathers of the church, was born in Syria, and brought up under the care of the Apostle John. About the year 67, he became bishop of Antioch. In this important station he continued above 40 years, both an honor and a safeguard to the Christian religion; undaunted in the midst of very tempestuous times, and unmoved with the prospect of suffering a cruel death. He taught men to think little of the present life; to value and love the good things to come; and never to be deterred from a course of piety and virtue, by the fear of any temporal evils whatever; to oppose only meekness to anger, humility to boasting, and prayers to curses and reproaches.

This excellent man was selected by the emperor Trajan, as a subject whose sufferings might be proper to inspire terror and discouragement in the hearts of the Christians at Rome. He was condemned to die for his faith in Christ, and ordered to be thrown among wild beasts to be devoured by them. This cruel sentence, far from weakening his attachment to the great cause he had espoused, excited thankfulness of heart, that he had been counted worthy to suffer for the sake of religion. "I thank thee, O Lord," said he, "that thou hast condescended thus to honor me with thy love; and hast thought me worthy, with thy apostle Paul, to be bound in chains."

On his passage to Rome he wrote a letter to his fellow Christians there, to prepare them to acquiesce in his sufferings, and to assist him with their prayers. "Pray for me," said he, "that God would give me both inward and outward strength, that I may not only say, but do well; that I may not only be called a Christian, but be found one." Animated by the cheering prospect of the reward of his sufferings, he said: "Now, indeed, I begin to be a disciple; I weigh neither visible nor invisible things, in comparison with an interest in Jesus Christ." With the utmost Christian fortitude he met the wild beasts assigned for his destruction and triumphed in death. -- Power of Religion.

### 002 -- WONDERFUL CONVERSION OT MARY LONES

We were requested to visit a young woman, nearly gone with consumption, who resisted every effort that was made to bring her to Christ. We went, trusting in the Lord for help. She received us respectfully, but seemed quite careless about her soul. The Spirit of the Lord soon touched her heart, and she became distressed on account of her sins; at one time while praying with her she began to plead in real earnest for herself and continued in prayer until she could say, "I am the Lord's and He is mine." A sweet peace settled down on her soul and soon after she received the clear witness that her sins were forgiven. Although she was very weak and could hardly speak above a whisper, yet, when the Lord set the seal of Bis Spirit to the work wrought in her soul, her shouts of victory could be heard through the entire building.

She soon began to yearn for entire sanctification, and her soul was greatly drawn out in prayer for the blessing. At one time we read to her the fourth chapter of Ist John and encouraged her to look to be made perfect in love, to believe for it and expect it every moment until it was given. "Oh!" said she, "that is just what 1 need, and I am praying for it all the while" -- although she did not know the name of the blessing she was seeking. She had many conflicts with the powers of darkness before she obtained this victory. At length the all-cleansing touch was given. It was about five o'clock one Sabbath evening a few weeks before her death. Her soul had been much drawn out in prayer all day for purity of heart. She said the Spirit fell on her and seemed to go through both soul and body. She had been confined to her bed and was so weak we thought she would never again stand on her feet; but when she received the blessing she not only had the use of her voice, but walked the floor back and forth, shouting aloud, "Glory to God." We were told that she had naturally a fiery disposition, but after this baptism she was all patience, resignation, love and praise. Her sufferings were very great toward the last, but not a murmur or complaint was ever heard. Neither tongue nor pen can describe some of the scenes witnessed in that little room. From the time that she received the blessing of perfect love, until her death, her sky was unclouded, her conversation in heaven, and her experience, although a young convert, was that of a mature Christian. Her light on the things of God and the state of deceived professors of religion was wonderful. She seemed to have an unclouded view of her heavenly inheritance and longed to depart and be with Christ. On one occasion, when we were singing --

Filled with delight, my raptured soul Would here no longer stay, Though Jordan's waves around me roll, Fearless, I launch away --

she raised her hand in triumph and repeated the word, "fearless, fearless," while glory unspeakable beamed from her countenance. At times, when talking or singing of her heavenly home, she appeared more like an inhabitant of heaven than of earth. She was truly the most beautiful, angelic-looking being we ever saw. She died in triumph; was conscious to the last, and whispered, "I walk through the valley in peace;" then pointing to each one that stood around her bed, she raised her hand, as if to say, "Meet me in Heaven." She then folded her hands on her breast, looked up, smiled, and was gone.

Glory to God and the Lamb forever; another safely landed. -- Brands From The Burning.

## 003 -- THE AWFUL DEATH OF SIR FRANCIS NEWPORT

Sir Francis Newport was trained in early life to understand the great truths of the gospel; and while in early manhood it was hoped that he would become an ornament and a blessing to his family and the nation, the result was far otherwise. He fell into company that corrupted his principles and his morals. He became an avowed infidel, and a life of dissipation soon brought on a disease that was incurable. When he felt that he must die, he threw himself on the bed, and after a brief pause, be exclaimed as follows: "Whence this war in my heart? What argument is there now to assist me against matters of fact? Do I assert that there is no hell, while I feel one in my own bosom? Am I certain there is no after retribution, when I feel present judgment? Do I affirm my soul to be as mortal as my body, when this languishes, and that is vigorous as ever? O that any one would restore unto me that ancient gourd of piety and innocence! Wretch that I am, whither shall I flee from this breast? What will become of me?"

An infidel companion tried to dispel his thoughts, to whom he replied. "That there is a God, I know, because I continually feel the effects of His wrath; that there is a hell I am equally certain, having received an earnest of my inheritance there already in my breast; that there is a natural conscience I now feel with horror and amazement, being continually upbraided by it with my impieties, and all my iniquities, and all my sins brought to my remembrance. Why God has marked me out for an example of His vengeance, rather than you, or any one of my acquaintance, I presume is because I have been more religiously educated, and have done greater despite to the Spirit of grace. O that I was to lie upon the fire that never is quenched a thousand years, to purchase the favor of Gods and be reunited to Him again! But it is a fruitless wish. Millions of millions of years will bring me no nearer to the end of my torments than one poor hour. O, eternity, eternity! Who can discover the abyss of eternity? Who can paraphrase upon these words -- forever and ever?"

Lest his friends should think him insane, he said: "You imagine me melancholy, or distracted. I wish I were either; but it is part of my judgment that I am not. No; my apprehension of persons and things is more quick and vigorous than it was when I was in perfect health; and it is my curse, because I am thereby more sensible of the condition I am fallen into. Would you be informed why I am become a skeleton in three or four days? See now, then. I have despised my Maker, and denied my Redeemer. I have joined myself to the atheist and profane, and continued this course under many convictions, till my iniquity was ripe for vengeance, and the just judgment of God overtook me when my security was the greatest, and the checks of my conscience were the least."

As his mental distress and bodily disease were hurrying him into eternity, he was asked if he would have prayer offered in his behalf; he turned his face, and exclaimed, "Tigers and monsters! are ye also become devils to torment me? Would ye give me prospect of heaven to make my hell more intolerable?"

Soon after, his voice failing, and uttering a groan of inexpressible horror, he cried out, "OH, THE INSUFFERABLE PANGS OF HELL!" and died at once, dropping into the very hell of which God gave him such an awful earnest, to be a constant warning to multitudes of careless sinners. --

## *004 -- POLYCARP, THE SAINTED CHRISTIAN FATHER*

Polycarp, an eminent Christian father, was born in the reign of Nero. Ignatius recommended the church of Antioch to the care and superintendence of this zealous father, who appears to have been unwearied in his endeavors to preserve the peace of the church, and to promote piety and virtue amongst men.

During the persecution which raged at Smyrna, in the year 167, the distinguished character of Polycarp attracted the attention of the enemies of Christianity. The general outcry was, "Let Polycarp be sought for." When he was taken before the proconsul, he was solicited to reproach Christ, and save his life: but with a holy indignation, he nobly replied: "Eighty and six years have I served Christ, who has never done me any injury: how then can I blaspheme my King and Savior?"

When he was brought to the stake, the executioner offered, as usual, to nail him to it; but he said, "Let me alone as I am: He who has given me strength to come to the fire, will also give me patience to abide in it, without being fastened with nails."

Part of his last prayer, at his death, was as follows: "O God, the Father of Thy beloved son, Jesus Christ, by whom we have received the knowledge of Thyself; O God of angels and powers, of every creature, and of all the just who live in Thy presence; I thank Thee that Thou hast graciously vouchsafed, this day and this hour, to allot me a portion amongst the number of martyrs. O Lord, receive me; and make me a companion of saints in the resurrection, through the merits of our great High Priest, the Lord Jesus Christ. I praise and adore Thee, through thy beloved Son, to whom, with Thee, and Thy Holy Spirit, be all honor and glory, both now and forever. Amen." -- Power of Religion.

## *005 -- THE MARTYR PATRICK HAMILTON*

On the first of March, 1528, some eight years before Tyndale was betrayed by a Romish spy, Archbishop Beaton condemned Patrick Hamilton to be burned because he advocated the doctrines of the Reformation and exposed the errors of popery.

The principal accusations were that he taught that it was proper for the poor people to read God's Word and that it was useless to offer masses for the souls of the dead. Hamilton admitted the truth of these charges, and boldly defended his doctrine. But his judges, Archbishop Beaton and the bishops and clergy associated with him in council, could not endure the truths presented by their prisoner, which indeed were greatly to their disadvantage; for a people before whom an open Bible is spread will soon test by it the lives and teachings of their pastors, and to abolish masses for the dead is to cut off a chief source of the revenues of Rome's priesthood. Hamilton therefore was quickly condemned, and in a few hours afterwards, to avoid any possibility of his rescue by influential friends, the stake was prepared before the gate of St. Salvador College.

When the martyr was brought to the stake, he removed his outer garments and gave them to his servant, with the words, "These will not profit me in the fire, but they will profit thee. Hereafter thou canst have no profit from me except the example of my death, which I pray thee keep in memory, for, though bitter to the flesh and fearful before man, it is the door of eternal life, which none will attain who denies Christ Jesus before this ungodly generation."

His agony was prolonged by a slow fire, so that his execution lasted some six hours; but, through it all, he manifested true heroism and unshaken faith in the truth of the doctrines which he preached. His last words were, "How long, O Lord, shall darkness brood over this realm? Bow long wilt thou suffer this tyranny of man? Lord Jesus, receive my spirit."

Thus, in the bloom of early manhood, died Scotland's first Reformation martyr, and his death was not in vain. A Romanist afterwards said, "The smoke of Patrick Hamilton infected all it blew upon." His mouth was closed, but the story of his death was repeated by a thousand tongues. It emboldened others to seek a martyr's crown, and stirred up many more to defend the truths for which he died, and to repudiate the hierarchy which found it necessary to defend itself by such means. "Humanly speaking," says the author of "The Champions of the Reformation," to whom we are chiefly indebted for the facts of our sketch, "could there have been found a fitter apostle for ignorant, benighted Scotland than this eloquent, fervent, pious man? Endowed with all those gifts that sway the heads of the masses, a zealous, pious laborer in season and out of season, what Herculean labors might he not have accomplished! What signal triumphs might he not have achieved! So men may reason, but God judged otherwise. A short trial, a brief essay in the work he loved and longed for, was permitted to him, and then the goodly vessel, still in sight of land, was broken in pieces. " -- Heroes and Heroines

## 006 -- REV. E. PAYSON'S JOYFUL EXPERIENCES AND TRIUMPHANT DEATH

He was asked, by a friend, if he could see any particular reason for this dispensation. He replied, "No; but I am as well satisfied as if I could see ten thousand reasons."

In a letter dictated to his sister he writes: "Were I to adopt the figurative language of Bunyan, I might date this letter from the land of Beulah, of which I have been for some time such a happy inhabitant. The celestial city is full in view. Its glories beam upon me; its breezes fan me; its odors are wafted to me; its sounds strike upon my ears, and its spirit is breathed into my heart. Nothing separates me from it but the river of death, which now appears as an insignificant rill, which can be crossed at a single step, whenever God shall give permission. The Sun of Righteousness has been gradually drawing nearer and nearer, appearing larger and brighter as He approached, and now fills the whole hemisphere, pouring forth a flood of glory, in which I seem to float like an insect in the beams of the sun, exulting, yet almost trembling, while I gaze on this excessive brightness, and wondering why God should deign thus to shine upon a sinful worm."

On being asked, "Do you feel reconciled?" he replied, "O, that is too cold; I rejoice; I triumph; and this happiness will endure as long as God himself, for it consists in admiring and adoring Him. I can find no words to express my happiness. I seem to be swimming in a river of pleasure, which is carrying me to the great fountain. It seems as if all the bottles in heaven were opened, and all its fullness and happiness have come down into my heart. God has been depriving me of one blessing after another, but as each one has removed, He has come in and filled up its place. If God had told me sometime ago, that He was about to make me as happy as I could be in this world, and that He should begin by crippling me in all my limbs, and removing from me all my usual sources of enjoyment, I should have thought it a very strange mode of accomplishing His purposes, now, when I am a cripple, and not able to move, I am happier than I ever was in my life before, or ever expected to be.

"It has often been remarked, that people who have passed into the other world cannot come back to tell us what they have seen; but I am so near the eternal world, that I can almost see as clearly as if I were there; and I see enough to satisfy me of the truth of the doctrines I have preached. I do not know that I should feel at all surer had I been really there."

"Watchman, what of the night!" asked a gray-headed member of his church. "I should think it was about noonday," replied the dying Payson.

The ruling passion being strong in death, he sent a request to his pulpit, that his people should repair to his sick-chamber. They did so in specified classes, a few at a time and received his dying message.

To the young men of his congregation, he said: "I felt desirous that you might see that the religion I have preached can support me in death. You know that I have many ties which bind me to earth; a family to which I am strongly attached, and a people whom I love almost as well; but the other world acts like a much stronger magnet, and draws my heart away from this."

"Death comes every night, and stands by my bedside in the form of terrible convulsions, every one of which threatens to separate the soul from the body. These grow worse and worse, till every bone is almost dislocated with pain. Yet, while my body is thus tortured, my soul is perfectly, perfectly happy and peaceful. I lie here and feel these convulsions extending higher and higher, but my soul is filled with joy unspeakable! I seem to swim in a flood of glory, which God pours down upon me. Is it a delusion, that can fill the soul to overflowing with joy in such circumstances? If so, it is a delusion better than any reality. It is no delusion. I feel it is not. I enjoy this happiness now. And now, standing as I do, on the ridge that separates the two worlds -- feeling what intense happiness the soul is capable of sustaining, and judging of your capacities by my own, and believing that those capacities will be filled to the very brim with joy or wretchedness forever, my heart yearns over you, my children, that you may choose life, and not death. I long to present every one of you with a cup of happiness, and see you drink it."

"A young man," he continued, "just about to leave the world, exclaimed, 'The battle's fought, the battle's fought, but the victory is lost forever!' But I can say, The battle's fought -- and the victory is won -- the victory is won forever! I am going to bathe in the ocean of purity, and benevolence, and happiness, to all eternity. And now, my children, let me bless you, not with the blessing of a poor, feeble, dying man, but with the blessing of the infinite God." He then pronounced the apostolic benediction.

A friend said to him, "I presume it is no longer incredible to you, that martyrs should rejoice and praise God in the flames and on the rack?"

"No," said he; "I can easily believe it. I have suffered twenty times as much as I could in being burned at the stake, while my joy in God so abounded as to render my sufferings not only tolerable, but welcome."

At another time, he said: "God is literally now my all in all. While He is present with me, no event can in the least diminish my happiness; and were the whole world at my feet, trying to minister to my comfort, they could not add one drop to my cup."

To Mrs. Payson, who observed to him, "Your head feels hot and seems to be distended"; he replied: "It seems as if the soul disdained such a narrow prison, and was determined to break through with an angel's energy, and I trust with no small portion of an angel's feeling, until it mounts on high."

"It seems as if my soul had found a new pair of wings, and was so eager to try them, that in her fluttering, she would rend. the fine network of the body in pieces."

## THE CLOSING SCENE

On Sabbath, October 21, 1827, his last agony commenced, attended with that labored breathing and rattling in the throat which rendered articulation extremely difficult. His daughter was summoned from the Sabbath-school, and received his dying kiss and "God bless you, my daughter." He smiled on a group of church members and exclaimed, with holy emphasis, "Peace, peace! victory!" He smiled on his wife and children and said, in the language of dying Joseph, "I am going, but God will surely be with you!"

He rallied from the death conflict and said to his physician "that although he had suffered the pangs of death, and got almost within the gates of Paradise, yet, if it was God's will that he should come back and suffer still more, he was resigned." He passed through a similar scene in the afternoon and again revived.

On Monday morning, his dying agonies returned in all their severity. For three hours every breath was a groan. On being asked if his sufferings were greater than on the preceding Sunday night, he answered, "incomparably greater." He said the greatest temporal blessing of which he could conceive would be one breath of air.

Mrs. Payson, fearing from the expression of suffering on his countenance that he was in mental distress, questioned him. He replied, "Faith and patience hold out." These were the last words of the dying Christian hero.

He gradually sunk away, till about the going down of the sun his chastened and purified spirit, all mantled with the glory of Christian triumph in life and death, ascended to share the everlasting glory of his Redeemer before the eternal throne. -- Fifty Years and Beyond.

## 007 -- THE AWFUL DEATH OF AN INFIDEL SON

"I will never be guilty of founding my hopes for the future upon such a compiled mess of trash as is contained in that book (the Bible), mother. Talk o] that's being the production of an Infinite mind; a boy ten years of age, if he was half-witted, could have told a straighter story, and made a better book. I believe it to be the greatest mess of lies ever imposed upon the public. I would rather go to hell (if there is such a place) than have the name of bowing to that impostor -- Jesus Christ -- and be dependent on his merits for salvation."

"Beware! Beware! my son, 'for God is not mocked,' although 'He beareth with the wicked long, yet he will not keep His anger forever.' And 'all manner of sin shall be forgiven men, except the sin against the Holy Ghost, which has no forgiveness.' And many are the examples, both in sacred and profane history, of men who have been smitten down in the midst of their sinning against that blessed Spirit."

"Very well, father, I'll risk all the cutting down that I shall get for cursing that book, and all the agonies connected therewith. Let it come, I'm not at all scared."

"O Father, lay not this sin to his charge, for he knows not what he does."

"Yes, I do know what I'm about, and what I say -- and mean it."

"John, do you mean to drive your mother raving distracted? Oh, my God! what have I done that this dreadful trial should come upon me in my old age?"

"Mother, if you don't want to hear me speak my sentiments, why do you always begin the subject? If you do not want to hear it, don't ever broach the subject again, for I shall never talk of that book, in any other way."

The above conversation took place between two fond parents and an only son, who was at home on a visit from college, and now was about to return. And the cause of this outburst was, the kind-hearted Christian parents had essayed to give him a few words of kind admonition, which, alas! proved to be the last. And the above were his last words which he spoke to them as he left the house.

How anxiously those fond parents looked after him as though something told them that something dreadful would happen. What scalding tears were those that coursed their way down these furrowed cheeks! Oh! that they might have been put in the bottle of mercy! Poor, wretched young man, it had been better for him had the avalanche from the mountain crushed him beneath its deadly weight ere those words escaped his lips. Little did he think that He who said, "Honor thy father and mother," and, "He that hardeneth his heart, and stiffeneth his neck, shall suddenly be destroyed, and that without remedy," was so soon going to call him to give an account for those words, so heart-rending to his aged parents, and so dreadful in the sight of a holy God. He had imbibed those dreadful principles from an infidel room-mate at college. Beware, young men, with whom you associate, lest you fall as did this unfortunate young man.

John B. left his home and hastened to the depot where he took the cars which were to bear him to M. where he was in a few months to finish his studies. The whistle blew, and away swept the cars "across the trembling plain." But alas!

they had gone but a few miles, when the cars, coming round a curve in a deep cut, came suddenly upon an obstruction on the track, which threw the engine and two of the cars at once from the rails.

As fate would seem to have it, the wicked son (John B.) was that moment passing between them. He was thrown in an instant from the platform, his left arm being "broken, and his skull fractured by the fall; and in an instant one of the wheels passed directly over both his legs near the body, breaking and mangling them in the most dreadful manner. Strange as it may seem, no one else was injured. The dreadful news soon reached his already grief-stricken parents; and ere long that beloved, yet ungrateful son, was borne back to them; not as he left, but lying upon a litter a poor, mangled, raving maniac. Why these pious parents were called to pass through this dreadful trial, He "whose ways are in the deep and past finding out," only knows; except that by this sad example of His wrath many might be saved. Many skillful physicians were called, but the fiat of the Almighty had gone forth, and man could not recall it. When the news reached the college, his class-mates hastened to see him. When they came, nature was fast sinking, but the immortal part was becoming dreadfully alive. Oh! that heart-rending scene. His reason returning brought with it a dreadful sense of his situation. His first words were, and oh, may never mortal hear such a cry as that again upon the shores of time:

"Mother! I'm lost! lost! lost! damned! damned! damned forever!" and as his class-mates drew near to the bed, among whom was the one who had poisoned his mind with infidelity, with a dreadful effort he rose in the bed and cried, as he fixed his glaring eyes upon him: "J__, you have brought me to this, you have damned my soul! May the curses of the Almighty and the Lamb rest upon your soul forever."

Then like a hellish fiend, he gnashed his teeth, and tried to get hold of him that he might tear him in pieces. Then followed a scene from which the strongest fled with horror. But those poor parents had to hear and see it all, for he would not suffer them to be away a moment. He fell back upon his bed exhausted, crying, "O mother! mother, get me some water to quench this fire that is burning me to death"; then he tore his hair and rent his breast; the fire had already begun to burn, the smoke of which shall ascend up for ever and ever. And then again he cried, "O mother, save me, the devils have come after me. O mother, take me in your arms, and don't let them have me." And as his mother drew near to him, he buried his face in that fond bosom which had nourished and cherished him, but, alas, could not now protect or shield from the storm of the Almighty's wrath, for he turned from her, and with an unearthly voice he shrieked, "Father! mother! father, save me; they come to drag my soul -- my soul to hell." And with his eyes starting from their sockets, he fell back upon his bed a corpse. The spirit had fled -- not like that of Lazarus, borne on the wings of a convoy of angels, but dragged by fiends to meet a fearful doom. May his dreadful fall prove a warning to those who would unwittingly walk in the same path. -- Earnest Christian, September, 1867

## 008 -- "CHILDREN, IS THIS DEATH? HOW BEAUTIFUL! HOW BEAUTIFUL!"

A preacher in Oregon, Rev. J. T. Leise, writes us as follows: "I thought it might be to the glory of God to give you an account of my mother's death. She died July 28, 1888, in the township of Winnebago City, Faribault County, Minnesota. About six months before her death I left home to enter the work of the Lord. At that time, and also for years, mother had what we often call an up-and-down experience. About July 1st, of the same year she died, I got word to return home to see her die. On my arrival I found mother very low, but having a strong faith in God. I said, 'Mother, you have a better experience than you have ever had.' 'Yes, Johnnie,' she said, 'about three months ago I got what I have longed for for years.' Mother's disease was of a dropsical character. With limbs swollen, she would suffer intensely; but her faith in Jesus never wavered. She would often speak of the glorious prospects in view. The morning she died, about four o'clock, a sister and I were sitting by her bed fanning her, when she suddenly opened her eyes and said, 'Children, is this death? How beautiful; how beautiful.' I said, 'Mother, you will soon be at rest. It won't be long before you shall have crossed over and are at home.' Mother never could sing to amount t o any. thing, but on this occasion she sang as if inspired from Heaven,

O I long to be there
And His glories to share
And to lean on my Savior's breast.

About four hours after we were around her bed having family worship, when, without a struggle, she passed away to be forever with the Lord. Amen-

## 009 -- "MA, I CAN'T DIE TILL YOU PROMISE ME."

At the close of a series of meetings in Springfield, Mass., a mother handed me a little girl's picture wrapped in two one-dollar bills, at the same time relating the following touching incident:

Her only child, at the age of six years, gave her heart to the Savior, giving, as the pastor with whom I was laboring said, the clearest evidence of conversion.

At once she went to her mother and said, "Ma, I have given my heart to Jesus and He has received me; now, won't you give your heart to Him?" (The parents were both unconverted at the time.) The mother replied, "I hope I shall some time, dear Mary." The little girl said, "Do it now, ma," and urged the mother, with all her childlike earnestness, to give herself to the Savior then

Finding she could not prevail in that way, she sought to secure a promise from her mother, feeling sure she would do what she promised; for her parents had made it & point never to make her a promise with. out carefully fulfilling it. So time after time she would say, "Promise me, me"; and the mother would reply, "I do not like to promise you, Mary, for fear I shall not fulfill."

This request was urged at times for nearly six years, and finally the little petitioner had to die to secure the promise.

Several times during her sickness the parents came to her bedside to see her die, saying to her, "You are dying now, dear Mary." But she would say, "No, ma, I can't die till you promise me." Still her mother was unwilling to make the promise, lest it should not be kept. She intended to give her heart to Jesus sometime, but was unwilling to do it "now."

Mary grew worse, and finally had uttered her last word on earth: her mother was never again to hear that earnest entreaty, "Promise me, ma."

But the little one's spirit lingered, as if it were detained by the angel sent to lead the mother to Jesus, that the long-sought promise might be heard before it took its flight.

The weeping mother stood watching the countenance of the dying child, who seemed to say, by her look, "Ma, promise me, and let me go to Jesus." There was a great struggle in her heart as she said to herself, "Why do I not promise this child? I mean to give my heart to Jesus; why not now? If I do not promise her now I never can."

The Spirit inclined her heart to yield. She roused her child and said, "Mary, I will give my heart to Jesus." This was the last bolt to be drawn; her heart was now open, and Jesus entered at once, and she felt the joy and peace of sins forgiven.

This, change was so marked, she felt constrained to tell the good news to her child, that she might bear it with her where she went to live with Jesus; so, calling her attention once more, she said, "Mary, I have give my heart to Jesus, and He is my Savior now."

For six years Mary had been praying to God and pleading with her mother for these words; and now, and they fell upon her ear, a peaceful smile lighted up her face, and, no longer able to speak, she raised her little, pale hand, and pointing upward, seemed to say, "Ma, we shall meet up there." Her life's work was done, and her spirit returned to Him who gave it.

The mother's heart was full o£ peace, though her loved one had gone. She now felt very anxious that her husband should have this blessing which she found in Christ.

The parents went into the room where the remains were resting, to look upon the face of her who slept so sweetly in death, when the mother said, 'Husband, I promised our little Mary that I would give my heart to Jesus, and He has received me. Now, won't you promise?"

The Holy Spirit was there. The strong man resisted for a while, then yielded his will, and taking the little cold hand in his, kneeled and said, "Jesus, I will try to seek Thee."

The child's remains were laid in the grave. The parents were found in the house of prayer -- the mother happy in Jesus, and the father soon having some evidence of love to Christ.

When I closed my labors in Springfield, Dr. Ide said to his congregation, "I hope you will all give Bro. Earle some token of your regard for his services before he leaves." As this mother heard these words, she said she could, as it were, see her little Mary's hand pointing down from heaven, and heard her sweet voice saying, "Ma, give him my two one-dollars."

Those two one-dollars I have now, wrapped around the picture of that dear child, and wherever I go, little Mary will speak for the Savior.

Reader, is there not some loved one now pointing down from heaven and saying to you, "Give your heart to Jesus"? Are you loving some earthly object more than Jesus? God may sever that tie -- may take away your little Mary, or Willie, or some dear friend. Will you not come to Jesus, without such a warning? -- Bringing in Sheaves

## *010 -- THE CHILD MARTYR*

The noted evangelist, E. P. Hammond, writes us from his home at Hartford, Conn., Aug. 11, 1898, and sends us the following reliable and very touching article for this work:

I have been surprised to notice how many children have died a martyr death rather than deny Jesus. I want to tell you about one of these young martyrs. In Antioch, where the disciples were first called Christians, a deacon from the church of Caesarea was called to bear cruel torture to force him to deny the Lord who bought him with His precious blood. While he was being tortured he still declared his faith, saying: "There is but one God and one mediator between God and man, Christ Jesus." His body was almost torn in pieces. The cruel emperor, Galerius, seemed to enjoy looking upon him in his suffering. At length this martyr begged his tormentors to ask any Christian child whether it was better to worship one God, the maker of heaven and earth, and one Savior, who had died for us, and was able to bring us to God, or to worship the gods many and the lords many whom the Romans served. There stood near by a Roman mother who had brought with her a little boy, nine years of age, that he might witness the sufferings of this martyr from Caesarea. The question was asked the child. He quickly replied, "God is one and Christ is one with the Father."

The persecutor was filled with fresh rage and cried out, "O base and wicked Christian, that thou hast taught this child to answer thus." Then turning to the boy, he said more mildly, "Child, tell me who taught thee thus to speak? Where did you learn this faith?"

The boy looked lovingly into his mother's face and said, "It was God that taught it to my mother, and she taught me that Jesus Christ loved little children, and so I learned to love Him for his first love for me."

"Let us see what the love of Christ can do for you," cried the cruel judge, and at a sign from him the officers who stood by with their rods, after the fashion of the Romans, quickly seized the boy and made ready to torture him.

"What can the love of Christ do for him now?" asked the judge, as the blood streamed from the tender flesh of the child. "It helps him," answered the mother, "to bear what his master endured for him when he died for us on the cross."

Again they smote the child, and every blow seemed to torture the agonized mother as much as the child. As the blows, faster and heavier, were laid upon the bleeding boy, they asked, "What can the love of Christ do for him now?"

Tears fell from heathen eyes as that Roman mother replied, "It teaches him to forgive his tormentors." The boy watched his mother's eyes and no doubt thought of the sufferings of his Lord and Savior, and when his tormentors asked if he would now serve the gods they served, he still answered, "I will not deny Christ. There is no other God but one, and Jesus Christ is the redeemer of the world. Be loved me and died for me, and I love him with all my heart."

The poor child at last fainted between the repeated strokes, and they cast the torn and bleeding body into the mother's arms, saying, supposing that he was dead, "See what the love of Christ has done for your Christian boy now."

As the mother pressed him to her heart she answered, "That love would take him from the wrath of man to the peace of heaven, where God shall wipe away all tears!"

But the boy had not yet passed over the river. Opening his eyes, he said, "Mother, can I have a drop of water from our cool well upon my tongue?"

As he closed his eyes in death the mother said, "Already, dearest, thou hast tasted of the well that springeth up unto everlasting life. Farewell! thy Savior calls for thee. Happy, happy martyr! for His sake may He grant thy mother grace to follow in thy bright path."

To the surprise of all, after they thought he bad closed his eyes and had breathed his last, he finally raised his eyes and looked to where the elder martyr was, and said in almost a whisper, "There is but one God, and Jesus Christ whom He has sent." And with these words upon his parched lips, he passed into God's presence, "where is fullness of joy, and to His right hand, where are pleasures forevermore."

Are you, my dear reader, a Christian? If not, you can become one now. That same Jesus who bled and died to save that little Roman boy, suffered on the cross for you, and He is ever ready to give you a new heart, so that you will love Him so much that you would be willing to die a death of suffering rather than deny Him.

## 011 -- THE SAD DEATH OF A LOST MAN

Near the town of K__, in Texas, there lived and prospered, a wealthy farmer, the son of a Methodist preacher, with whom the writer was intimately acquainted. He was highly respected in the community in which he lived. He was a kind-hearted and benevolent man; but, however, had one great fault -- he was very profane. He would utter the most horrible oaths without, seemingly, the least provocation. On several occasions, I remember having seen him under deep conviction for salvation, during revival meetings. On one occasion, during a camp-meeting, he was brought under powerful conviction. He afterwards said he was suddenly frightened, and felt as if he wanted to run away from the place. Just one year from that time, another camp-meeting was held at the same place, and he was again brought under conviction, but refused to yield; after which he was suddenly taken ill, and died in three days. I was with him in his last moments. He seemed to be utterly forsaken of the Lord from the beginning of his sickness. The most powerful medicines had no effect on him whatever. Just as the sun of a beautiful Sabbath morning rose in its splendor over the eastern hills, he died -- in horrible agony. All through the night previous to his death, he suffered untold physical and mental torture. He offered the physicians all his earthly possessions if they would save his life. He was stubborn till the very last; and would not acknowledge his fear of death until a few moments before he died; then, suddenly he began to look, then to stare, horribly surprised and frightened, into the vacancy before him; then exclaimed, as if he beheld the king of terrors in all of his merciless wrath, "My God!" The indescribable expression of his countenance, at this juncture, together with the despairing tones in which he uttered these last words, made every heart quake. His wife screamed, and begged a brother to pray for him; but he was so terror-stricken that he rushed out of the room. The dying man continued to stare in dreadful astonishment, his mouth wide open, and his eyes protruding out of their sockets, till at last with an awful groan,

*"Like a flood with rapid force,
Death bore the wretch away."*

His little three-year-old son, the idol of his father's heart, was convulsed with grief. This little boy, then so innocent, grew up to be a wicked young man, and died a horrible death. Oh how sad! When we reflect that in hell there are millions of fathers and sons, mothers and daughters, husbands and wives, hopelessly lost, given over forever to the mad ravages of eternal, pitiless wrath, ever frightened by real ghosts, tortured by serpents and scorpions, gnawed by the worm that never dies; and when we reflect that this, the future state of the wicked, will never abate its fury but, according to the natural law of sin, degradation and wretchedness, will grow worse and more furious as the black ages of eternity roll up from darker realms, we turn for relief from the sad reverie to the Man of Sorrows, who tasted death for every man, then to the beautiful city. whose builder and maker is God, to the bliss of the glorified who will shine as the stars for ever and ever; then with renewed efforts we continue with gratitude to work out our own, and the salvation of others, with fear and trembling. -- The Ambassador

## 012 -- THE COURAGE AND TRIUMPHANT DEATH OF ST. LAURENCE THE MARTYR

Laurentius, usually called St. Laurence, was archdeacon under Sextus, and when that bishop was led out to execution, Laurence accompanied and comforted him. As they parted from each other for the last time, Sextus warned his faithful follower that his martyrdom would soon come after his own: that this prophecy was true is indicated by the tradition that has been handed down to us telling of his subsequent seizure and cruel death.

The Christian church of Rotor, even at this early period, had in its treasury considerable riches -- both in money, and in gold and silver vessels used at the services of the church. All these treasures were under the watchful eye of Laurence, the archdeacon. Besides maintaining its clergy, the church supported many poor widows and orphans; nearly fifteen hundred of these poor people, whose names Laurence kept upon his list, lived upon the charity of the church. Sums of money were also constantly needed to help struggling churches which had been newly established in distant parts of the world.

Macrianus, governor of Rome under the emperor Valerian, had heard of these riches, and longed to seize them; he therefore sent soldiers to arrest Laurence, who was soon taken and dragged before the governor. As soon as Macrianus' pitiless eyes rested upon the prisoner, he said harshly:

"I hear that you who call yourselves Christians possess treasures of gold and silver, and that your priests use golden vessels at your services. Is this true?"

Laurence answered: "The church, indeed, has great treasures."

"Then bring those treasures forth," said Macrianus. "Do not your sacred books tell you to render unto Caesar the things that are Caesar's? The emperor has need of those riches for the defense of the empire; therefore you must render them up."

After reflecting deeply for a few moments, Laurence replied: "In three days I will bring before you the greatest treasures of the church."

This answer satisfied the governor; so Laurence was set free, and Macrianus impatiently awaited the time when the expected stores of gold and silver should be placed before him.

On the appointed day Macrianus, attended by his officers, came to the place where the Christians usually assembled. They were calmly received by Laurence at the entrance and invited to pass into an inner room.

"Are the treasures collected?" was the first question of Macrianus.

"They are, my lord," replied Laurence; "will you enter and view them?"

With these words he opened a door and displayed to the astounded gaze of the governor, the poor pensioners of the church, a chosen number -- a row of the lame, a row of the blind, orphans and widows, the helpless and the weak. Astonished by the sight, the governor turned fiercely upon Laurence, saying: "What mean you by this mockery? Where are the treasures of gold and silver you promised to deliver up?"

"These that you see before you," replied the undaunted Laurence, "are the true treasures of the church. In the widows and orphans you behold her gold and silver, her pearls and precious stones. These are her real riches. Make use of them by asking for their prayers; they will prove your best weapon against your foes."

Enraged and disappointed at not securing the hoped-for gold (which had been carried to a place of safety during the three days that had elapsed), the governor furiously commanded his guards to seize Laurence and take him to a dungeon. There, terrible to relate, a great fire was built upon the stone floor, and a huge gridiron placed upon it; then the martyr was stripped of his clothing and thrown upon this fiery bed, to slowly perish in the scorching heat.

The cruel tyrant gazed down upon this dreadful sight to gratify his hatred and revenge; but the martyr had strength and spirit to triumph over him even to the last. Not a murmur escaped him, but with his dying breath he prayed for the. Christian church at Rome, and for the conversion of the entire empire to God; and so, lifting up his eyes to heaven, he gave up the ghost.

A Roman soldier, named Romanus, who looked on at the sufferings of St. Laurence, was so much affected by the martyr's courage and faith that he became a convert to Christianity. As soon as this was known the soldier was severely scourged, and afterward be. headed. -- Foxe's Book of Martyrs

## *013 -- TRIUMPHANT DEATH OF GEORGE EDWARD DRYER*

This saint of God went to heaven from Readsburg, Wis., Feb. 1, 1896. His sister, Mrs. Evaline Dryer Green, sends us the following:

Dear readers, come with me for a little while as I look on memory's walls. See, there are many things written there! Here is one story, sweet and sacred, almost too sacred to relate; yet as" with hushed voices we talk of this, our hearts shall melt and we shall feel that heaven is drawing nigher.

I remember my baby brother -- though I was a child of but four years when he came into our home. I well remember that little face as I saw it first. I remember the chubby brown hands when he was a wee boy, always in mischief then. 1 was a frail girl, and he soon outgrew me. Then those sweet years of home life-and later the glad home comings when I was away at school. On my return George was always the first to wave his hand and shout for joy -- perhaps toss his hat high in the air and give a certain "whoop" and three cheers that I loved to hear. We were right loyal friends, my brother and I. And then -- ah, its here I'd wish to draw the vail, and forget. We thought he would accomplish his ambitions -- so strong, so full of life! But we will only glance at those long months of suffering and hasten to the last. Nearly eighteen months of weariness from coughing, and there he lay, the picture of patient endurance, saying from his heart's depths,

*"Farewell, mortality -- Jesus is mine*
*Welcome, eternity -- Jesus is mine!"*

Often he would call me near him and say, "Oh, sister, the Lord does so save me!" To the doctor, the boys of his own age, to neighbors, and all who came, he testified how Jesus saved him, through and through.

The last hours were drawing near. One of the Lord's servants came and prayed. George prayed for father, mother, brothers and sisters. A little later in the evening a sweat, deathly cold, covered him. We thought he was going then -- the poor, weak body seemed all but gone, while the spirit grew even more bright. Ah, that picture! That high, marble-white brow, either cheek glowing with fever intense, great, expressive blue eyes, that peered earnestly, joyfully, all about him and upward. Those dear hands were lifted high, while he said, with heaven lighting his face,

*"Angels now are hovering round us."*

(Even now I feel to say, as I did then, "O death, where is thy sting? O grave, where is thy victory?")

Again he came back to us -- to spend one more night of suffering on earth, and to work for God and eternity. We watched all night, while he praised God, often saying 'under his breath, between awful fits of coughing, "Precious Jesus!" Toward morning he asked a dear sister to sing "I Saw A Happy Pilgrim."

Finally the morning came; a dark, rainy morning in February. The gray light was just dawning when we all gathered about his bed. We repeated beautiful texts to him, and verses of hymns that he most loved, and encouraged him to the very river's brink. His last spoken words were, "Eva, come on this side." Then, peacefully he closed his eyes and grew so still.

"And with the morn, those angel faces smile, Which I have loved long since -- and lost a while."

## *014 -- "FIVE MINUTES MORE TO LIVE"*

A young man stood before a large audience in the most fearful position a human being could be placed-on the scaffold! The noose had been adjusted around his neck. In a few moments more he would be in eternity. The sheriff took out his watch and said, "If you have anything to say, speak now; as you have but five minutes more to live." What awful words for a young man to hear, in full health and vigor!

Shall I tell you his message to the youth about him? He burst into tears and said with sobbing: "1 have to die! I had only one little brother. He had beautiful blue eyes and flaxen hair. How I loved him! I got drunk -- the first time. I found my little brother gathering strawberries. I got angry with him, without cause; and killed him with a blow from a rake. I knew nothing about it till I awoke on the following day and found myself closely guarded. They told me that when my little brother was found, his hair was clotted with his blood and brains. Whisky had done it! It has ruined me! I have only one more word to say to the young people before I go to stand in the presence of my Judge. Never, Never, NEVER touch anything that can intoxicate!"

Whiskey did it! The last words of this doomed young man make our heart ache, and we cry out to God, "How long, how long shall our nation be crazed with rum? When, oh when, will the American people wake up?" Oh that the professed people of God would vote as they pray. What about the licensed saloon that deals out this poison that sends millions reeling and crazed with drink to hell? What about the multitudes of innocent people who are killed by inches and sacrificed to the god of rum? We protect and license a man who deals out death and destruction, and hang a man who gets drunk and kills his neighbor. Who was most to blame -- this young man, or the saloon-keeper who made him crazy, or the government that gave the saloon-keeper license not only to make crazy but to ruin soul and body? God help us to decide this question in the light of the coming judgment. Amen.

## 015 -- BLACK DAYS AND WHITE ONES -- A RESCUE STORY

We are thankful to God that we have had the privilege of helping to launch the Rescue Home in Grand Rapids, Mich. We induced the Salvation Army to open a home in our city by furnishing the buildings free of rent the first year, and by helping in other ways. Capt. Duzau, the first in charge, led not only the subject of the sketch to God, but most of the other girls that passed through the home have been saved from a life of shame, and I am told by good authority that most all of the girls who enter the various rescue homes of the Army are saved. We quote the following from the War Cry:

Alice's life had always been a sad one -- at least, as far as she could remember. Perhaps the first three years of babyhood life had been as pleasant and happy as if she had been born in a more comfortable home But Alice couldn't be sure about this, and no one else could speak for her.

Certainly there was misery and unhappiness from one day on -- misery that lasted for nearly fifteen years of girlhood life. That was the day which came shortly after her third birthday, when Alice ceased to be a baby.

She couldn't remember much about it, but it seemed like a big, round, black spot, big enough to shut out all the sunlight from life. The day itself was dark and gloomy, but that wasn't the worst. Some strange men Alice had never seen before came to the little house -- and they were all dressed in black -- and they took away something in a long, black box -- and Alice never saw her mother again after that day. No wonder it seemed to the child -- the youngest one of the five thus suddenly left motherless -- like something black and awful.

Besides, after that, life was bitterly hard for the one who was still the youngest, but no longer watched over with care that even a three-year-old baby needs. Things at home which had been in some ways bad enough before were worse now; and, from that time on, the child grew up in an atmosphere of such moral degradation that it is a wonder she did not fall sooner and sin more deeply than was the case. Two of her sisters lived an openly sinful life, and assuredly the brother for whom she went to keep house as soon as she was old enough, was no better. A companion of this brother came to the house one day; when he went away he was as light-hearted and careless as ever, but he left behind him such a burden of shame and sorrow and disgrace as poor Alice felt she could not carry.

This girl of seventeen went to her two sisters with the weight of sorrow and wrong, to the two sisters who should have stood in the place of mother to her.

"Nonsense," said Kate, "why, you'll get used to it!" Bettina was a little more sympathetic, but even more discouraging. "I never thought you'd feel like that," she said, "but it's too late to mend matters now. It could have been helped yesterday, but not today. What's done can't be undone. There isn't a respectable woman in the world whom speak to you now!" Alice walked away as if in a dream. "What's done can't be undone," she kept repeating to herself, as if to fasten the direful statement upon her mind and memory. Occasionally the words changed, and she repeated, "It's too late to mend matters now."

It was the old argument, used so successfully in scores and hundreds and thousands of cases -- the argument that one step down the ladder of disgrace involves the whole distance, that there is no hope, no way of escape, after the first wrong-doing.

"There's no help for it -- you are doomed now, anyway-no respectable woman could speak to you -- you might as well take what pleasure you can out of this life." In almost every case, someone is sure to come with this temptation of utter hopelessness, and the young girl whose better nature is fighting against the horror of the whole thing, calls on that better nature to yield the battle. "It is no use trying to be good," she says despairingly.

So it was with Alice Sawyer. She knew of no one in the village to whom she could go for help, or even Christian advice, and she gave up the struggle. "It isn't my fault," she said to herself once when her half dormant conscience spoke out and would be heard. "There simply isn't any way out for me, or if there is, I can't find it, and that's the same thing."

Weeks passed by, during which no one would have suspected that Alice Sawyer felt any repugnance toward the careless, irregular sort of life she was leading. "There, I knew she'd get used to it soon enough," exclaimed Kate one day.

But Bettina said nothing. Deep down in her heart there was a sort of sorrow for her youngest sister, but it was a sorrow she did not know how to put into words.

After a time Alice went away from home and found her way to the city of Grand Rapids. Like many others, she imagined that it would be easy to hide her shame in the midst of a crowd, and as soon as she arrived in the city she began her search for work.

She wanted to be lost, but instead she was found-found by the One who came to seek and to save that which was lost.

Almost at the beginning of her search for work, Alice discovered that one part at least of the disheartening prophecy was untrue, because she came across an earnest Christian lady, who not only "spoke to her," but even took her into her own home for the night.

The next day this lady brought her to the Salvation Army Rescue Home in Grand Rapids. Alice wanted to stay, and was very grateful for the opportunity. Yet it all seemed so strange, so unexpected, that it took the poor child some time to realize that "the way out" of her sin and misery had, actually been found, and that the door was open before her into paths of new life and hope.

Kneeling by her bedside one night, Alice claimed fur herself the power of that uttermost salvation which alone can take away the bitterness from the memory of such a past as hers, and which alone can make it possible to sing,

*He breaks the power of canceled sin,*
*He sets the prisoner free:*
*His blood can make the foulest clean,*
*His blood avails for me.*

That night marked the last of Alice's unhappy days, the "black ones" as she sometimes called them in contrast to the "white ones" of the new life which then began. Her one sorrow was for those left behind in the village home, without any knowledge of Christ, and she prayed for them all, especially for her father, then seventy-one years old.

"It will take something to touch my father's heart," she said one day to the Captain of the Home; "but I am praying for him, and I believe he will give his heart to God."

That "something" which should touch her father's heart came sooner than was expected by some.

Alice had to go to the hospital, and after she had been there a short time it became evident that she would never be able to go out again. But she had no fear, and was sorry only because she had hoped to be able to go to others with the story of that wonderful salvation which had availed for her.

On the first evening of her stay in the hospital the Captain and Lieutenant of the Rescue Home went with her and stayed a few hours. As they were saying goodnight to her and to the nurse who was to have her in charge, Alice suddenly dropped on her knees by the bedside.

It was indeed a striking picture. On the one side the two Salvationists in their uniforms, on the other side the nurse in hers, while by the bedside knelt the girl of eighteen who had been saved in time from a life of misery and sorrow. It seemed as if the very light of heaven were striking through, illuminating the scene with divine radiance and blessing. It may indeed have been so, for Alice was rapidly nearing the very gates of heaven.

Suddenly the summons came -- such a summons always is sudden at the last, even when the possibility has been in view for some time.

Word was sent to the Rescue Home, and the Captain came at once to the hospital. "I do love you, Captain," said Alice. Then, with her eyes steadfastly fixed on the face of the one who had lead her into the light of salvation through Jesus, the girl passed quietly, peacefully away to that land where there is no more pain, for the "former things are passed away."

This scene might do very well as a beautiful ending to a story which began in sadness and gloom. It was indeed a bright, white, glorious day in Alice's experience, but it did not mark the end of her work on earth.

The "something" which was to touch her father's heart did reach and touch that man of seventy-one through his youngest daughter's death.

At the simple funeral service, held in the Rescue Home, he came forward like a child, knelt sobbing by the coffin and asked God to help him meet his Alice in the great, wonderful land beyond the grave. -- Adjutant Elizabeth M. Clark

## 016 -- TRIUMPHANT DEATH OF MRS. MARGARET HANEY

Mrs. Margaret Haney, of Greenville, Mich., died of cancer, May 31, 1896, aged 53 years. She was converted fifteen years ago in a meeting held by Bro. S. B. Shaw. Sister Haney was born in Canada. She was an excellent Christian. A few days before she died she said to one of the sisters, "Do you know that I love Jesus?" and to another sister she said, "He fills my soul with glory." Tuesday before she died she waved her hands and praised the Lord while Sister Taylor was reading, "I go to prepare a place for you," etc. A few hours before she passed away I said, "Sister Haney, do you know Jesus?" and she nodded her head, after she could speak no more. She arranged her temporal matters for her departure, selected the text for her funeral (Rev. 14: 13) and asked Bro. D. G. Briggs to preach her funeral sermon. The funeral was held at Greenville, June 2. The Comforter was present to give hope and cheer to sorrowing friends. Sister Haney will not only be missed in our class, but all over the city, and especially in her home by her husband and children. -- Mrs. A. Hoadley

## 017 -- LAST HOURS ON EARTH OF THE NOTED FRENCH INFIDEL, VOLTAIRE

When Voltaire felt the stroke that he realized must terminate in death, he was overpowered with remorse. He at once sent for the priest, and wanted to be "reconciled with the church." His infidel flatterers hastened to his chamber to prevent his recantation; but it was only to witness his ignominy and their own. He cursed them to their faces; and, as his distress was increased by their presence, he repeatedly and loudly exclaimed:

"Begone! It is you that have brought me to my present condition. Leave me, I say; begone! What a wretched glory is this which you have produced to me!"

Hoping to allay his anguish by a written recantation, he had it prepared, signed it, and saw it witnessed. But it was all unavailing. For two months he was tortured with such an agony as led him at times to gnash his teeth in impotent rage against God and man. At other times, in plaintive accents, he would plead, "O Christ! O Lord Jesus!" Then, turning his face, he would cry out, "I must die -- abandoned of God and of men!"

As his end drew near, his condition became so frightful that his infidel associates were afraid to approach his bedside. Still they guarded the door, that others may not know how awfully an infidel was compelled to die. Even his nurse repeatedly said, "For all the wealth of Europe she would never see another infidel die." It was a scene of horror that lies beyond all exaggeration. Such is the well-attested end of the one who had a natural sovereignty of intellect, excellent education, great wealth, and much earthly honor. We may all well exclaim with Balsam, "Let me die the death of the righteous, and let my last end be like his. -- The Contrast Between Infidelity and Christianity

## 018 -- DYING WORDS OF SAMUEL HICK

Many of our readers no doubt have heard of "Sammy Hick, the Village Blacksmith." His eccentricities and devotion to God are widely known, not only in England, his native land, but in other countries as well. His biographer says:

In 1825, Mr. Hick gave up business and devoted the remainder of his days to the work of the Lord. Everywhere he became very popular. In London he drew crowds to hear him, and he was the means of doing much good. In speaking in the pulpit or on the platform, he was loud and vehement; on warming up with his subject he was much given to gesticulation and stamping, making the platform tremble under him; in fact, on one occasion he stamped the platform down. "Just at the moment of applying his subject," says Rev. J. Everett, "and saying, 'Thus it was that the prophets went,' that part of the platform on which he stood gave way, and he instantly disappeared. Fortunately no injury was done."

And now the time for his dissolution drew near. About a month before he died he told his friends he was "going home." He wished Mr. Dawson to preach his funeral sermon from Isaiah 48: 18; he also desired that his death should be advertised in the Leeds paper, and that a sack of meal should be baked into bread and two cheeses purchased for the use of those who came to witness the interment. "My friends will all come," said he, "there will be a thousand people at my funeral." By Martha's desire, however, Mr. Dawson succeeded in "persuading him off" this baking and cheese purchasing business, especially as his means were small. That dry, hearty humor to which he was so much given showed itself even in his last hours. A friend who prayed with him in his last illness asked the Lord to "make his bed in his affliction." "Yes," responded Sammy, "and shake it well, Lord." Remembering that the stairs were narrow, and the windows of the room small, he said to those about him, "As soon as I die, you must take the body down and lay it out; for you will not be able to get the coffin either down-stairs or out of the windows." Then after singing I'll praise my Maker while I've breath:

*And when my voice is lost in death,*
*Praise shall employ my nobler powers,*

he said faintly, "I am going, get the sheets ready"; and on Monday, at 11 p. m., Nov. 9th, 1829, in the 71st year of his age, he took his departure. On the following Sunday he was buried in Aberford Churchyard, and about a thousand persons attended the funeral; many of whom after taking their last look at the coffin, turned away exclaiming, "If ever there was a good man, Sammy Hick was one." -- Life Stories Of Remarkable Preachers

## *019 -- THE SAINTED SUSANNA WESLEY*

"The Mother of Methodism" was born in London in 1669, and was the youngest child of Dr. Samuel Annesley, an able and prominent minister, who paid every attention to the education of his favorite daughter. When Susanna was twenty years of age she and her husband, Samuel Wesley, a graduate of Exeter College and a curate in London, began married life on an income of sixty pounds a year. The young husband was a diligent student and devoted to his work; his beautiful wife, a person of fine manners. Had Susanna Wesley not been a person of very strong will, she could not have borne all the trials, privations and hardships incident to her long and toilsome life. Not only did poverty often stare the rapidly increasing family in the face, but in 1702 their home was destroyed by fire and other troubles fast followed. Mr. Wesley, owing debts which he could not pay, was put into prison, where he remained three months before his friends succeeded in releasing him. A still greater calamity was awaiting them. In 1709 Epworth Rectory was burned to the ground, and some of the children narrowly escaped with their lives. Their books, which had been purchased with great self-denial, twenty pounds in money and their clothing were all gone. A month later Mrs. Wesley's nineteenth and last child was born. The rectory was after a time rebuilt and the scattered family reunited.

Notwithstanding her manifold household duties Mrs. Wesley found time for a vast amount of literary work. Not only did she conduct a household school, which she continued for twenty years, but she prepared three text-books for the religious training of her children.

She also held Sunday evening services in the rectory for her children and servants. Others asked permission to come, and often two hundred were present.

The letters she wrote to her children give some insight into her pure and noble character. When John entered school at London many letters passed between mother and son. She advised him what books to read. "Imitation of Christ" and "Rules for Holy Living and Dying" made lasting impressions upon him. When he was first asked to go to America to preach the gospel he hesitated, wishing to remain near his aged mother. When he consulted her she replied, "Had I twenty sons I should rejoice were they all so employed, though I should never see them again." What must have been her feelings as she witnessed the grand work done by his son before she was called away.

"Children, as soon as I am released sing a psalm of praise to God," was her last uttered request. The words of her son Charles, "God buries the workmen, but the work goes on," are true, and though this model mother has long since passed away, the grand work of her sons still goes forward. -- Traits of Character

### 020 -- "OH! I HAVE MISSED IT AT LAST!"

Some time ago, a physician called upon a young man who was ill. He sat for a little while by the bedside, examining his patient, and then he honestly told him the sad intelligence that he had but a very short time to live. The young man was astonished; he did not expect it would come to that so soon. He forgot that death comes "in such an hour as ye think not." At length he looked up into the face of the doctor, and, with a most despairing countenance, repeated the expression, "I have missed it -- at last."

"What have you missed?" inquired the tenderhearted, sympathizing physician.

"I have missed it -- at last," again he repeated.

"Missed what?"

"Doctor, I have missed the salvation of my soul."

"Oh, say not so -- it is not so. Do you remember the thief on the cross?"

"Yes, I remember the thief on the cross. And I remember that he never said to the Holy Ghost, 'Go thy way.' But I did. And now He is saying to me, 'Go your way.'" He lay gasping a while, and looking up with a vacant, starting eye, he said, "I was awakened and was anxious about my soul a little time ago. But I did not want to be saved then. Something seemed to say to me, 'Don't put it off, make sure of salvation.' I said to myself, 'I will postpone it.' I knew I ought not to do it. I knew I was a great sinner, and needed a Savior. I resolved, however, to dismiss the subject for the present. Yet I could not get my own consent to do it until I had promised to take it up again, at a time not remote and more favorable. I bargained away, resisted and insulted the Holy Spirit. I never thought of coming to this. I meant to have made my salvation sure, and now I have missed it -- at last."

"You remember," said the doctor, "that there were some who came at the eleventh hour."

"My eleventh hour," he rejoined, "was when I had that call of the Spirit. I have had none since -- shall not have. I am given over to be lost. Oh! I have missed it! I have sold my soul for nothing -- a feather -- a straw -- undone forever!" This was said with such indescribable despondency, that nothing was said in reply. After lying a few moments, he raised his head, and looking all around the room as if for some desired object, he buried his face in the pillow, and again exclaimed in agony and horror, "Oh! I have missed it at last!" and died.

Reader, you need not miss your salvation, for you may have it now. What you have read is a true story. How earnestly it says to you, "NOW is the accepted time!"

"Today, if ye will hear His voice, harden not your hearts" (Heb. 3: 7, 8). -- The Fire Brand

# 021 -- "VICTORY! TRIUMPH! TRIUMPH!" WERE JOHN S. INSKIP'S LAST WORDS

This great evangelist of full salvation was greatly used in bringing Christians from a life of wandering in the wilderness of doubts and fears to the promised land of perfect rest. For many years he was at the head of the great holiness movement in this country. His biographer says:

"The agents whom God employs for special work, are marked men -- men who seem, by special enduement, to be leaders; and who at once, by their superior adaptation, command public attention and take their place, by general consent, in the front ranks. Such a character was Rev. John S. Inskip."

He was a great sufferer for many weeks before he died. On one occasion Mrs. Inskip said: "My dear, religion was good when you were turned from your father's home; it was good in the midst of labor, trials and misrepresentations; it has been good in the midst of great battles, and when the glorious victory came; does it now hold in the midst of this great suffering?" He pressed her hand, and with uplifted eyes, and a hallowed smile, responded, "Yes, oh yes! I am unspeakably happy." This was followed by "Glory! glory!" During his sickness he requested many of his friends to sing and pray with him. He was "always cheerful and his face radiant with smiles and bright with the light of God. His biographer says:

The last song sung, on the day of his departure, was, "'The Sweet Bye And Bye." While singing that beautiful and appropriate hymn, the dying man pressed his loving wife to his breast, and then, taking her hands in his, raised them up together, and with a countenance beaming with celestial delight, shouted, "Victory! Triumph! Triumph:" These were his last words on earth.

He ceased to breathe at 4 p. m., March 7, 1884 But so peacefully and imperceptibly did he pass away, that those who watched by him could scarcely perceive the moment when he ceased to live. On that day the Christian warrior, the powerful preacher, the tender husband, the world-renowned evangelist, was gathered to his fathers, and rested from his toil. And thou art crowned at last."

The intelligence of his death spread throughout all the land with great rapidity, and though not unexpected, it produced a profound impression upon all. Letters of Christian sympathy for the afflicted widow came pouring in from all parts of the country. The general feeling was, that a great and useful man had fallen -- one whose place in the holiness movement of the country could not easily be filled. -- Life of John S. Inskip

# 022 -- THE WONDERFUL COURAGE OF THE MARTYR PHILIP, BISHOP OF HERACLEA

Philip, bishop of Heraclea, in Asia Minor, who lived in the third century, had in almost every act of his life shown himself to be a good Christian.

An officer, named Aristomachus, being sent to shut up the Christian church in Heraclea, Philip told him that the shutting up of buildings made by hands could not destroy Christianity; for the true faith dwelt not in the places where God is adored, but in the hearts of His people.

Being denied entrance to the church in which he used to preach, Philip took up his station at the door, and there exhorted the people to patience, perseverance and godliness. For this he was seized and carried before the governor, who severely reproved him, and then said: "Bring all the vessels used in your worship, and the Scriptures which you read and teach the people, and surrender them to me, before you are forced to do so by tortures." Philip listened unmoved to this harsh command, and then replied "If you take any pleasure in seeing us suffer, we are prepared for the worst you can do. This infirm body is in your power; use it as you please. The vessels you demand shall be delivered up, for God is not honored by gold and silver, but by faith in His name. As to the sacred books, it is neither proper for me to part with them, nor for you to receive them." This answer so much enraged the governor, that he ordered the venerable bishop to be put to the torture.

The crowd then ran to the place where the Scriptures and the church plate were kept. They broke down the doors, stole the plate, and burned the books; after this they wrecked the church. When Philip was taken to the market-place, he was ordered to sacrifice to the Roman gods. In answer to this command, he made a spirited address on the real nature of the Deity; and said that it appeared that the heathens worshipped that which might lawfully be trodden under foot, and made gods of such things as Providence had designed for their common use. Philip was then dragged by the mob through the streets, severely scourged, and brought again to the governor; who charged him with obstinate rashness, in continuing disobedient to the emperor's command. To this he boldly replied that he thought it wise to prefer heaven to earth, and to obey God rather than man. The governor then sentenced him to be burned, which was done accordingly, and he expired singing praises to God in the midst of the fire. -- Foxes Book, of Martyrs

# 023 -- "I CAN SEE THE OLD DEVIL HERE ON THE BED WITH ME."

There lived at one time in our neighborhood a man whom we will call Mr. B___. He was intelligent, lively, a good conversationalist, and had many friends. But Mr. B loved tobacco and strong drink, and was not friendly to Christianity. He would not attend church and would laugh and make fun of religion, and some of his neighbors he would call Deacon so-and-so for fun.

But Mr. B___ was growing old. His head was frosted over with many winters and he had long since passed his three score and ten years.

At the close of a wintry day, in a blinding snowstorm, a neighbor called at our home saying Mr. B___ wished to see my husband. Knowing Mr. B___ was ill, my husband was soon on his way. On entering the sick room, he asked what he wished of him. He replied, "O, I want you to pray for me." "Shall I not read a chapter from the Bible to you first?" was asked. He assented. The chapter selected was the fifth of St. John. While reading, Mr. B___ would say, "I can see the old devil here on the bed with me, and he takes everything away from me as fast as you read it to me, and there are little ones on each side of me." After reading, prayer was offered for him, and he was told to pray for himself. He said: "I have prayed for two days and nights and can get no answer. I can shed tears over a corpse, but over this Jesus I cannot shed a tear. It is too late, too late! Twenty-five years ago, at a camp-meeting held near my home, was the time that I had ought to have given my heart to Jesus. Oh!" he cried, "see the steam coming up! See the river rising higher and higher! Soon it will be over me and I will be gone."

The room was filled with companions of other days; not a word was spoken by them. Fear seemed to have taken hold of them; and some said after that, "I never believed in a hell before, but I do now. O, how terrible!"

Mr. B___ lived but a short time after this and then died as he had lived, a stranger to Jesus, with no interest in His cleansing blood. -- E. A. Rowes

## 024 -- "GOD HAS CALLED ME TO COME UP HIGHER."

Mrs. Gafford was dying, away from father, mother, brothers and sisters. Not one of her relatives knew of her illness. She mentioned this fact to me, and requested me to tell her people how kind her husband's family had been to her, and that she had had everything that could be done for her. Mrs. Gafford was a noted teacher, and was a graduate from the Normal College, South Nashville. She had been married but two months before her death occurred, which was on the same day that her marriage took place. Mr. Gafford's youngest brother came for me, saying, "Sister Chloe says she is dying and wants to see you." As I entered the room, she said, "Mrs. Moore, God has called me to come home. I have had a happy, beautiful home on this earth, but God has one for me that will last forever." When Bro. Harrel came, she said, "Bro. Harrel, God has called me to come up higher. He says my life's work is done." Bro. Harrel said, "We need you so much here, I am going to ask God to spare you to us." Mrs. Gafford replied, "The Lord's will be done." Bro. Harrel then read to her from the Bible. She commented on each passage, saying, "The Lord has been all this to me." As he read "When thou passest through the waters, I will be with thee; and through the rivers, they shall not overflow thee," she said, "Bro. Harrel, death is the deep waters, God is with me." Then, putting her arms around her mother-in-law's neck, she said, "God has sent me here to die to win you to heaven." She then began to sing "The Unclouded Day" and "Home, Sweet Home"; and soon after left us to live with God. As .Mr. Gafford, her husband's father, had died several years before, they did not know each other on this earth, but I am sure that they have met up yonder. -- Prepared for this book by Mrs. T. C. Moore, White's Bend, Tenn.

## 025 -- CARRIE CARMEN'S VISION OF THE HOLY CITY

When Carrie Carmen, with whom the author was personally acquainted, as pastor, came to the "river's margin," perfectly conscious, she gazed upward, and exclaimed, "Beautiful! beautiful! beautiful"

One asked, "What is so beautiful?"

"Oh, they are so beautiful."

"What do you see?"

"Angels; and they are so beautiful."

"How do they look?"

"Oh, I can't tell you, they are so beautiful."

"Have they wings?"

"Yes; and hark! hark! they sing the sweetest of anything I ever heard."

"Do you see Christ?"

"No; but I see the Holy City that was measured with the reed whose length and breadth and height are equal, and whose top reaches to the skies; and it is so beautiful I can't tell you how splendid it is." Then she repeated the verse beginning "Through the valley of the shadow I must go."

She then spoke of the loneliness of her husband, and prayed that he might have grace to bear his bereavement, and that strength might be given him to go out and labor for souls. (They were expecting soon to enter the ministry.) She also prayed for her parents, asking that they might make an unbroken band in the beautiful city. She closed her eyes and rested a moment, and then looked up with beaming eyes and said: "I see Christ, and oh, He is so beautiful."

Her husband asked again, "How does He look?"

"I can't tell you; but He is so much more beautiful than all me rest." Again she said, "I see the Holy City." Then, gazing a moment, she said, "So many!"

"What do you see, of which there are so many?"

"People."

"How many are there?"

"A great many; more than I can count."

"Any you know?"

"Yes, a great many."

"Who?"

"Uncle George and a lot more. They are calling me. They are beckoning to me."

"Is there any river there?"

"No; I don't see any."

Her husband then said, "Carrie, do you want to go and leave me?"

"No; not until it is the Lord's will that I should go. I would like to stay and live for you and God's work. His will be done." Presently she lifted her eyes and said, "Oh, carry me off from this bed."

Her husband said, "She wants to be removed from the bed." But his father said, "She is talking with the angels."

When asked if she were, she replied, "Yes." She then thanked the doctor for his kindness to her, and asked him to meet her in heaven. She closed her eyes, and seemed to be rapidly sinking away.

Her husband kissed her and said, "Carrie, can't you kiss me?"

She opened her eyes and kissed him, and said: "Yes; I can come back to kiss you. I was part way over." She said but little more, but prayed for herself and for her friends. Frequently she would gaze upward and smile, as though the sights were very beautiful." -- Christ Crowned Within

## *026 -- THE AWFUL END OF A BACKSLIDER*

The following is a short account of the life and death of William Pope, of Bolton, in Lancashire. He was at one time a member of the Methodist Society, and was a saved and happy man. His wife, a devoted saint, died triumphantly. After her death his zeal for religion declined, and by associating with back-slidden professors he entered the path of ruin. His companions even professed to believe in the redemption of devils. William became an admirer of their scheme, a frequenter with them of the public-house, and in time a common drunkard.

He finally became a disciple of Thomas Paine, and associated himself with a number of deistical persons at Bolton, who assembled together on Sundays to confirm each other in their infidelity. They amused themselves with throwing the Word of God on the floor, kicking it around the room, and treading it under their feet. God laid His hand on this man's body, and he was seized with consumption.

Mr. Rhodes was requested to visit William Pope. He says: "When I first saw him he said to me, 'Last night I believe I was in hell, and felt the horrors and torment of the dammed; but God has brought me back again, and given me a little longer respite. The gloom of guilty terror does not sit so heavy upon me as it did, and I have something like a faint hope that, after all I have done, God may yet save me.' After exhorting him to repentance and confidence in the Almighty Savior, I prayed with him and left him. In the evening he sent for me again. I found him in the utmost distress, overwhelmed with bitter anguish and despair. I endeavored to encourage him. I spoke of the infinite merit of the great Redeemer, and mentioned several cases in which God had saved the greatest sinners, but he answered, 'No case of any that has been mentioned is comparable to mine. I have no contrition; I cannot repent. God will damn me: I know the day of grace is lost. God has said of such as are in my case, "I will laugh at your calamity, and mock when your fear cometh,"'

I said, 'Have you ever known anything of the mercy and love of God?' 'Oh, yes,' he replied; 'many years ago I truly repented and sought the Lord and found peace and happiness.' I prayed with him after exhorting him to seek the Lord, and had great hopes of his salvation; he appeared much affected, and begged I would represent his case in our Society and pray for him. I did so that evening, and many hearty petitions were put up for him."

Mr. Barraclough gives the following account of what he witnessed. He says: "I went to see William Pope, and as soon as he saw me he exclaimed, 'You are come to see one who is damned forever!' I answered, 'I hope not; Christ can save the chief of sinners.' He replied, 'I have denied Him, I have denied Him; therefore hath He cast me off forever! I know the day of grace is past, gone -- gone, never more to return!' I entreated him not to be too hasty, and to pray. He answered, 'I cannot pray; my heart is quite hardened, I have no desire to receive any blessing at the hand of God,' and then cried out, 'Oh, the hell, the torment, the fire that I feel within reel Oh, eternity.' eternity! To dwell forever with devils and damned spirits in the burning lake must be my portion, and that justly!'

On Thursday I found him groaning under the weight of the displeasure of God. His eyes roiled to and fro; he lifted up his hands, and with vehemence cried out, 'Oh, the burning flame, the hell, the pain I feel! I have done, done the deed, the horrible, damnable deed!' I prayed with him, and while I was praying he said with inexpressible rage, 'I will not have salvation at the hand of God! No, no! I will not ask it of Him.'

After a short pause, he cried out, 'Oh, how I long to be in the bottomless pit -- in the lake which burneth with fire and brimstone!' The day following I saw him again. I said, 'William, your pain is inexpressible.' He groaned, and with a loud voice cried out, 'Eternity will explain my torments. I tell you again, I am damned. I will not have salvation.' He called me to him as if to speak to me, but as soon as I came within his reach he struck me on the head with all his might, and gnashing his teeth, cried out, 'God will not hear your prayers.'

At another time he said, 'I have crucified the Son of God afresh, and counted the blood of the covenant an unholy thing! Oh, that wicked and horrible deed of blaspheming against the Holy Ghost! which I know I have committed!' He was often heard to exclaim, 'I want nothing but hell! Come, O devil, and take me!' At another time he said, 'Oh, what a terrible thing it is! Once I might, and would not: now I would and must not.' He declared that he was best satisfied when cursing. The day he died, when Mr. Rhodes visited him, and asked the privilege to pray once more with him, he cried out with great strength, considering his weakness, 'No!' and passed away in the evening without God."

Backslider, do you know you are in danger of the fires of hell? Do you know you are fast approaching the

*"Line by us unseen*
*That crosses every path,*
*That marks the boundary between*
*God's mercy and His wrath."*

You are, and unless you turn quickly, you with William Pope will be writhing in hell through all eternity. God says, "The backslider in heart shall be filled with his own ways." But He says again, "Return, ye backsliding children, and I will heal your backslidings." Oh, come back and be healed before God shall say of you, "He is joined to his idols, let him alone." -- Remarkable Narratives

## *027 -- THE ADVICE OF ETHAN ALLEN, THE NOTED INFIDEL, TO HIS DYING DAUGHTER*

Though the following biographic note may be familiar to some, it may yet be useful to many. Ethan Allen was a professed infidel. He wrote a book against the divinity of our blessed Lord. His wife was a Christian, earnest, cheerful and devoted. She died early, leaving an only daughter behind, who became the idol of her father. She was a fragile, sensitive child, and entwined herself about the rugged nature of her sire, as the vine entwines itself about the knotty and gnarled limbs of the oak. Consumption marked this fair girl for its own; and she wasted away day by day, until even the grasshopper became a burden.

One day her father came into her room and sat down by her bedside. He took her wan, ethereal hand in his. Looking her father squarely in the face, she said:

"My dear father, I'm going to die." "Oh! no, my child! Oh! no. The spring is coming and with the birds and breezes and the bloom, your pale cheeks will blush with health." "No; the doctor was here today. I felt I was nearing the grave, and I asked him to tell me plainly what I had to expect. I told him that it was a great thing to exchange worlds; that I did not wish to be deceived about myself, and if I was going to die I had some preparations I wanted to make. He told me my disease was beyond human skill; that a few more suns would rise and set, and then I would be borne to my burial. You will bury me, father, by the side of my mother, for that was her dying request. But father, you and mother did not agree on religion. Mother often spoke to me of the blessed Savior who died for us all. She used to pray for both you and me, that the Savior might be our friend, and that we might all see Him as our Savior, when He sits enthroned in His glory. I don't feel that Z can go alone through the dark valley of the shadow of death. Now, tell me, father, whom shall I follow, you or mother? Shall I reject Christ, as you have taught me, or shall I accept Him, as He was my mother's friend in the hour of her great sorrow?"

There was an honest heart beneath that rough exterior. Though tears nearly choked his utterance, the old soldier said:

"My child, cling to your mother's Savior; she was right. I'll try to follow you to that blessed abode."

A serene smile over-spread the face of the dying girl, and who can doubt there is an unbroken family in heaven.

## 028 -- "MA, I SHALL BE THE FIRST OF OUR FAMILY OVER YONDER."

Asa Hart Alling, eldest son of Rev. J. H. and Jennie E. Alling, of Rock River Conference, was born Dec. 20, 1866, in Newark, Kendall County, Ill.; and died in Chicago, April 19, 1881. He was converted and united with the church at Morris when eleven. His conversion was clear and well defined, and his Christian life eminently satisfactory. He was regularly present at worship, and frequently took part. He would invariably close his prayer by asking the Lord to keep him "from bad boys." He assisted cheerfully in the fulfillment of his own prayer, and made choice of the more noble youths of his own age. And while most boys were devoting their spare time to fun and rude sport, he was applying himself to works of benevolence and humanity, and numbers of aged and infirm people living near Simpson church will bear record of the good deeds by his youthful hands. In the public school he took high rank, and led his classmates. For his years he was well advanced. Friday, April 15, he complained of being ill, but insisted upon going to school. He returned in distress, took to his bed, and did not leave it. He was smitten with cerebro-spinal meningitis, and was at times in agony. Through it all he proved himself a hero and a Christian conqueror. Be realized that his sickness would terminate fatally, and talked about death with composure.

He put his arms about his mother's neck, and gently drawing her face close to his own, said, "Ma, I shall be the first of our family over yonder, but I will stand on the shore and wait for you all to come." He requested his mother to sing for him, "Pull for the shore." She being completely overcome with grief could not sing. He said, "Never mind, ma; you will sing it after I am gone, won't you?" To a Christian lady who came to see him, he said, "You sing for me. Sing 'Hold the fort:'" She sang it. "Now sing 'Hallelujah: 'Tis done.'" He fully realized that the work of his salvation was done, and he was holding the fort till he should be called up higher. He bestowed his treasures upon his brother and sisters. He gave his Bible to his brother Treat; and as he did so said to his father, "Pa, tell aunty, who gave me this Bible, that I died a Christian." His last hours of consciousness were rapidly closing. He remarked, "Ma, I shall not live till morning; I am so tired, and will go to sleep. If I do not wake up, good-bye; good-bye all." A short time afterward he fell asleep. He was not, for God had taken him. He had reached the shores of eternal life for which he had pulled so earnestly and with success. His funeral was attended by a large concourse of people, who thronged the church. The services were conducted by several of the Chicago pastors, and were very impressive and instructive. We all felt as if we had lost a treasure, and heaven had gained a jewel. -- G. A. Vanhorne

## *029 -- "TAKE THEM AWAY -- TAKE THEM AWAY."*

"Some years ago a neighboring family, consisting of father, mother, and five or six children that God had entrusted to their care, were all seemingly without a thought of eternity -- all for the world and the things of the world. But soon the dark shadows began to gather. The father was taken sick. He grew worse and worse and soon it was said that he was seriously ill. In a few short days the message came to me saying, "Come quick, Mr. S. is dying." I went immediately to his bedside, and found him talking and trying to draw back from some apparition that he evidently saw, saying, "Take them away! Take them away!" It seemed to be the demons or the wicked spirits tormenting him while yet alive."

The above was recently sent us for publication by Mrs. M. E. Holland, Bentonville, Ark. May God help all our readers, if not already free from evil spirits, to call on God to take them away at once -- not wait until they are called to die. The time to get rid of the devil is when he first makes his appearance, or when the soul becomes conscious of his presence. May God help our readers to realize that "The Lord knoweth how to deliver the godly out of temptation." "Now all these things happened unto them for ensamples: and they are written for our admonition, upon whom the ends of the world are come. Wherefore let him that thinketh he standeth take heed lest he fall. There hath no temptation taken you but such as is common to man: but God is faithful, who will not suffer you to be tempted above that ye are able; but will with the temptation also make a way of escape, that ye may be able to bear it. Wherefore, my dearly beloved, flee from idolatry. I speak as to wise men; judge ye what I say" (1 Cor. 10: 11-12).

## *030 -- A DYING MAN'S REGRETS*

A minister once said to a dying man, "If God should restore you to health, think you that you would alter your course of life?" He answered: "I call heaven and earth to witness, I would labor for holiness as I shall soon labor for life. As for riches and pleasure and the applause of men, I account them as dross. Oh! if the righteous Judge would but reprieve and spare .he a little longer, in what spirit would I spend the remainder of my days! I would know no other business, aim at no other end, than perfecting myself in holiness. Whatever contributed to that -- every means of grace, every opportunity of spiritual improvement, should be dearer to me than thousands of gold and silver. But, alas! why do I amuse myself with fond imaginations? The best resolutions are now insignificant, because they are too late."

Such was the language of deep concern uttered by one who was beginning to look at these things in the light of the eternal world, which, after all, is the true light. Here we stand on the little molehills of sublunary life, where we cannot get a clear view of that other world; but, oh! what must it be to stand on the top of the dark mountain of death, and take an outlook upon our surroundings, knowing that from the top of that mountain, if angel pinions do not lift us to the skies, we must take a leap into the blackness of darkness!

Reader, when your soul shall pass into eternity, is it an angel or a fiend that shall greet you on your entrance there? if you want a well-grounded hope of heaven, live for it! live for it! -- The Manna.

## *031 -- THE TRANSLATION OF THE SAINTED FRANCES E. WILLARD*

Early on February 17, the last day God let us have her with us, she remembered it was time for her "letter from home," as she loved to call our official paper, The Union Signal, and sweetly said, "Please let me sit up and let me have our beautiful Signal." She was soon laid back upon her pillows, when, taking Dr. Hills' hand in hers, she spoke tender, appreciative words about her friend and physician, of which the last were these, "I say, God bless him; I shall remember his loving kindness through all eternity."

A little later Mrs. Hoffman, National Recording Secretary of our society, entered the room for a moment. Miss Willard seemed to be unconscious, but as Mrs. Hoffman quietly took her hand she looked up and said, "Why, that's Clara; good Clara; Clara, I've crept in with mother, and it's the same beautiful world and the same people, remember that -- it's just the same."

"Has my cable come?" she soon asked; "Oh, how I want to come": and when, a few moments later, a message of tenderest solicitude and love was received from dear Lady Henry, I placed it in her hand. "Read it, oh read it quickly -- what does it say?" were her eager questions, and as I read the precious words I heard her voice, "Oh, how sweet, oh, how lovely, good -- good!"

Quietly as a babe. in its mother's arms she now fell asleep, and though we knew it not "the dew of eternity was soon to fall upon her forehead." "She had come to the borderland of this closely curtained world."

Only once again did she speak to us, when about noon the little thin, white hand- that active, eloquent hand -- was raised in an effort to point upward, and we listened for the last time on earth to the voice that to thousands has surpassed all others in its marvellous sweetness and magnetic power, it was like the lovely and pathetic strain from an Aeolian harp on which heavenly zephyrs were breathing, and she must even then have caught some glimpse of those other worlds for which she longed as she said, in tones of utmost content, "How beautiful it is to be with God."

As twilight fell, hope died in our yearning heart, for we saw that the full glory of another life was soon to break o'er our loved one's "earthly horizon." Kneeling about her bed, with the faithful nurses who had come to love their patient as a sister, we silently watched while the life immortal, the life more abundant, came in its fullness to this inclusive soul, whose wish, cherished from her youth, that she might go, not like a peasant to a palace, but as a child to her Father's home, was about to be fulfilled. A few friends who had come to the hotel to make inquiries joined the silent and grief-stricken group. Slowly the hours passed with no recognition of the loved ones about her. There came an intent upward gaze of the heavenly blue eyes, a few tired sighs, and at the "noon hour" of the night Frances Willard was

"Born into beauty
And born into bloom,
Victor immortal
O'er death and the tomb."

-- The Beautiful Life of Frances E. Willard

## 032 -- "IT IS EASIER TO GET INTO HELL THAN IT WILL BE TO GET OUT."

In the village of Montgomery, Mich., in the spring of 1884, an infidel, husband of a spiritualist, was stricken down with disease. He had such a hatred for the cause of Christ that he had requested previous to his death that his body should not be 'carried to a church for funeral services, or any pastor be called upon to officiate. As he was nearing the shores of eternity, he turned his face toward the wall and began to talk of his future prospects. His wife saw that he was troubled in spirit and endeavored to comfort and console him by telling him not to be afraid; that his spirit would return to her and they would commune together then as now. But this gave him no comfort in this awful hour. With a look of despair, he said, "I see a great high wall rising around me, and am finding out at last, when it is too late, that it is easier to get into hell than it will be to get out," and in a few moments his spirit had departed from this world to receive its reward. My sister-in-law was present at the time and heard the conversation. -- Written for this book by Rev.

W. C. Muffit, Cleveland, Ohio.

## 033 -- THE BELOVED PHYSICIAN WALTER C. PALMER'S SUNLIT JOURNEY TO HEAVEN

His biographer, Rev. George Hughes, says: At 5:15 p. m., July 20, 1883, his ransomed spirit entered the triumphal chariot and, under a bright angelic escort, sped away to the world of light and blessedness. There was no dark river to cross -- no stormy billows to intercept his progress. It was a translation from the terrestrial to the celestial -- the work of a moment, but covered with eternal resplendency. Heaven's pearly gates were surely opened wide to admit this battle-scarred veteran, laden with the spoils and honors of a thousand battles. The light of a conqueror was in his eye. His countenance was radiant. His language was triumphant. The angelic escort was near.

The expanded vision was rapturously fixed on immortal objects and scene. The ear was saluted with the songs of angels and redeemed spirits. The blood-washed soul was filled with high expectancy. Every avenue of the inner being was swept with rapture. Hallelujahs burst momentarily from his lips. The aspects of such a departure were gorgeous indeed -- no other word will express it. The splendors of the eternal state were gathered to a focus, and burned intensely around the couch of the Christian warrior as he breathed his earthly farewell. Such a departure was the allotment of the beloved physician.

The place designated was wondrously attractive. A few steps only from his cottage-home, the grand old ocean was ceaselessly rolling his billows upon the strand, making solemn music, offering a deep-toned anthem of praise to the Creator. The clear blue heavens above were resplendent. The sun was declining, but glorious in his decline.

But the moral surroundings of the period set for this departure were still more gorgeous. Not far away was the hallowed grove, the place of holy song and Gospel ministration, where multitudes congregated. And there, too, the "Janes Tabernacle," where such indescribable triumphs had been won. "The voice of salvation and rejoicing was in the tabernacles of the righteous." Even now we seem to hear the forest resounding with prayer and praise. Surely holy angels must have delighted to hover o'er the scene, glad to join the hallowed songs.

And what is that we see? In yonder cottage there is one newly born into the kingdom of heaven. The first song of the new life is breaking upon the ears of surrounding friends, Hallelujahs rule the hour.
In a little tent there is a child of God who has just entered "Beulah Land!" He is inhaling its pure atmosphere. The fragrance of the land delights him. He is basking in the meridian rays of the "Sun of righteousness." What a heavenly glow there is upon his countenance! How the Beulah-notes burst from his lips!

Hark! yonder is the shout of victory! What does it mean? Ah, one of God's dear saints has been sorely buffeted of Satan; but "Strong in the strength which God supplies Through His eternal Son," she has just said, authoritatively, in overcoming faith, "Get thee behind me, Satan!" And, lo! the enemy is discomfited -- he flies ingloriously from the field! Jesus, in the person of His tempted one, has driven the arch-foe to his native hell.

And so we might go on in this field survey. At each step new wonders would rise upon our view. Heaven and earth were surely keeping jubilee in the sacred inclosure.

Can we conceive of a grander spot, in either hemisphere, from which a good man might make his transition from world to world? Nay! Is it not written, "My times are in Thy hand"? And are not the places too at the Divine disposal? Did not Jehovah conduct (Moses) His servant of old to the Mount of transition, and Himself perform the funeral-rites and interment? And so secure, so hidden from the rude gaze of men the entombment, that the ages have not discovered the burial-place.

Is it too much to think that the God of glory put forth His hand to designate the place, so full of natural and moral attractions, for the departure of His honored servant, Dr. Palmer. And then what a quiet hour -- just as the sun was declining and the soft evening shades were being stretched forth! What an evening, after such a day!

All day long the beloved one had been quietly reclining upon his couch. The tokens of his convalescence were cheering. A new light had been given to his languid eye. A radiant smile illumined his whole countenance. Inspiring words dropped from his lips. Loving friends, who had kept sleepless vigils around him, rejoiced with great joy.

The day had been a festive one. The table of the Lord had been spread before him, and he had feasted upon its dainties. At the foot of his couch had been suspended "The Silent Comforter" (meaning perhaps, the Bible, or some publication containing God's promises) -- silent, yet voiceful, telling of the riches of the kingdom of heaven.

It was open at the passage for the day, reading thus:

"But now thus saith the Lord that created thee, O Jacob, and He that formed thee, O Israel, Fear not: for I have redeemed thee, I have called thee by thy name; thou art mine.
"When thou passest through the waters, I will be with thee: and through the rivers, they shall not overflow thee -- When thou walkest through the fire, thou shalt not be burned; neither shall the flame kindle upon thee. For I am the Lord thy God, the Holy One of Israel, thy Savior" (Isaiah 43: 1-3).

What beautiful words -- beautiful words of life! His eye and his heart drank in the Father's message -- a message of perfected redemption -- of joyous adoption into the royal family, and the conferment of a royal name -- of defense against destroying forces, the overflowing waters and the consuming flame -- of exalted spiritual relationship, "I am thy God, thy Savior." O, wondrous message spoken by Isaiah's fire-touched lips! Well might that prostrate one rise into new life as he gazed upon the glittering pages. Indeed, he had during the weeks of his suffering taken refuge in the precious Word, so that the wicked one had not dared to approach him!

About two weeks before his release from earth, Mrs. Palmer said to him, "My dear, Satan has not troubled you much of late." Raising his arm, with emphatic voice he exclaimed, "No! he has not been allowed to come near me!"

So now, he was sweetly reposing in the Divine Word as opened to his view on the page of the "Silent Comforter."

So strong was the doctor's returning pulse that those who were performing tender ministries were encouraged to have him attired and seated in an easy chair where he could look upon the ocean and be invigorated by its breezes. Indeed, he walked out and took his seat on the upper piazza. The beloved of his life was by his side, and in a letter written to a friend subsequent to the departure of her dear husband, beautifully describes what transpired at this particular juncture:

"About three in the afternoon, he walked out on the second-story balcony, sat there a half-hour or more, and seemed unusually joyous. He talked of the beautiful landscape before him, and the grand old ocean. Seeing our dear friend Mr. Thornley, who had so kindly relieved us of the care of the morning meetings, come out of his cottage on the opposite side of the park, in front of our summer cottage, our loved one waved his hand again and again, with smiles of affectionate recognition. He then went into the room and wrote a business letter to his son-in-law, Joseph F. Knapp, and read it to me in a strong voice, and conversed freely.

"About five o'clock he proposed lying down to rest. His head had scarcely reached the pillow, when I was startled by seeing those large blue eyes open wide, as if piercing the heavens. Two or three struggles, as if for breath, followed. "Raise me higher," he said, as I put my arm about him, holding him up. A moment's calm ensued, I said, "Precious darling, it's passing over." The dear one, putting his finger on his own pulse, looking so sweetly, said in a low tone, "Not yet" -- and almost in the same breath, in a clear, strong voice, said, "I fear no evil, for Thou art with me." After a moment's pause, he continued, "I have redeemed thee; thou art mine. When thou pass -- "Here his loved voice failed. The precious spirit was released to join the glorified above."

## 034 -- "GOOD-BY! I AM GOING TO REST."

Through the kindness of T. L. Adams, of Magdalena, New Mexico, we furnish our readers with this incident: In the year 188-, in Milan, Tenn., Ella Bledsoe, daughter of Dr. Bledsoe, lay dying from a painful, wasting flux. Being near neighbors, Ella and my sister had been together much of the time, and from close association had learned to love each other very tenderly.

Ella had now been ill for about nine days. Her Christian father had heretofore kept her under the influence of opiates to ease her pain, but not willing that she should pass out of this world stupefied by these drugs, he had ceased to administer them.

When sister Dorrie and I heard that Ella was dying we at once prayed to God that she might not pass away without leaving a dying testimony. She was a Christian, a member of the C. P. Church, as was also her father. We hastened to her bedside and found her tossing from side to side on her dying couch in the painful agonies of the "last enemy."

My sister approached her, and sitting on the side of the bed, she took one of her hands in her own, and said, "Ella, are you afraid to die?" It seemed for a moment all that life offers to a young girl rushed in before her youthful gaze, and she replied, "I hate to die." Then turning, like Hezekiah, with her face to the wall for a few moments, doubtless in communion with her Heavenly Father, she turned back and said to sister, "Good-bye; I am going to rest," and extending her hand to me she said, "Good-bye. Meet me at rest."

She then called her family up to her. bedside, one by one, and kissed them and bade them "good-bye," requesting and exhorting them to meet her

"Where the weary are at rest."

This was an affecting scene, one that impressed al.' that were present with the reality of the joys of the Christian religion, and that when all things around us fade away, this religion enables us to rejoice even in the face of death. Thank God! "The wicked is driven away in his wickedness: but the righteous hath hope in his death" (Prov. 14: 32). "For we know, that if our earthly house of this tabernacle were dissolved, we have a building of God, an house not made with hands, eternal in the heavens" (2 Cor. 5:1). "And I heard a voice from heaven, saying unto me, Write, Blessed are the dead which die in the Lord from henceforth; Yea, saith the Spirit. that they may rest from their labors; and their works do follow them" (Rev. 14:13).

## 035 -- "THE FIENDS, THEY COME; OH! SAVE ME! THEY DRAG ME DOWN! LOST, LOST, LOST!"

The following incident is concerning a young lady, who, under deep conviction for sin, left a revival meeting to attend a dance which had been gotten up by a party of ungodly men, for the purpose of breaking up the meeting. She caught a severe cold at the dance and was soon on her death bed. In conversation with a minister, she said, "Mr. Rice, my mind was never clearer. I tell you all today that I do not wish to be a Christian. Don't want to go to heaven -- would not if I could. I would rather go to hell than heaven, they need not keep the gates closed." "But you don't want to go to hell, do you Jennie?" was asked. She replied, "No, Mr. Rice. O, that I had never been born. I am suffering now the agonies of the lost. If I could but get away from God; but no, I must always see Him and be looked upon by Him. How I hate Him -- I cannot help it. I drove His Spirit from my heart when He would have filled it with His love; and now I am left to my own evil nature -- given over to the devil for my eternal destruction. My agony is inexpressible! How will I endure the endless ages of eternity? O, that dreadful, unlimited, unfathomable eternity." When asked by Mr. Rice how she got into that despairing mood, she replied, "It was that fatal Friday evening last winter when I deliberately stayed away from the meeting to attend the dance. I felt so sad, for my heart was tender -- I could scarcely keep from weeping. I felt provoked to think that my last dance, as I felt it to be for some cause, should be spoiled. I endured it until I became angry, then with all my might I drove the influence of the Spirit away from me, and it was then that I had the feeling that Be had left me forever. I knew that I had done something terrible, but it was done. From that time I have had no desire to be a Christian, but have been sinking down into deeper darkness and more bitter despair. And now all around, and above and beneath me are impenetrable clouds of darkness. O, the terrible gloom; when will it cease?" She then sank away and lay like one dead a short time. But she raised her hand slightly, her lips quivering as if in the agonies of death, her eyes opened with a fixed and awful stare, and then gave such a despairing groan that sent the chill blood to every heart. "Oh, what horror," whispered the sufferer. Then turning to Mr. Rice, she said, "Go home now and return this evening. I don't want you to pray for me. I don't want to be tormented with the sound of prayer." About four o'clock she inquired the time, and upon being told exclaimed, "O, how slowly the hours wear away. This day seems an age to me. O, how will I endure eternity?" In about an hour she said, "How slowly the time drags. Why may I not cease to be?" About seven P. M. she sent for Mr. Rice. As he approached her bed Jennie said to him, "I want you to preach at my funeral. Warn all of my young friends against the ball-room. Remember everything I have said and use it." He replied, "How can I do this? Jennie, how I do wish you were a good Christian, and had a hope of eternal life."! 'Now, Mr. Rice, I don't want to hear anything about that. I do not want to be tormented with the thought. I am utterly hopeless; my time is growing short; my fate is eternally fixed/ I die without hope because I insulted the Holy Spirit so bitterly. He has justly left me alone to go down to eternal night. He could not have borne with me any longer and followed farther and retained His divine honor and dignity. I wait but a few moments, and as much as I dread it, I must quit these mortal shores. I would delay, I would linger -- but no! The fiends, they come; O save me! They drag me down! Lost! lost! lost!" she whispered as she struggled in the agonies of death. A moment more and she rallied and with glazed eyes she looked upon her weeping friends for the last time, then the lids sank partly down and pressed out a remaining tear as she whispered, "Bind me, ye chains of darkness! Oh! that I might cease to be, but still exist. The worm that never dies, the second death." The spirit fled, and Jennie Gordon lay a lifeless form of clay. -- The Unequal Yoke, by J. H. Miller

## *036 -- "OH, PAPA, WHAT A SWEET SIGHT! THE GOLDEN GATES ARE OPENED."*

Through the kindness of L. B. Balliett, M. D., we furnish our readers with this touching incident: Lillian Lee, aged ten, when dying spoke to her father thus: "Oh! papa, what a sweet sight! The golden gates are opened and crowds of children come pouring out. Oh! such crowds. And they ran up to me and began to kiss me and call me by a new name. I can't remember what it was." She lay and looked upwards, her eyes dreaming. Her voice died into a whisper as she said, "Yes, yes, I come, I come!"

## *037 -- "I AM GOING TO DIE. GLORY BE TO GOD AND THE LAMB FOREVER."*

These were the last words of the sainted Ann Cutler, one of Mr. Wesley's workers in whom he had great confidence. She was converted under Rev. Wm. Bramwell, who wrote the following account:

Ann Cutler was born near Preston, in Lancashire, in the year 1759. Till she was about twenty-six years of age, though she was very strict in her morals and serious in her deportment, yet she never understood the method of salvation by Jesus Christ till the Methodist local preachers visited that neighborhood. After hearing one of them she was convinced of sin, and from that time gave all diligence to obtain mercy. In a short time she received pardon, and her serious deportment evinced the blessing she enjoyed. It was not long before she had a clearer sight into her own heart; and, though she retained her confidence of pardon, she was yet made deeply sensible of the need of perfect love. In hearing the doctrine of sanctification, and believing that the blessing is to be received through faith, she expected instantaneous deliverance, and prayed for the power to believe. Her confidence increased until she could say, "Jesus, thou wilt cleanse me from all unrighteousness!"

In the same year of her finding mercy (1785) the Lord said, "I will; be thou clean." She found a sinking into humility, love and dependence upon God. At this time her language was, "Jesus, Thou knowest I love Thee with all my heart. I would rather die than grieve Thy Spirit. O! I cannot express how much I love Jesus!" After this change something remarkable appeared in her countenance -- a smile of sweet composure. It was noticed by many as a reflection of the divine nature, and it increased to the time of her death. In a few months she felt a great desire for the salvation of sinners, and often wept much in private; and, at the same time, was drawn out to plead with God for the world in general She would frequently say, "I think I must pray. I cannot be happy unless I cry for sinners. I do not want any praise, i want nothing but souls to be brought to God. I am reproached by most. I cannot do it to be seen or heard of men. I see the world going to destruction; and I am burdened till I pour out my soul to God for them."

Her great devotion to God is shown in the following account of her sickness and death by Mrs. Highfield:

I will endeavor to give you a few particulars relative to the death of Ann Cutler. I would have done it sooner had not the affliction of my family prevented. While she was with us, it seemed to be her daily custom to dedicate herself, body and soul, to God.

She came to Macclesfield, very poorly of a cold, on the fifteenth of December. Being our preaching night, she had an earnest desire to have a prayer-meeting; but I told her on account of preaching being so late as eight o'clock, and the classes having to meet after, it would not be convenient. But she was very importunate, and said she could not be happy without one; adding, "I shall not be long here, and I would buy up every opportunity of doing something for God, for time is short." Knowing she had an uncommon talent for pleading for such souls as were coming to God, we got a few together, to whom she was made a blessing. A few days before her death, she often said, "Jesus is about to take me home. I think I shall soon have done with this body of clay; and O how happy shall I then be when I cast my crown before Him, lost in wonder, love and praise!" About three o'clock on Monday morning (the day of her death) she began to ascribe glory to the ever-blessed Trinity, and continued saying, "Glory be to the Father, glory be to the Son, and glory be to the Holy Ghost," for a considerable time. About seven o'clock the doctor, with those about her, thought she was just gone; but, to our great surprise she continued in this state till between ten and eleven o'clock in the forenoon. She then lifted herself up and looked about her, and spoke just so as to be heard, and was very sensible; she seemed perfectly composed, but her strength nearly gone. About three o'clock she looked at her friends and said, "I am going to die"; and added, "Glory be to God and the Lamb forever!" These were her last words. Soon afterwards the spirit left this vale of misery. So died our dear and much-valued friend, Ann Cutler.

## 038 -- "I HAVE TREATED CHRIST LIKE A DOG ALL MY LIFE AND HE WILL NOT HELP ME NOW."

About twenty years ago, when we were holding revival meetings at G___, Mr. B___, a well-to-do farmer living near the town, was in the last stages of consumption. He was a wicked man; all of his life having been spent in laying up treasures on earth. At the time we visited him, he was about sixty years old. The pastor of the Methodist church, whom we were assisting, had not as yet called on him because he was so ungodly. The pastor said to me one day, "I am waiting until Mr. B___ is near his end, hoping he will then allow me to talk to him about his soul."

Several days before Mr. B___'s death, in company with the pastor of the Methodist church, we visited this man and talked with him about his moral condition. His mind was very dark and full of unbelief. We talked earnestly with him about the saving of his soul, but left him without receiving much encouragement.

In a day or two we called on him again and found him more willing to converse, but he still seemed to be fur away from God. We plead with him and urged him to call on God to have mercy on him for Jesus' sake.

"I cannot: I have never spoken the name of Jesus, only when using it in profanity, and I have used it that way all of these years. I have treated Christ like a dog all of my life and He will not hear me now. I would give all I am worth if I could only feel as you say you feel." was his reply.

We told him that God was no respecter of persons, that He never turned any away that came to Him for pardon. He continued, "I cannot get any feeling. What can 1 do? My heart is so hard." Our heart ached for him. He was afraid to die without faith in God, but he seemed to have no ability to repent.

Before we left the town, he went to meet his God, so far as we know, unprepared, as he gave no evidence of salvation. He had treasures on earth; but, alas, that did not avail him anything when he came to face eternity.

Reader, how are you treating the Christ on whom you must depend if you are ever saved? God grant that your experience may not be like his. Editor.

## 039 -- "JESUS WILL TAKE CARE OF ME."

These were the last words uttered by Ella Gilkey, as she passed away from earth to live with Him who said, "Suffer little children, and forbid them not, to come unto me; for of such is the kingdom of heaven."

In the winter of 1860-61 I was holding a series of meetings in Watertown, Mass., during which a large number found Jesus precious -- many believing they found Him in my room; thus rendering that room ever memorable and dear to me.

Among those who there gave themselves to the Savior was Ella. Coming in one morning, with tears on her face, she said, "Mr. Earle, I came up here to give my heart to Jesus. I feel that I am a great sinner. Will you pray for me?" I replied, "I will pray for your Ella, and I can pray in faith if you see that you are a sinner; for Jesus died for sinners."

After pointing out the way of salvation I asked her if she would kneel down by my side and pray for herself, and, as far as she knew, give herself to Jesus, to be His forever. She said, "I will; for I am a great sinner."

Could one so young, and kind to everybody, be a great sinner? Yes, because she had rejected the Savior until she was twelve years old; and when the Holy Spirit had knocked at the door of her heart, she had said, '.'No, not yet. Go Thy way for this time."

We kneeled down, and after I had prayed, she said, "Jesus, take me just as I am. I give myself to Thee forever. I will love and serve Thee all my life."

The door of her heart was now open and Jesus entered and took possession. The tears were gone from her face, which was now covered with smiles.

And I believe holy angels in that room witnessed the transfer of her heart to Jesus, and then went back to heaven to join in songs of thanksgiving; for "joy shall be in heaven over one sinner that repenteth."

Ella then went down stairs, her face beaming with joy as she thought of her new relation to Jesus, and said to her mother, "I have given myself to Jesus, and He has received me. O, I am so happy!"

Little did we think that in a few days she would be walking the "golden streets" with the blood-washed throng.

Like the Redeemer, who, when at her age, said to His mother, "Wist ye not that I must be about My Father's business?" she seemed to long to be doing good.

" 'What can I do for Christ,' she said,
'Who gave His life to ransom me
I'll take my cross, and by Him led,
His humble, faithful child will be.' "

Among other subjects of prayer there was one which particularly weighed upon her heart; it was for the conversion of an older brother. One day, after earnestly praying that this dear brother might be led to accept the Savior, she said to her mother, "O, I think he will be a Christian!" At another time she said, "I would be willing to die if it would bring him to Jesus."

Could she speak from her bright home above, I believe she would say to this brother, and to all who are delaying,

*"Delay not, delay not: why longer abuse
The love and compassion of Jesus, thy God
A fountain is opened: how canst thou refuse
To wash and be cleansed in His pardoning blood?"*

Anxious to obey her Savior in all things, she obtained permission from her parents to present herself to the church for baptism; and, in the absence of a pastor, I baptized her, with several others, a few weeks after her conversion.

The next Tuesday after her baptism she was present at our evening meeting and gave her last public testimony for Jesus. When an opportunity was given for any one to speak, Ella arose, and, turning to the congregation, said, in a clear, earnest tone, "If there are any here who have not given their hearts to Jesus, do it now."

As I sat in my room at her father's that night, after meeting, I heard her voice mingling with his, in songs of praise, until near the midnight hour. Less than three days after this, Ella was called away from us, to sing in heaven the song of Moses and the Lamb.

As death drew near, she said to her parents, "I am going home," and commenced singing her favorite hymn,

*"O, happy day, that fixed my choice
On Thee, my Savior, and my God
Well may this glowing heart rejoice,
And tell its raptures all abroad."*

"Yes," she whispered, "it was a happy day." Then putting her arm around her father's neck, whose heart seemed almost broken, she said, "Don't care for me, father; Jesus will take care of me."

These were her last conscious words; the smile of affection lingered a little longer on her face, the look of love in her eyes, and its pressure in her hand. and then her spirit took its flight, mid angel guards and guides, leaving behind her the clearest evidence of love to Jesus, and a worthy example of fidelity to Him, though she had followed Him but one short month.

On the first Sabbath of February I gave the hand of fellowship to a large number of new members, and Ella would have been with them had she lived. It so happened that near the place where she would have stood there was a vacant spot. I directed the attention of the large assembly to that opening and asked, "Where is Ella today?" For a moment all was still, and the entire congregation appeared to be bathed in tears, when I said, "Jesus seems to say, 'I have given Ella the hand of fellowship up here.'"

A few days after her death, her parents, in looking over her portfolio, found she had written, unknown to any one, in the middle of a blank book, as if intended only for God's eye, the following deed, which shows her depth of purpose and complete dedication to Christ:

"December 21, 1860. -- This day I have given my heart to the Savior, and have resolved to do just what He tells me to do, and to take up my cross daily and follow Him -- my eyes to weep over sinners, and my mouth to speak forth His praise and to lead sinners to Christ. -- Ella J. Gilkey."

And in the vestry of the church at Watertown these words, printed in large type, and handsomely framed, now hang upon the wall, where all who enter may read them; so that, in the hours of Sabbath school and in the prayer meeting and social gathering, Ella, though in heaven, still speaks, and continues her work for Jesus. -- Bringing in Sheaves.

## *040 -- A DYING GIRL'S REQUEST*

An evangelist said: "A little girl of eight years was sent on an errand by her parents. While on her way she was attracted by the singing of a gospel meeting in the open air, and drew near. The conductor of the meeting was so struck with the child's earnestness that he spoke to her and told her about Jesus. She being the child of Roman Catholics, did not know much about Him, but the gentleman told her of His love to her. On returning home, her father asked her what had detained her. She told him, and he cruelly beat her, forbidding her to go to any such meeting again. About a fortnight afterward she was sent on another errand, but she was so taken up with what she had previously heard about Jesus that she forgot all about her message. She saw the same gentleman, who again told her more about the Savior. On her return home she again told her father, as before, where she had been, and that she had not brought what she had been sent for, but that she had brought Jesus. Her father was enraged, and kicked the poor little creature until the blood came. She never recovered from this brutal treatment. Just before she breathed her last she called to her mother and said, 'Mother, I have been praying to Jesus to save you and father.' Then pointing to her little dress she said, 'Mother, cut me a bit out of the blood-stained piece of my dress.' The mother, wondering, did so. 'Now,' said the dying child, 'Christ shed His blood for my sake, and I am going to take this to Jesus to show Him that I shed my blood for His sake.' Thus she died, holding firmly the piece of her dress stained with her own blood. The testimony of that dear child was the means of leading both father and mother to Christ."

## *041 -- QUEEN ELIZABETH'S LAST WORDS -- "ALL MY POSSESSIONS FOR A MOMENT OF TIME"*

Queen Elizabeth ascended the English throne at the age of twenty-five, and remained in power for forty-five years. She was a Protestant, but was far from being a true Christian in her life. She persecuted the Puritans for many years and her cruelty was manifested all through her public life. She died in 1603, seventy years old. Her last words were, "All my possessions for a moment of time."

We take the following from Schaff's Encyclopedia: With Elizabeth, Protestantism was restored, and -- in spite of occasional resistance from within, the Spanish Armada and papal deposition from without (1570) became the permanent religion of the large majority in the land. Two periods stand out in the history of the church under Elizabeth. In the early part of the reign the divorce of the National Church from the Roman Catholic see was consummated; in the latter part its position was clearly stated in regard to Puritanism, which demanded recognition, if not supremacy, within its pale. The queen was no zealous reformer, but directed the affairs of the church with the keen sagacity of a statesmanship which placed national unity and the peace of the realm above every other consideration. In the first year of her reign the Acts of Supremacy and Uniformity were passed. By the former, all allegiance to foreign prince or prelate was forbidden; by the latter, the use of the liturgy enforced. The royal title of "Defender of the Faith and Supreme Head of the Church" was retained, with the slight alteration of "Head" to "Governor." But the passage was struck out of the Litany which read, "From the tyranny of the Bishop of Rome and all his detestable enormities, good Lord deliver us." The queen retained, against the protest of bishops, an altar, crucifix, and lighted candles in her own chapel, disapproved of the marriage of the clergy, interrupted the preacher who spoke disparagingly of the sign of the cross, and imperiously forced her wishes upon unwilling prelates.

## *042 -- DYING TESTIMONY AND VISION OF MISS LILA HOMER*

We are indebted to her pastor, Rev. B. C. Matthews, for this sketch:

Miss Lila Homer, a member of the Methodist Church at Dardanelle, Arkansas, died in the Lord at her home, October 3rd, 1895. She had just entered her twenty-fifth year March 19th, 1895.

She was converted at the early age of ten years. Just before her death she had a glimpse of the invisible world. Knowing that she was the Lord's handmaiden, and that her disease would allow her to be rational to the end, I thought she might be able to see the angels and tell us something of what she saw, so I said, "Lila, when the angels come for you, let us know." In a short while she whispered to her sister, "Tell Bro. Matthews to come closer," and then said, "Bro. Matthews, I saw some angels but they were so far away that I could not recognize anyone." I asked her if they had wings, to which she replied, "They had no wings, but were all arrayed in white and looked just like people." After a while she said, "I saw a great host of angels, but there were more babies than any others. I saw grandpa and ma Homer and Aunt Joe." In a short while she turned to her sister, Miss Jodie, and said, "O, Joe, tell Emma Lawrence that Daisy Conger is the sweetest angel." Miss Joe then asked her if Daisy looked bright and happy, to which she replied, "O, yes, so bright and happy. Tell the Conger girls to be good and meet Daisy." On Thursday morning, just before she fell asleep, she said to her mother, "I won't get to go to the Sulphur Springs, mamma, but I will go to an everlasting spring, where flowers never wither." In reply to this her mother said, "Lila, I can't go with you." "No, mamma," she said, "but you can come, and I will be waiting for you all." She talked to each member of the family separately and sent a message by them to her absent brother. After thanking her friends for their kindness, she quietly breathed her last.

## 043 -- DREADFUL MARTYRDOM OF ROMANUS

Romanus, a native of Palestine, was deacon of the church of Caesarea, at the time of the commencement of Diocletian's persecution, in the fourth century. He was at Antioch when the imperial order came for sacrificing to idols, and was much grieved to see many Christians, through fear, submit to the idolatrous command, and deny their faith in order to preserve their lives.

While reproving some of them for their weakness, Romanus was informed against, and soon after arrested. Being brought to the tribunal, he confessed himself a Christian, and said he was willing to suffer anything they could inflict upon him for his confession. When condemned, he was scourged, put to the rack, and his body torn with hooks. While thus cruelly mangled, he turned to the governor and thanked him for having opened for him so many mouths with which to preach Christianity; "for," he said, "every wound, is a mouth to sing the praises of the Lord." He was soon after slain by being strangled. -- Foxe's Book of Martyrs.

## 044 -- JOHN CASSIDY AND THE PRIEST

Any one who has sailed past the new Mole into Gibraltar Bay will have noticed the long, yellow-washed building standing high upon the south front, and has been told it is the military naval hospital. In one of the wards of this hospital, about a year before the commencement of the Crimean War, there lay private of the Thirty-third Regiment, John Cassidy by name, who had been seized by a fatal attack of dysentery. He felt that death was near; and calling to him the hospital sergeant, he said, "Morris, I shan't be long, and I want to make my peace before I go. Will you send for the priest?"

"There is no need to send for him," replied Morris, who was an earnest Christian; "haven't I told you that Jesus, the blessed Savior, is ready to receive you just now, and make you fit for heaven, if you'll only ask Him?"

"But I'm so weak, I haven't got any strength to pray," said the poor fellow; "it's far easier to let the priest do it; and he'll only charge five shillings. You must go to the pay-master, Morris, to get the money, and give it to him as soon as he comes. And don't be long about it; for I feel that I haven't many hours before me. I'd like to die in my own religion; and you'll see how comfortable I'll be when the priest has performed the offices."

The sergeant thought it best for John to prove for himself what a broken reed he was leaning on, and accordingly sent at once for the priest. He came, received the money, and directed four candles to be brought, which he lighted, and placed two at the head and two at the foot of the bed. He then took some "sacred oil" and put it on the brow and cheeks and lips of the dying man, and on various parts of his body. Afterwards he sprinkled him freely with "holy water" and then, waving a censor over the bed until the air was heavy with the perfume, he pronounced absolution and solemnly declared that John Cassidy was ready for death.

"But I don't feel ready, sir," said John, looking up piteously into his face. "I don't feel a bit different after all you have done."

"But you ought to feel different," replied the priest angrily. "You must trust the church; and I tell you, in her name, that you are now a saved man."

"Well, sir," persisted John, "yet men that are saved, and are ready for heaven, feel happy, and I don't. There was a man that Sergeant Morris talked to in this ward. He died the other day, and he was so happy! He said he saw angels coming to take him away, and he wasn't afraid to die; and I thought you'd make me feel like that; but I'm quite frightened."

Strange language for a priest to hear, and most unwelcome. Straightening himself to his fullest height, he stood over the bed, and extending his hand in a threatening manner toward the dying man, he exclaimed, "I give you this warning, John Cassidy, that if you listen to that heretic sergeant you will be damned."

John quailed for a moment before the fearful words; and then as the weight of unforgiven sin pressed upon his heart, and he felt that the priest had no power -- as he once believed -- to cleanse it away, he cried out in the bitterness of his soul, "I can not be worse than I am, sir; that's certain; so please go away, and let me take my chance!" And as the priest seemed still inclined to linger, and to remonstrate, he raised himself partly on his pillow, and with strange energy persisted, "Don't stay any longer, sir! I haven't many minutes left, and I can't afford to lose any of them in arguing; so have pity on a dying man and go at once."

The priest merely said on leaving the room, "John Cassidy, I warn you! You are forsaking your own mercy."

John was almost exhausted by the agitation and disappointment of the interview; but as he lay quite still, too weak for words, the sergeant came and sat by his bedside, and read to him such passages as the following:

"There is one mediator between God and man, the man Christ Jesus." "Behold the Lamb of God, which taketh away the sin of the world!" "By Him all that believe are freely justified from all things." "Neither is there salvation in any other; for there is none other name under heaven given among men whereby we must be saved." "The blood of Jesus Christ, His Son, cleanseth us from all sin."

The sergeant added no words of his own, but sat by the dying man, silently praying that the utterance of this Divine Word might give light to lighten the darkness of that departing soul. In a little while, a low murmur caused him to bead his ear close to the lips of his dying comrade; and he caught the words as they came in faint, gasping utterance, "No other name! It was a mistake -- to think any priest could get me to heaven -- but Jesus Christ can -- and I think he will-I'm happy -- 1 am not frightened now -- good-bye, Morris -- tell all the poor fellows -- about -- the blood -- cleanseth." No more words, only a shiver and sigh, and then a look of calm on the tired, worn face; and Sergeant Morris gently closed the eyes of the dead soldier, murmuring as he did so, "Thanks be unto God, Who giveth us the victory through our Lord Jesus Christ." -- Christian Family Almanac For 1874.

### 045 -- "I AM IN THE FLAMES -- PULL ME OUT, PULL ME OUT!"

Mr. W___, the subject of this narrative, died in J___, New York, about the year 1883, at the age of seventy-four. He was an avowed infidel. He was a good neighbor in some respects, yet he was very wicked and made a scoff of Christianity. About seven years previous to his death he passed through a revival. The Spirit strove with him, but he resisted to the last.

One Sabbath after this, Mr. N -, who relates this sketch, was on his way to church and passed Mr. W 's house, who was standing by the gate. He said, "Come with me to church, Mr. W___." The infidel, holding out his hand, replied, "Show me a hair on the palm of my hand and I will show you a Christian." During his last sickness, Mr. N called on him often and sat up with him several nights, and was with him when he died. The infidel was conscious of his near approaching end and of the terrors of his lost condition. He said once to Mr. N___, who, as a local worker, held meetings in school houses around, "Warn the world not to live as I have lived, and escape my woe." At another time when visited by a doctor, he was groaning and making demonstrations of great agony. The doctor said, "Why do you groan, your disease is not painful?" "O, doctor," said he, "it is not the body but the soul that troubles me." On the evening of his death, Mr. N -came at ten o'clock. A friend of his was there also. As he entered the room he felt that it was filled with an awful presence as if he were near the region of the damned. The dying man cried out, "O God, deliver me from that awful pit!" It was not a penitential prayer, but the wail of a lost soul. About fifteen minutes before his death, which was at twelve, he exclaimed, "I am in the flames -- pull me out, pull me out!" He kept repeating this until the breath left his body. As the bodily strength failed his words became more faint. At last Mr. N__ put his ear down close to catch his departing whispers, and the last words he could hear were, "Pull me out, pull me out!" "It was an awful scene," said he. "It made an impression on me that I can never forget. I never want to witness such a scene again." I was talking with my friend years after, and he said those words, "I am in the flames -- pull me out, pull me out!" were still ringing in his ears. -- Written for this book by Rev. C. A. Balch, Cloverville, N. Y.

## 046 -- THE TRIUMPHANT TRANSLATION OF BISHOP PHILIP WILLIAM OTTERBEIN

Bishop Otterbein, founder of the United Brethren Church, ended a ministry of sixty-two years in great peace. Rev. Dr. Kurtz, of the Lutheran Church, for many years a devoted personal friend of the distinguished preacher, offered at his bedside the last audible prayer, at the close of which the bishop responded, "Amen, amen! it is finished." Like good old Simeon, who was spared to take the babe of Bethlehem in his arms, he could say, "Lord, now lettest thou thy servant depart in peace, according to Thy word: for mine eyes have seen Thy salvation." His grief-stricken friends, thinking he was dying, had gathered about him to take the last look ere he smote with his sandals the waters of death's river, but, rallying again for a moment, as if to finish his testimony, and to give still greater assurance of victory, he said, "Jesus, Jesus, I die, but Thou livest, and soon I shall live with Thee." Then, turning to his friends, he continued, "The conflict is over and past. I begin to feel an unspeakable fullness of love and peace divine. Lay my head upon my pillow and be still." All was quiet. He awaited the approach of heaven's chariot; nor did he wait in vain. "A smile, a fresh glow, lighted up his countenance, and, behold, it was death. " -- From Life to Life.

## 047 -- "THERE'S MAGGIE AT THE GATE!"

"I shall go to him, but he shall not return to me." (2 Sam. 12: 23.)

An aged Christian woman -- a ripe old saint-recently "fell asleep in Jesus." She had some few years before parted with her favorite daughter, whose name was Maggie. Just before she breathed her last, Maggie had said to her mother, "Mother, when you come to heaven, I shall be at the gate waiting for you. I shall be the first to bid you welcome" And her spirit soared to the realms of bliss.

And now the dear old woman was passing away She looked forward with joy to welcome her loved ones; for faith in Jesus Christ takes all the sting from death. And she could not help thinking of her dear Maggie, and of her parting words, "I shall be at the gate of heaven waiting for you."

Her eldest daughter was nursing her in her last moments. The end was fast approaching, but she was quite conscious.

"Mother," said her daughter, "shall I sing your favorite hymn?"

"Yes," said the dying saint, "'Waiting and Watching for Me.'"

And she sang the first stanza of Marianne Farningham's popular hymn --

*"When my final farewell to the world I have said,*
*And gladly lie down to my rest*
*When softly the watchers shall say, ' She is dead,'*
*And fold my pale hands o'er my breast:*
*And when with my glorified vision at last,*
*The walls of that City I see,*
*Will any one then at the beautiful gate*
*Be waiting and watching for me?"*

Just as the singer was repeating the words,

"Will any one then at the beautiful gate -- "
Her mother sprang up as if she saw her beloved daughter close at hand, and exclaimed: "There's Maggie at the gate!"

These were her last words. Her spirit departed "to be with Christ, which is far better."

Reader, have you any loved ones in heaven? Are you on the road that leads to that beautiful and holy place? Are you sure that you are fitted for the holy society of heaven? Have you made vows to those beyond the vale that you would surrender all to Christ and so constantly keep all of His holy commandments that they will meet you at the gate and rejoice to welcome you to the endless bliss of heaven? Or have you forgotten to pay those vows so solemnly made to your loved ones and God? If so, hasten to pay them. Do it now, or you may forever lose heaven and the society of those loved on earth. Will you do it? Will you do it -- now? -- Rev. A. Smith, Utica, N. Y.

## 048 -- "IT WAS THE CURSED DRINK THAT RUINED ME."

To one of the Bellevue cells there came one morning a woman bearing the usual permit to visit a patient. She was a slender little woman with a look of delicate refinement that sorrow had only intensified, and she looked at the physician, who was just leaving the patient, with clear eyes which had wept often, but kept their steady, straight-forward gaze.

"I am not certain," she said. "I have searched for my boy for a long while, and I think he must be here. I want to see him."

The doctor looked at her pityingly as she went up to the narrow bed where the patient lay, a lad of hardly twenty, with his face buried in the pillow. His fair hair, waving' crisply against the skin, browned by exposure, had not been cut, for the hospital barber who stood there had found it so far impossible to make him turn his head.

"He's lain that way ever since they brought him in yesterday," said the barber, and then moved by something in the agitated face before him, turned his own way. The mother, for it was quite plain who this must be, stooped over the prostrate figure. She knew it as mothers know their own, and laid her hand on his burning brow.

"Charley," she said softly, as if she had come into his room to rouse him from some boyish sleep, "mother is here."

A wild cry rang out that startled even the experienced physician:

"For God's sake take her away! She doesn't know where I am. Take her away!" The patient had started up and wrung his hands in piteous entreaty.

"Take her away!" he still cried, but his mother gently folded her arms about him and drew his head to her breast. "Oh, Charley, I have found you," she said through her sobs, "and I will never lose you again."

The lad looked at her a moment. His eyes were like hers, large and clear, but with the experience of a thousand years in their depths; a beautiful, reckless face, with lines graven by passion and crime. Then he burst into weeping like a child.

"It's too late! It's too late!" he said in tones almost inaudible.

"I'm doing you the only good turn I've done you, mother. I'm dying and you won't have to break your heart over me any more. It wasn't your fault. It was the cursed drink that ruined me, blighted my life and brought me here. It's murder now, but the hangman won't have me, and save that much disgrace for our name."

As he spoke he fell back upon his pillow; his face changed and the unmistakable hue of death suddenly spread over his handsome features. The doctor came forward quickly, a look of anxious surprise on his face.

"I didn't know he was that bad," the barber muttered under his breath, as he gazed at the lad still holding his mother's hand. The doctor lifted the patient's head and then laid it back softly. Life had fled.

"It's better to have it so." he said in a low voice to himself, and then stood silently and reverently, ready to offer consolation to the bereaved mother, whose face was still hidden on her boy's breast. She did not stir. Something in the motionless attitude aroused vague suspicion in the mind of the doctor, and moved him to bend forward and gently take her hand. With an involuntary start he hastily lifted the prostrate form and quickly felt the pulse and heart, only to find them stilled forever.

"She has gone, too," he softly whispered, and the tears stood in his eyes. "Poor soul! It is the best for both of them."

This is one story of the prison ward of Bellevue, and there are hundreds that might be told, though never one sadder or holding deeper tragedy than the one recorded here. New York Press.

## 049 -- THE TRANSLATION OF WILLIE DOWNER

This saint of God went to heaven from Greenville, Michigan, in the spring of 1883, in the eighteenth year of his age. We had the privilege of meeting him many times, and at his request often sang and prayed with him. During our stay in his town, God was pleased to fill him with the Spirit and from that time he lived a devoted saint of God, walking in all the commandments of God blamelessly. Much of his time was spent in earnest prayer for souls. He was often greatly burdened for the desolation of Zion. For about five years he was a helpless cripple. He was one of the greatest sufferers we ever saw, yet in the midst of his pain he rejoiced in the privilege of suffering for his Savior. He never murmured nor complained. He was one of the most useful Christians in that community, although entirely confined to his home. Everybody realized the power and presence of God when in his company. Like most of the saints of God, he was poor in this world's goods, yet rich in faith, an heir to an inheritance that fadeth not away. He lived in a very humble little home on earth, but now dwells in a mansion with the heavenly host. The dear Lord was pleased to give him a glimpse of his heavenly home before his departure from the shores of time. To comfort him in the midst of his indescribable suffering the Lord gave him a vision of himself, and he saw his crippled and helpless form lifeless sometime before he passed over. He often had glimpses of heaven and frequently spoke of seeing his Savior and the angels of God. Willie lived in the land of Beulah in sight of the New Jerusalem. He was the only child of a widowed mother and of course was her constant care. May the dear Lord help all who read this to live a holy life and like our brother Willie walk in all the light that shines on their pathway and thus please God. May we all like him take to heart the worth of immortal souls that throng the broad way to eternal death, is our earnest prayer. Amen. -- Editor.

## 050 -- THE DYING EXPERIENCE OF A WEALTHY MAN

He had spent his life amassing a fortune of $75,000, but had never given any special attention to his soul's salvation.

When he came to die his wealth was no satisfaction to him, but, on the contrary, it cost him great anguish to fully realize that he had spent his life in amassing wealth to the neglect of his soul. In this dying condition he called in his brother-in-law to pray for him, who said he called so loudly for mercy that he could scarcely hear himself pray or fix his thoughts on anything. After the prayer was over, he took his hand in both of his, and said as he shook it,

"Good-bye, John. Pray for me. I shall never see your face again." And he never did.

After he had gone away, a neighbor came in and saw the condition he was in, and said something must be done. "I would suggest that we do something to quiet his mind and fears," and so he recommended a game of cards. He replied, "Cards for a dying man! How contemptible; going into eternity. These are not what I want. I want mercy!"

A little later his son came into his room and said, "Father, what arrangements, if any, do you wish to make in regard to the property?" He said, "I have given all my life to gain property; I cannot take a dollar with me. The law and the family will have to take care of that: I want to take care of my soul. Property avails nothing; I want mercy!"

And so he died, calling upon God for mercy; but he left no evidence that he found it. An illustration of giving a life for the gain of property to the loss of the soul. -- The Word.

## 051 -- LAST WORDS OF JOHN HUS, THE MARTYR

The great Bohemian reformer and martyr, John Hus, was born in 1369. He was burned at the stake as a heretic in Constance, Germany, July 6, 1415. When arriving at the place of execution, he prayed, "Into Thy hands, O Lord, do I commit my spirit. Thou hast redeemed me, O most good and faithful God. Lord Jesus Christ, assist and help me, that, with a firm and present mind, by Thy most powerful graces I may undergo this most cruel and ignominious death, to which I am condemned for preaching the truth of Thy most holy gospel."

When the wood was piled up to his very neck, the Duke of Bavaria asked him to recant. "No," said Hus, "I never preached any doctrine of an evil tendency, and what I taught with my lips, I now seal with my blood." The fagots were then lighted and the martyr sung a hymn so loud as to be heard through the crackling of the flames.

## 052 -- LAST TESTIMONY OF AUGUSTUS M. TOPLADY

Augustus M. Toplady died in London, August 11th, 1778, at the age of thirty-eight. He was the author of that good old hymn,

*Rock of Ages, cleft for me,*
*Let me hide myself in Thee;*
*Let the water and the blood,*
*From Thy wounded side which flowed,*
*Be of sin the double cure --*
*Save from wrath and make me pure."*

He had everything before him to make life desirable, yet when death drew near, his soul exulted in gladness. He said, "It is my dying avowal that these great and glorious truths which the Lord in rich mercy has given me to believe and enabled me to preach, are now brought into practical and heartfelt experience. They are the very joy and support of my soul. The consolations flowing from them carry me far above the things of time and sense. So far as I know my own heart, I have no desire but to be entirely passive." Frequently he called himself a dying man, and yet the happiest man in the world; adding, "Sickness is no affliction, pain no curse, death itself no dissolution; and yet how this soul of mine longs to be gone; like a bird imprisoned in its cage, it longs to take its flight. Had I wings like a doves then would I fly away to the bosom of God, and be at rest forever."

Within an hour before he expired he seemed to awake from a gentle slumber, when he exclaimed, "O, what delights! Who can fathom the joys of the third heaven? What a bright sunshine has been spread around me! I have not words to express it. I know it cannot be long now till my Savior will come for me, for surely no mortal man can live," bursting as he said it into a flood of tears, "after glories that God has manifested to my soul. All is light, light, light -- the brightness of His own glory. O come, Lord Jesus, come; come quickly." Then he closed his eyes and fell asleep, to be awakened with others of like precious faith on that great day "when the Lord Jesus shall be revealed from heaven with His mighty angels, to be glorified with His saints and admired in all them that believe." -- The Contrast Between Infidelity and Christianity.

## 053 -- "BE GOOD AND MEET ME IN HEAVEN."

The subject of this sketch, Mary J. Whitaker Wiggins, was born in VanBuren Co., Iowa, February 5th, 1853, and died at Weaubleau, Mo., September 4th, 1897.

She united with the Christian Church when a little girl of thirteen summers. She was ever noted for her continuous piety and faithful attendance at all of her church services and duties, though she was of a quiet, retiring disposition. If Mary was ever absent from her church-meeting, the inquiry went around, "Is she sick?" or else, "Who in the neighborhood is sick?"

When she lay dying, her family, husband and eight children, besides her brothers and other sympathizing friends, stood by her bedside. She had ever taught them by her exemplary, godly life how Christians should live; and now she showed them how triumphantly a Christian may die. All that evening as her life was fading away her faith in Christ showed forth so vividly that it seemed to those standing around to be more like an entering into life than a departing from it. She conversed freely and rationally of her final change. She was so ready and so confident that she would soon be with a sainted mother and child and others, that the weeping ones were consoled in their grief by her prospective joy. She assured us all that no cloud of doubt existed. She said to her pastor and brother, "I will be absent from our next church meeting on earth, but I will be in heaven." Her parting words to her husband and weeping children were, "Be good and meet me in heaven."

After she could speak no more, while those around her, at her request, were singing the words, " I am going home, to die no more," she raised her feeble hands and clapped them two or three times.

Thus she died! Her triumphant death was a fitting close to the devoted Christian life which this loving sister and wife and godly mother had lived. Let me too die the death of the righteous. -- J. Whitaker, D. D.

The attending physician, G. B. Viles, deposes that he was present at her death and that she was not delirious but remarkably rational up to her death.

## 054 -- THE AWFUL DEATH OF A PROFLIGATE

The following account of an affecting, mournful exit, and the reflections that accompany it, are solemn and impressive. We shall present them to the reader in the words of Doctor Young, who was present at the melancholy scene:

Is not the death-bed of a profligate a prime school of wisdom? Are we not obliged, when we are invited to it? for what else should reclaim us? The pulpit? We are prejudiced against it. Besides, an agonizing profligate, though silent, out-preaches the most celebrated the pulpit ever knew. But, if he speaks, his words might instruct the best instructors of mankind. Mixed in the warm converse of life, we think with men; on a death-bed, with God.

There are two lessons of this school written, as it were, in capitals, which they who run may read. First, he that, in this his minority, this field of discipline and conflict, instead of grasping the weapons of his warfare, is forever gathering flowers, and catching at butterflies, with his unarmed hand, ever making idle pleasure his pursuit; must pay for it his last reversion: and on opening his final account (of which a death-bed breaks the seal), shall find himself a beggar, a beggar past beggary; and shall passionately wish that his very being were added to the rest of his loss. Secondly, he shall find that truth, divine truth, however, through life, injured, wounded, suppressed, is victorious, immortal: that, though with mountains overwhelmed, it will, one day, burst out like the fires of Etna; visible, bright and tormenting, as the most raging flame. This now (oh, my friend!) I shall too plainly prove.

The sad evening before the death of the noble youth, whose last hours suggested these thoughts, I was with him. No one was present but his physician and an intimate friend whom he loved and whom he had ruined. At my coming in he said, "You and the physician are come too late. I have neither life nor hope. You both aim at miracles. You would raise the dead!" "I-leaven," I said, "was merciful --" "Or," exclaimed he, "I could not have been thus guilty. What has it not done to bless and to save me! I have been too strong for omnipotence! I have plucked down ruin!" I said, "The blessed Redeemer --" "Hold! hold! you wound me! That is the rock on which I split -- I denied His name!"

Refusing to hear anything from me or take anything from the physician he lay silent, as far as sudden darts of pain would permit, till the clock struck, then with vehemence he exclaimed, "Oh! time! time! it is fit thou shouldst thus strike thy murderer to the heart! How art thou fled forever! A month! Oh, for a single week -- I do not ask for years; though an age were too little for the much I have to do." On my saying we could not do too much, that heaven was a blessed place -- "So much the worse. 'Tis lost! 'Tis lost! Heaven is to me the severest place of hell!"

Soon after, I proposed prayer -- "Pray, you that can. I never prayed. I cannot pray -- nor need I. Is not heaven on my side already? It closes with my conscience. Its severest strokes but second my own." Observing that his friend was much touched at this, even to tears (who could forbear? I could not), with a most affectionate look he said, "Keep those tears for thyself. I have undone thee -- dost thou weep for me? That is cruel What can pain me more?"

Here his friend, too much affected, would have left him. "No, stay -- that thou mayst hope; therefore hear me. How madly I have talked! How madly hast thou listened and believed. But look on my present state, as a full answer to thee, and to myself. This body is all weakness and pain; but my soul, as if stung up by torment to greater strength and spirit, is full powerful to reason; full mighty to suffer. And that which thus triumphs within the jaws of immortality, is, doubtless, immortal. And as for a Deity, nothing less than an Almighty could inflict what I feel."

I was about to congratulate this passive, involuntary confessor, on his asserting the two prime articles of his creed, extorted by the rack of nature, when he thus very passionately exclaimed, "No, no[ let me speak on. I have not long to speak. My much injured friend, my soul, as my body, lies in ruins; in scattered fragments of broken thought. Remorse for the past throws my thought on the future. Worse dread of the future strikes it back on the past. I turn and turn and find no ray. Didst thou feel half the mountain that is on me thou wouldst struggle with the martyr for his stake, and bless heaven for the flames; that is not an everlasting flame; that is not an unquenchable fire."

How were we struck! Yet, soon after, still more. With what an eye of distraction, what a face of despair, he cried out, "My principles have poisoned my friend; my extravagance has beggared my boy; my unkindness has murdered my wife! And is there another hell? Oh! thou blasphemed, yet indulgent, Lord God, hell itself is a refuge, if it hide me from Thy frown!" Soon after his understanding failed. His terrified imagination uttered horrors not to be repeated, or ever forgotten. And ere the sun (which, I hope, has seen few like him) arose, the gay, young, noble, ingenious, accomplished and most wretched Altamont expired.

If this is a man of pleasure, what is a man of pain? How quick, how total, is the transit of such persons! In what a dismal gloom they set forever! How short, alas, the day of their rejoicing. For a moment they glitter, they dazzle. In a moment, where are they? Oblivion covers their memories. Ah, would it did! Infamy snatches them from oblivion. In the long-living annals of infamy their triumphs are recorded. Thy sufferings, poor Altamont, still bleed in the bosom of the heart-stricken friend -- for Altamont had a friend. He might have had many. His transient morning might have been the dawn of an immortal day. His name might have been gloriously enrolled in the records of eternity. His memory might have left a sweet fragrance behind it, grateful to the surviving friend, salutary to the succeeding generation. With what capacity was he endowed, with what advantages for being greatly good. But with the talents of an angel a man may be a fool. If he judges amiss in the supreme point, judging right in all else but aggravates his folly; as it shows him wrong, though blessed with the best capacity of being right. -- Power of Religion.

### 055 -- "YOU'LL BE A DUKE, BUT I SHALL BE A KING."

A consumptive disease seized the eldest son and heir of the Duke of Hamilton, which ended in his death. A little before his departure from the world, he lay ill at the family seat near Glasgow. Two ministers came to see him, one of them at his request prayed with him. After the minister had prayed, the dying youth put his hand back and took his Bible from under his pillow and opened it at the passage, "I have fought a good fight, I have finished my course, I have kept the faith; henceforth there is laid up for me a crown of righteousness, which the Lord, the Righteous Judge, shall give me at that day; and not to me only, but unto all them also that love His appearing." "This, sirs," said he, "is all my comfort." As he was lying one day on the sofa, his tutor was conversing with him on some astronomical subject, and about the nature of the fixed stars. "Ah," said he, "in a little while I shall know more of this than all of you together." When his death approached, he called his brother to his bedside, and addressing him with the greatest affection and seriousness, he closed with these remarkable words, "And now, Douglas, in a little time you'll be a duke, but I shall be a king." -- Cheever.

### 056 -- "I DIE IN PEACE; I SHALL SOON BE WITH THE ANGELS."

Miss Maggie Shaw, of Ida, Ill., sends us a clipping from the Earnest Christian giving a brief sketch of the life and death of Rev. J. M. Morris, from which we take the following:

Father Morris was born in Campbell Co., Virginia, Feb. 15, 1807, died at Mores Creek, Cal., Feb. 4, 1891. He was eighty-four years old, lacking eleven days.

When twelve years old his father died. He was left the main support of his mother. He got only thirty days schooling all told. By the aid of shell bark hickory as a substitute when out of candles, he devoted his evenings to study. He went through English grammar, arithmetic and part way through an advanced algebra without a teacher. When a man he was rarely surpassed in sound biblical learning and doctrine.

In early life he was deprived of attending church and Sunday school, but he was impressed with the necessity of a change of heart.

We give in his own words his experience:

"When a lone boy, having hardly ever heard any one pray or preach, while all alone in the cotton field with my hoe in hand, I became powerfully convicted that I was a sinner. I tried to pray as best I could, when the Lord came down in mighty power and blessed my soul. I did not know what to do or say, but God put it into my mind to praise His name, and there, with hoe in hand, both arms outstretched, I shouted 'Glory to God!' All looked beautiful; the sun and sky never looked so bright as when I was alone in that cotton patch with no one near but God."

As he would get shouting happy in relating this experience in meetings the holy fire would spread, and all would go home saying, "We had a good meeting; Morris was in the cotton patch today."

He crossed the plains in 1857 with ox teams to Trinity County, California. Going into a hotel in the mines, he demolished the bar where the grog was sold and preached in the bar room, as it was called, for two years, where a class of twenty-five or thirty was formed.

Leaving the Trinity mines, he, with the family, removed to Napa County, California, where he ever after made, to a great extent, his home, being absent from time to time a few years east, on account of ill health of some of the family. He preached and labored as colporteur in California, more or less, for thirty years.

He crossed the plains three times with ox teams and four times by rail. He preached in Iowa, Missouri and Kansas, at intervals after coming to California. In the winter of 1867, on the Delaware reserve in Kansas, he preached through a month's revival for the Missionary Baptists when they were not able to obtain a minister of their own, and there were thirty or forty gloriously converted to God. The greater part of those converted under his ministry had gone on to glory to welcome him to the immortal shores, and how oft have we heard him say, "My company has gone on before."

Disposing of all his little earthly effects in his last sickness; and giving the most minute orders about his burial, he said, "I die in peace with all men, I shall soon be with the angels. All I want is to be a little twinkling star." On calling Mother Morris, he said, "The other day you came to my bed and said, 'I want you to get well and pray as you used to once.' I have not been able to pray since, and I shall never be any better, but I want you to write to all the grandchildren and tell them I'd rather leave this request of their grandmother as a legacy to them than all the gold of Ophir." He made us promise him that we would bury him on the farm he had lived on for twelve years, in a plain coffin, no flowers or parade.

For thirty days we had watched day and night, taking four persons each night. All agreed that they did not know that anyone was capable of suffering so muck as he did, but his patience and resignation were so great, he would say, "I am in the hands of the great God of the universe, He knows best." Then he would say, "Oh, help me to be patient. The will of the Lord be done." After suffering thus for thirty days from asthma, lung trouble and something like la grippe he drew his last breath like he was going to sleep, in his right mind, without a struggle or a groan.

## *057 -- DEATH-BED SCENE OF DAVID HUME, THE DEIST*

David Hume, the deistical philosopher and historian, was born at Edinburgh in 1711. In 1762 he published his work, Natural Religion. Much of his time was spent in France, where he found many kindred spirits, as vile and depraved as himself. He died in Edinburgh in 1776, aged sixty-five years. Rev. E. P. Goodwin, in his work on Christianity and Infidelity, shows Hume to be dishonest, indecent and a teacher of immorality. Rev. Robert Hall, in his Modern Infidelity, says:

"Infidelity is the joint offspring of an irreligious temper and unholy speculation, employed, not in examining the evidences of Christianity, but in detecting the vices and imperfections of confessing Christians. It has passed through various stages, each distinguished by higher gradations of impiety; for when men arrogantly abandon their guide, and willfully shut their eyes on the light of heaven, it is wisely ordained that their errors shall multiply at every step, until their extravagance confutes itself, and the mischief of their principles works its own antidote.

"Hume, the most subtle, if not the most philosophical, of the deists; who, by perplexing the relations of cause and effect, boldly aimed to introduce a universal skepticism and to pour a more than Egyptian darkness into the whole region of morals."

Again in McIlvaine's Evidences:

"The nature and majesty of God are denied by Hume's argument against the miracles. It is Atheism. There is no stopping place for consistency between the first principle of the essay of Hume, and the last step in the denial of God with the abyss of darkness forever. Hume, accordingly, had no belief in the being of God. If he did not positively deny it, he could not assert that he believed it. He was a poor, blind, groping compound of contradictions. He was literally 'without God and without hope,' 'doting about questions and strifes of words,' and rejecting life and immortality out of deference to a paltry quibble, of which common-sense is ashamed.

"There is reason to believe that however unconcerned Hume may have seemed in the presence of his infidel friends, there were times when, being diverted neither by companions, nor cards, nor his works, nor books of amusements, but left to himself, and the contemplation of eternity, he was anything but composed and satisfied.

"The following account was published many years ago in Edinburgh, where he died. It is not known to have been ever contradicted. About the end of 1776, a few months after the historian's death, a respectable-looking woman, dressed in black, came into the Haddington stage-coach while passing through Edinburgh. The conversation among the passengers, which had been interrupted for a few minutes, was speedily resumed, which the lady soon found to be regarding the state of mind persons were in at the prospect of death. An appeal was made, in defense of infidelity, to the death of Hume as not only happy and tranquil, but mingled even with gaiety and humor. To this the lady said, 'Sir, you know nothing about it; I could tell you another tale.' 'Madam,' replied the gentleman, 'I presume I have as good information as you can have on this subject, and I believe what I have asserted regarding Mr. Hume has never been called in question.' The lady continued, 'Sir, I was Mr. Hume's housekeeper for many years, I was with him in his last moments; and the mourning I now wear is a present from his relatives for my attention to him on his death bed; and happy would I have been if I could have borne my testimony to the mistaken opinion that has gone abroad of his peaceful and composed end. I have, sir, never till this hour opened my mouth on this subject, but I think it a pity the world should be kept in the dark on so interesting a topic. It is true, sir, that when Mr. Hume's friends were with him he was cheerful and seemed quite unconcerned about his approaching fate; nay, frequently spoke of it to them in a jocular and playful way; but when he was alone, the scene was very different; he was anything but composed, his mental agitation was so great at times as to occasion his whole bed to shake. And he would not allow the candles to be put out during the night, nor would he be left alone for a minute, as I had always to ring the bell for one of the servants to be in the room before he would allow me to leave it. He struggled hard to appear composed, even before me. But to one who attended his bedside for so many days and nights and witnessed his disturbed sleeps and still more disturbed wakings -- who frequently heard his involuntary breathings of remorse and frightful startings, it was no difficult matter to determine that all was not right within. This continued and increased until he became insensible.

I hope to God I shall never witness a similar scene.

## 058 -- TRIUMPHANT DEATH OF JOHN CALVIN

Calvin's unremitting labors favored the inroads of a variety of distressing diseases, which he suffered from for many years, but bravely battled against or disregarded, hating nothing so much as idleness. On February 6, 1564, he preached, with difficulty, his last sermon. After that he left his house but a few times, when he was carried on a litter to the council-hall and the church. Once a deputation from the council visited him on his sick-bed and received his exhortation to use their authority to the glory of God. And several times the clergy of the city and neighborhood gathered around him. In the midst of intense sufferings his spirit was calm and peaceful, and he occupied himself with the Bible and in prayer. When Farel, in his eightieth year, heard of his sickness, he wrote from Neufchatel that he would visit him, to which Calvin replied, in a letter dated May 2, "Farewell, my best and most right-hearted brother, and since God is pleased that you should survive me in this world, live mindful of our friendship, of which, as it was useful to the church of God, the fruit still awaits us in heaven. I would not have you fatigue yourself on my account. I draw my breath with difficulty, and am daily waiting till I altogether cease to breathe. It is enough that to Christ I live and die; to His people He is gain in life and death. Farewell again, not forgetting the brethren." Such words show that love as well as zeal had a place in Calvin's heart.

On the 27th of May, as the sun was setting, he fell asleep in Jesus. He was buried on the banks of the Rhone, outside of the city where he had so long labored in behalf of the religion of the Lord Jesus Christ. He asked that no monument might be placed upon his grave; and the spot where, some thirty years ago, the black stone was erected, is only conjectured to be his burial-place.

Prof. Tulloch well says of Calvin, "He was a great, intense and energetic character, who more than any other even of that great age has left his impress on the history of Protestantism."

His clear intellect and his logical acumen, together with his concise and crisp diction, make his works, even in the present day, a power in the church of God. He was needed in the church just as truly as Luther, Knox or Wesley, and we thank God for the gift of such a man. -- Heroes and Heroines.

### 059 -- "I WANT STRENGTH TO PRAISE HIM ABUNDANTLY! HALLELUJAH! – JOHN HUNT

We turn now to the remarkable story of the conversion of Fiji. This name is given to a group of islands, some two hundred and twenty-five in number, scattered over an area of two hundred and fifty by three hundred and seventy miles, of which about one hundred and forty are inhabited. The population in 1893 was 125,442. The largest of these islands, Vitu Levu, is about the same size as Jamaica. The story of this fair and fertile group, long the habitation of cruelty, is one of intense interest. That a Lincolnshire plowboy, who grew up to manhood with no educational advantages, should, before his thirty-sixth year, be the chief instrument in the conversion to Christianity and civilization of one of the most barbarous races of cannibals on the face of the earth is one of the most remarkable events in the annals of Christian missions....

Such devotion, however, could not fail of its glorious reward. A great religious awakening took place. Among the converts was the Queen of Vitu. "Her heart," says Mr. Hunt, "seemed literally to be broken, and, though a very strong woman, she fainted twice under the weight of a wounded spirit. She revived only to renew her strong cries and tears, so that it was all that we could do to proceed with the service. The effect soon became more general. Several of the women and some of the men literally roared for the disquietude of their hearts. As many as could chanted the Te Deum. It was very affecting to see upward of a hundred Fijians, many of whom were a few years ago some of the worst cannibals in the group, and even in the world, chanting, 'We praise Thee, O God; we acknowledge Thee to be the Lord,' while their voices were almost drowned by the cries of broken-hearted penitents." * *

Mr. Hunt's continuous toil at length told seriously upon his health. The man of iron strength, who had come up to London from the fields of Lincolnshire only twelve years before, was evidently dying. Of him, too, might it be truly said, "The zeal of thine house hath eaten me up." The converts from heathenism, with sad faces, flocked to the chapel and prayed earnestly for the missionary. "O Lord," Elijah Verant cried aloud, "we know we are very bad, but spare Thy servant. If one must die, take me! take ten of us! but spare Thy servant to preach Christ to the people!"

As he neared his end the missionary confidently committed his wife and babes to Gods but was sorely distressed for Fiji. Sobbing as though in acute distress, he cried out, "Lord, bless Fiji! save Fiji! Thou knowest my soul has loved Fiji; my heart has travailed for Fiji!" Then, grasping his friend Calvert by the hand, he exclaimed again, "O, let me pray once more for Fiji! Lord, for Christ's sake, bless Fiji! save Fiji!" Turning to his mourning wife, he said, "If this be dying, praise the Lord!" Presently, as his eyes looked up with a bright joy that defied death, he exclaimed, "I want strength to praise Him abundantly!" and with the note of triumph, "Hallelujah!" on his lips, he joined the worship of the skies. -- The Picket Line of Missions.

## *060 -- THE GREAT DANGER IN NOT SEEKING THE LORD WHILE HE MAY BE FOUND*

At one time during a prayer-meeting in about the year 1890, my attention was directed towards an unsaved lady who was present, who appeared to be trifling. The pastor in charge of the meeting made the remark that as a watchman upon the walls of Zion, he felt that there was danger for someone there; he could not understand why he was impressed with this thought, and repeated that he felt drawn out to say that there was danger and someone there ought to get saved, then and there.

This irreligious lady appeared unconcerned and oblivious to his remarks, and laughed when the minister shook hands with her at the close of the meeting. Just as she was preparing to leave the church she was taken very ill, so ill that she could not go home, neither could she be taken home by friends. Everything that could be done for her relief was done, but in less than one short hour she passed into eternity. Before she died, she tore her hair, cast aside the trashy gew-gaws that adorned her person and of which heretofore she had been very fond, and throwing up her hands she cried aloud for mercy, exclaiming "Oh, Lord, have mercy on me! Oh, Lord, help me!" In this distress of body and soul she passed into the great eternity without leaving any hope to those that stood round her dying bed. This sad experience shows the danger of putting off the day and hour of salvation. "For in such an hour as ye think not, the Son of Man cometh. " -- Written for this book by Julia E. Strait, Portlandville, N. Y.

# Part Two - Testimonies 61 to 120

### *061 -- LAST WORDS OF JOHN HOOPER, BISHOP AND MARTYR*

This great preacher and reformer was born in Somersetshire, in 1495, and died at the stake Feb. 9, 1555, in Gloucester. He was a great scholar and writer, and a diligent study of the scriptures and the works of Zwingli and Bullinger on the Pauline epistles convinced him of the errors of the papal church and made him an ardent advocate of the reformation.

Foxe says of him, "In his sermons he corrected sin and sharply inveighed against the iniquity of the world and the corrupt abuses of the church. The people in great flocks and companies came daily to hear him, insomuch that the church would oftentimes be so full that none could enter further than the doors.."

Hooper and Rogers were the first to be cited under Mary. On Aug. 29, 1553, the former was thrown into prison, where he received harsh treatment, and contracted sciatica. In January, 1555, he was condemned on three charges -- for maintaining the lawfulness of clerical marriage, for defending divorce and for denying transubstantiation. He called the mass "the iniquity of the devil." He was sentenced to die at the stake in Gloucester, whither he was conveyed. He met his death firmly and cheerfully. To a friend bewailing his lot, the martyr replied in the oft-quoted words, "Death is bitter and life is sweet, but alas! consider that death to come is more bitter, and life to come is more sweet." In another conversation he said, "I am well, thank God; and death to me for Christ's sake is welcome." His martyrdom was witnessed by a large throng of people. The martyr was forbidden to address the crowd. A real or pretended pardon being promised if he would recant, he spurned it away, saying, "If you love my soul, away with it." His agony was greatly prolonged and increased by the slow progress of the fire on account of the green fagots, which had to be rekindled three times before they did their work. -- Religious Encyclopedia.

### *062 -- LAST WORDS OF THE GREAT COMMENTATOR, MATTHEW HENRY*

Matthew Henry, a distinguished non-conformist divine and biblical commentator, born Oct. 28, 1662, at Broad Oak, Flintshire, England; died June 22,

1714, at Nantwich, England. He received his education under his father's (Rev. Philip Henry) roof, and in an academy at Islington. On the return journey from a visit to Chester he was seized with apoplexy and died. His old intimate friend, Mr. Illidge, was present, who had been desired by Sir Thomas Delves and his lady to invite him to their house, at Doddington, whither their steward was sent to conduct him. But he was not able to proceed any further, and went to bed at Mr. Mottershed's house, where he felt himself so ill that he said to his friends, "Pray for me, for now I cannot pray for myself." While they were putting him to bed, he spoke of the excellence of spiritual comforts in a time of affliction, and blessed God that he enjoyed them. To his friend, Mr. Illidge, he addressed himself in these memorable words: "You have been used to take notice of the sayings of dying men -- this is mine: That a life spent in the service of God, and communion with Him, is the most comfortable and pleasant life that one can live in the present world." He had a restless night, and about five o'clock on Tuesday morning he was seized with a fit, which his medical attendants agreed to be an apoplexy. He lay speechless, with his eyes fixed, till about eight o'clock, June 22, 1714, and then expired. -- Memoirs of the Rev. Matthew Henry.

### 063 -- "I CAN'T DIE! I WON'T DIE!"

Mrs. Phoebe Palmer, the noted and devoted holiness evangelist, is the authority for the following:

E___ had a friend who did not believe that the injunctions, "Come out from among them and be ye separate," "Be not conformed to the world," and kindred passages, have anything to do with the external appearance of the Christian. She was united in church fellowship with a denomination which does not recognize these things as important, and she had been heard to speak contemptuously of those contracted views that would induce one, in coming out in a religious profession, to make such a change in external appearance as to excite observation.

We should be far from favoring an intimation that E 's friend was hypocritical; she was only what would be termed a liberal-minded professor, and was no more insincere than thousands who stand on what would be termed an ordinary eminence in religious profession. The wasting consumption gradually preyed upon the vitals of this friend, and E___, who lives in a distant city, went to see her. E___, though not at the time as fully devoted as she might have been, was concerned to find her friend as much engaged with the vanities of the world and as much interested about conforming to its customs as ever, and she ventured to say, "I did not suppose you would think so much about these things now."

Her friend felt somewhat indignant at the remark, and observed, "I do not know that I am more conformed to the world than yourself, and the denomination to which you belong regards these things as wrong, but our people do not think that religion has anything to do with these little matters."

The hand of withering disease continued relentlessly laid on E 's friend, and as she drew nearer eternity her blissful hopes of immortality and eternal life seemed to gather yet greater brightness. Her friends felt that her piety was more elevated than that of ordinary attainment. Again and yet again her friends gathered around her dying couch to hear her last glowing expressions and to witness her peaceful departure. Such was her composure that she desired her shroud might be in readiness so that she might, before the mirror, behold her body arrayed for its peaceful resting place.

Her friend E___ was forced to leave the city a day or two before her dissolution, and called to take her final farewell. "We shall not meet again on earth," said the dying one, "but doubtless we shall meet in heaven. On my own part I have no more doubt than if I were already there, and I cannot but hope that you will be faithful unto death. We shall then meet." They then bade each other a last adieu.

The moment at last came when death was permitted to do his fearful work. The devoted friends had again gathered around the bed of the dying fair one to witness her peaceful exit. Respiration grew shorter and shorter and at last ceased, and they deemed the spirit already in the embrace of blissful messengers who were winging it to paradise. A fearful shriek! and in a moment they beheld her that they had looked upon as the departed sitting upright before them with every feature distorted.

Horror and disappointment had transformed that placid countenance so that it exhibited an expression indescribably fiendish. "I can't die!" vociferated the terrified, disappointed one. "I won't die!" At that moment the door opened and her minister entered. "Out of the door, thou deceiver of men!" she again vociferated, fell back and was no more.

"Not every one that saith unto Me, Lord, Lord, shall enter into the kingdom of heaven, but he that doeth the will of my Father which is in heaven." (Mat. 7:21.)

## *064 -- "VICTORY! ETERNAL VICTORY!" WERE THE LAST WORDS OF MOTHER COBB*

The sainted Eunice Cobb, better known as "Mother Cobb," was born at Litchfield, Connecticut, Feb. 13, 1793.

Mother Cobb was converted in the twenty-fourth year of her earthly life. After walking with God on earth for sixty years, He took her to Himself, to reign with

Him forever in the courts above, on the 3rd of January, 1877, in the eighty-fourth year of her age.

We select the following from an account of her life and death published in the "Marengo Republican":

"Died, at the residence of Mrs. M. T. Johnson, Jan. 3, 1877, Mrs. Eunice Cobb.

"During a pilgrimage of forty years with this people she ever exhibited an earnest zeal in the service of her Lord and Master. To her, religion was more than a name -- a profession; it was a reality, a power revealed in the heart, that led, controlled and adorned her whole life and being. She stopped at the Fountain, not only to drink, but to wash and be made whiter than snow. She avoided everything that had the appearance of conformity to the world, and deemed it an honor to be called 'singular' for Christ's sake. Filled with a holy enthusiasm for the salvation of souls, she devoted a large portion of her time to this work, visiting from house to house, and talking and praying with all with whom she came in contact -- instant in season and out of season. No work was so pressing but what there was time for prayer, and no public worship so imposing but that at its close she would earnestly, and with the most tender and thrilling appeals, exhort the unconverted to accept Christ, the believer to a higher, holier life.

"She was truly a godly woman, abundant in labors and in fruits.

"Mother Cobb, as she was known, was loved and respected by everybody, for she loved everybody, regardless of name or sect. Though fallen asleep, she yet lives in the hearts of those who have been saved by her instrumentality or blessed by her counsel. We have no words that can do full justice to the eminently devoted Christian life and character of this mother in Israel. It has been fittingly said of her, that her life is a grand commentary on the thirteenth chapter of First Corinthians, and this, to those who knew her, will be the most appropriate testimony of her Christian worth -- the best epitaph that can be inscribed to her memory.

"Many friends called to see her, and to all she testified to her perfect faith in Christ, and of His grace, not only to sustain but to cheer in a dying hour. Heaven itself seemed open to her, and a holy ecstasy filled her soul. Her last words were 'Victory! Victory! Eternal victory? -- Sixty Years' Walk With God.

### 065 -- "THERE IS LIGHT ALL AROUND ME."

The noted evangelist, Mrs. Grace Weiser Davis, writes of her mother's translation, to The Christian Standard, for July 10, 1898, as follows:

For five months past I have canceled all engagements and been a witness of the triumphs of the power of God to save amid suffering and to cast out all fear that hath torment. My mother left us July 20, aged fifty-nine years and seven months. She was born in York, Pa. She was converted at the same time as my father, just previous to my birth, in a revival that continued almost one year. Our home was always hospitably thrown open to ministers of the gospel. Mother would give them the best she could get and then apologize because it was no better. Hundreds can testify to the ministrations of this combination of Mary and Martha.

After father's death, mother retained her homestead in York, Pa., but spent her time largely between my sister and myself, at least eight months of the year being in my home.

We brought mother to Bradley Beach, hoping for a prolongation of the precious life. She was cheerful and planning for a continued life here. We Shrank from telling her the truth, but God Himself gloriously revealed it to her. The doctor and ministers bore testimony to my own that it was the most glorious death bed we ever witnessed.

One day my mother prayed, "Dear Lord, prepare me for the country to which I am going:" Before the close of the day she was shouting the praises of God. From that time on she talked of her coming translation and her faith so gloriously triumphant.

On Sabbath, June 27, she had a day of wonderful exaltation. She said, "I have always hoped and trusted in God, but now I have a fuller realization than ever before." As we all wept, she said, "I don't realize that this is death. It is His will, and is all right." To the doctor she said, "Just think, doctor, to be forever with the Lord." No one could come into my mother's room thereafter without being spoken to by her upon this glory that was filling her soul. To me she said, "Grace, God has given you gifts that few others possess; let us pray that God will make you a weight of glory in the world. God has blest you, and will still more." One afternoon she said, "I am homesick for heaven." To the doctor, "Sometimes my way has seemed dark', but it was like the Ferris wheel -- it always came round to a point of light." Again she said, "I believe I will get awake sometime and find myself in a strange country, to which I shall be translated!' "Mother, it will not be so strange. Your father and mother and husband and little boy are there, and we are on the way," I answered.

To one lately married she said, "You are just beginning life; it pays to begin right. Everything you do for God is on compound interest -- compound interest. It will be doubly repaid you. I commenced to serve Him in early life, and consecrated my children to Him in infancy, and they are all Christians, and I am so happy."

As I kissed her one day she said, "We will rejoice together in Jesus in heaven." Her favorite words were, "Surely goodness and mercy shall follow me," etc.; her favorite hymn, "Jesus, Lover of My Soul." The night previous to her death she said, "There is light all around me."

Until the last she gave evidence of hearing, seeing and understanding. I knelt within fifteen minutes of her translation and said, "Mother, though you walk through the valley of the shadow of death, you need fear no evil, for God is with you. Surely goodness and mercy shall follow you, and you are going to dwell in the house of the Lord forever." There came a responsive smile. In a few minutes she drew a gentle breath and was translated.

## 066 -- "YOU CANNOT RUN AWAY FROM THE SPIRIT OF GOD."

Several years ago, a gentleman, apparently in great haste, entered a certain city in one of the southern states on horseback, rode up to the hotel, alighted, and introduced himself as follows:

"I have been trying to run away from the Spirit of God, but it has followed me all of these many miles that I have traveled, and it is with me now. I had Christian training, and as I heard the gospel proclaimed from time to time I became deeply convicted of sin; but I was very rebellious and determined not to yield. The Spirit said, 'You must be born again,' but I said, 'I will not be born again.' I purchased this horse, a good, strong beast at the time, and I have worn it down poor, as you see; but I have not succeeded in outrunning the Spirit of God. I feel that I am about to die, and I have a request to make. I want you to sell this horse and bury me here in the street by this sign post, and put up a slab by my grave bearing this inscription, 'You cannot run away from the Spirit of God.' "

The man soon died. Physicians examined him and said there was no disease about him, but that he died of mental agony.

His strange request was granted, and the slab bearing this silent warning preached many a sermon to passers-by, and resulted in a revival of religion in the city of Tuscaloosa, Alabama. -- Written for this book by Mary E. Jenks, McBain, Mich.

## 067 -- JOHN WESLEY'S LAST WORDS -- "THE BEST OF ALL IS, GOD IS WITH US."

This holy man of God went to heaven March 2, 1791, in the eighty-eighth year of his life. He had preached the gospel sixty-five years. Shortly before his death, Mr.

Wesley said, "I will get up"; and whilst they arranged his clothes, he broke out singing in a manner which astonished all about him,

*"I'll praise my Maker while I've breath,
And when my voice is lost in death,
Praise shall employ my nobler powers:
My days of praise shall ne'er be past,
While life, and thought, and being last,
Or immortality endures.
Happy the man whose hopes rely On Israel's God;
He made the sky,
And earth and seas, with all their train;
His truth forever stands secure,
He saves the oppressed.
He feeds the poor,
And none shall find His promise vain."*

Once more seated in his chair, he said in a weak voice, "Lord, Thou givest strength to those who can speak and to those who cannot. Speak, Lord, to all our hearts, and let them know that Thou loosest tongues." And then he sang,

*"To Father, Son and Holy Ghost,
Who sweetly all agree."*

Here his voice failed. After gasping for breath he said, "Now, we have done all." He was then laid on the bed from whence he rose no more. After resting a little, he called to those who were with him to "Pray and praise." Soon after this he said, "Let me be buried in nothing but what is woolen, and let my corpse be carried in my coffin into the chapel." Again calling upon them to pray and praise, he took each by the hand, and, affectionately saluting them, bade them farewell. After attempting to say something which they could not understand, he paused a little, and then, with all the remaining strength he had, said, "The best of all is, God is with us." And again, lifting his hand, he repeated the same words in holy triumph, "The best of all is, God is with us." Being told that his brother's widow had come, he said, "He giveth His servants rest," thanked her as she pressed his hand, and affectionately tried to kiss her. After they had moistened his lips he repeated his usual grace after a meal -- "We thank Thee, O Lord, for these and all Thy mercies; bless the church and king, grant us truth and peace, through Jesus Christ our Lord." And, after a little pause, "The clouds drop fatness. The Lord is with us; the God of Jacob is our refuge." He then called to them to pray, and seemed to join fervently in their petitions. Most of the following night he repeatedly tried to repeat the hymn he had sung, but could only say, "I'll praise, I'll praise." On Wednesday morning his end was near. Joseph Bradford prayed with him about ten o'clock in the morning, whilst eleven friends knelt round the bed. "Farewell," said the dying man, and it was the last word he spoke.

Immediately after, without a groan or a sigh, he passed away. His friends stood round his bed and sang, "Waiting to receive thy spirit, Lo! the Savior stands above; Shows the purchase of His merit, Reaches out the crown of love." -- Kenyon's Life of John Wesley

## 068 -- LITTLE WILLIE LEONARD'S TRANSLATION TO HEAVEN

The following account of the death of Willie Leonard, aged only six years, will be of added interest to many who have read the little book One Year With Jesus, written a few years ago by Mrs. Anna Leonard, of Manton, Michigan, and in which she speaks of Willie. It is taken from a letter written by his mother at the time, seventeen years ago, to a friend who is glad to share it with others.

One day, about two weeks before Willie died, he came in from his play and said, "Mamma, seems to me I wouldn't want to die." When asked why, he said, "O, I wouldn't want to leave you folks here; but then I suppose I would be very happy in heaven, and, mamma, I would watch over you." His mamma clasped him in her arms; she loved him, oh! so much. She felt that the angels were beckoning to him while she talked with him of the joys that awaited him in heaven and that they would meet him there. He then said, "Mamma, I don't want any little lamb on my tomb stone, but I want a little boy lying on the grass as you have seen me lie in the summer time when I was tired out with play." (He never saw nor heard of anything of the kind; but such a stone now marks his grave.) He was taken sick with scarlet fever, of a diphtherial form, and lived but two days. He was such a patient little sufferer through it all! When asked if he was not a pretty sick little boy, he replied, "No, not very sick; but I think Jesus is going to take me to heaven to live," and an angelic look of holy rapture came over his face, with such a radiant smile. His papa was called and as he talked with him about it, that same glorious smile again illuminated his face. He then talked about the disposal of his toys, books, Sabbath school cards and papers (even remembering the writer, so many miles away, "For," said he, "I love her," and the memory is precious as she writes of him today).

He then spoke of a new hat, which he said he would not need now, and his mamma talked with him of the beautiful crown awaiting him in heaven, although her heart seemed bursting with grief. "Willie," said she, "no one can see Jesus when He comes except the one He comes after, so when you see Him will you tell me?" "Yes," he replied, "if I can talk, and if not I will point to Him." He then said he wanted them all to come to heaven. When his little brother told him that his papa had gone after the doctor he said, "O, I would rather that Jesus would take me to heaven than for Dr. Taplin to make me well!" In a few hours he was quite restless and delirious.

I now quote from the letter verbatim: "As we laid him back on his pillow, his eyes remained wide-open and fixed. We felt his feet and found them cold. I hastened and warmed flannels and wrapped them. We chafed his hands, although his finger-nails were blue. How could we believe that our Willie was dying-Willie our hope, our pride, the joy of our home, yes, our very idol! But so it was, and as we gathered round his bed we wept as only parents can weep at such times, and talked loving words to his inanimate form. He was lying very still, when all at once one little hand was raised and he pointed upward for a moment as his dear lips moved in an effort to speak. 'Willie,' I cried aloud, 'do you see Jesus?' His hand was laid again by his side, he breathed shorter and less frequently a few times and then ceased forever. In his last moments he remembered the signal agreed upon between him and me, and pointed me to Jesus.

"When the body that was so beautiful and dear to us was lowered into the silent grave and the earth fell with a hollow sound upon the box below, it seemed as if I could not rise above the shock, when I felt as it were a light breath fan my cheek and a sweet voice seemed to say, 'Mamma, I am not there; don't cry. I am happy.' My tears dried in an instant, and I cannot now think of him as anywhere but in that beautiful heaven where he longed to go. " -- Furnished for this work by Mrs. Eva Simkins, Lester, Mich.

## 069 -- LAST WORDS OF REV. H. Y. HUMELBAUGH

This hero of faith met and vanquished the last foe early on the morning of October 13, 1868. He was a member of Pennsylvania Conference, and spent thirteen years in itinerant work.

When his physician visited him the last time he inquired, "Doctor, what do you think of me?" "You are very ill, sir," was the reply. "Well, I did not expect that," said Mr. Humelbaugh, "but it is all right. I have tried to live a religious life, and now I can say, 'Saved by grace; saved by the grace of God.'" When asked if the gospel he had preached to others comforted his own heart, he quickly answered, "Oh, yes; oh, yes. I was afraid if I did get well I would have to give up preaching, but the Lord has arranged all that now." As the shadows thickened his faith seemed to lay hold of the Redeemer with an all-conquering grasp, and he exclaimed, "O Jesus, receive my spirit. Glory to God for a religion that saves in the dying hour." A friend, approaching his bedside, said, "Well, Brother Humelbaugh, you are going home." "Home! yes; blessed be God, I'm in the old ship sailing for -- glory to God! Glory to God for experimental religion." Lifting both hands, he continued, "Let people say what they choose against experimental religion, thank God it saves in a dying hour." Then, turning to his grief-stricken wife, he sought most tenderly to console her. "Oh, Fanny, weep not for me; I will soon rest, forever rest, from all my troubles. Oh, lead a holy life; train up our children in the fear of the Lord -- in experimental religion -- and tell them to be humble."

Addressing his physician again, he said, "Oh, doctor, what a beautiful land lies just before my eyes." Then in holy ecstasy he cried out: "O King of terrors! end of time! Oh, all is bright! I'll soon be at home. Farewell, pulpit; this is the end of my preaching." Kissing his little son, he said, "God bless you, my boy." With the confidence of Israel's sweet singer, he repeated to himself, "Though I walk through the valley of the shadow of death, I will fear no evil, for Thou art with me." So nearly exhausted was he that he omitted the last sentence, but when some one finished it he replied, "They comfort me; yes, bless God, they comfort me." A few minutes later his pulse was still. He had passed from life to life. -- From Life to Life.

### *070 -- LAST WORDS OF CHARLES IX., KING OF FRANCE -- "I AM LOST; I SEE IT WELL."*

This wicked king died May 30, 1574. His character was a compound of passion, acuteness, heartlessness and cunning. (He was, of course, a Roman Catholic.) The massacre of St. Bartholomew, August 24, 1572, was the culmination of a series of treacheries towards the Huguenots which greatly disgraced his reign. He died a young man. During his last hours he said, "Oh, my nurse, my nurse! What blood, what murders, what evil counsels have I followed! Oh, my God, pardon me and have mercy on me if Thou canst. I know not what I am! What shall I do? I am lost; I see it well."

### *071 -- "THOUGH I WALK THROUGH THE VALLEY OF THE SHADOW OF DEATH, I WILL FEAR NO EVIL."*

Sister Sarah A. Cook, known to many of our readers by her writings and evangelistic work, gives an account of the last days of her sister, who died in England during the spring of 1864. She says in her book, Wayside Sketches:

I was called to the sick bed of my eldest sister, Eliza, living in Melton Mowbray, Leicestershire. I found her suffering from intermittent fever and general prostration. Always delicate, with a mind too active for the frail tenement in which it dwelt, during the first stage of the sickness there seemed a strong clinging to life. Very happy in her marriage relationship -- with many interests -- a circle of loving friends, and an earnest worker in the cause of the Redeemer, life was full of attraction. Then the thought would come of her husband's loneliness without her, and she said, "I would be quite willing to go, but Harry would miss me so much"; but faith triumphed over nature and a little later she said, "The Lord could make Harry a happy home if He should take me."

Day by day the attraction heavenward became stronger. Once, when all was fixed for the night, and I was about leaving the room, she called me to her, and looking earnestly into my face she said, "Sarah, don't you pray for my recovery." Reminding her how much we all loved her and how glad we should be to keep her with us, she answered, "And I love you all very much; but it is so much better to depart and be with Jesus." While with her through the day, and listening to the doctor's cheery and hopeful words, I would think she might recover; but in prayer I could never take hold for her health -- could only breathe out, "Thy will, O Lord, not mine, be done."

The prayer of faith, in which at times our Father enables His children to take hold for the healing of the body, was never given. In His infinite love and wisdom He was calling her home, "Where no storms ever beat on that beautiful strand, While the years of eternity roll."

Every afternoon she liked for about an hour to be left entirely alone. The fever would then be off, and she chose it as the best time for secret communion with the Lord. Opening the door one day, after the hour had passed, she sat upright in bed, her face radiant with joy as she exclaimed, "O, I have had such a view of God's love!" Stretching out her hands, she said. "It seems to me like a boundless ocean, and as though I were lost in that boundless ocean of love!" When suffering from extreme prostration, her favorite lines would be:

*"Christ leads us through no darker rooms
Than He went through before;
He that would to His kingdom come.
Must enter by that door."*

"Do you," said a dear friend to her one day, "have any fear of death?" "Oh, no," she answered, "I don't know that I have ever thought of it." The word death was never on her lips. The "valley of the shadow" was all bridged over. She did not see it, for the eye of faith swept over it, and was on Him who is the resurrection and the life. "To be with Jesus" was her oft-repeated expression; repeating on Friday, with tenderest, deepest joy, the whole of that beautiful hymn:

*"Forever with the Lord,
Amen, so let it be;
Life from the dead is in that word,
'Tis immortality.
"Here in the body pent,
Absent from Him I roam;
Yet nightly pitch my moving tent
A day's march nearer home."*

The Sabbath dawned, her last day on earth. Seeing the end was very near, I hesitated about leaving her to meet her Bible-Class at the chapel, a large class of young women. I had been teaching them every Sabbath afternoon. "Would you like me, dear, to take your class this afternoon?" I asked. "Yes," she answered with some surprise in her voice, "why not? And tell them all I have loved and prayed for them very much." It was a melting time as we all together realized how near the parting was.

Our lesson that day was the words of comfort our Savior had spoken to His disciples, recorded in the 14th of John Returning from the school with the class, they all passed by the open door to take a last look at their loved teacher. Wonderfully all through the day these words were applied to my heart, "If ye loved me ye would rejoice, because I go unto my father"; until the thought of her exceeding blessedness in being so near the presence of Jesus swallowed up all thoughts of sorrow at losing her. Hour after hour passed as the "silver cord was loosening."

An aunt, Mrs. Tuxford, remarked, "You have had seven weeks of peace." "I have had seven weeks of perfect peace," she answered. Her peace flowed like a river all through the day; at times she spoke words of fullest trust. With her head leaning on the bosom of her husband, the last words that our listening ears caught were, "Though I walk through the valley of the shadow of death, I will fear no evil, for Thou art with me." -- Wayside Sketches.

## 072 -- "I AM READY, FOR THIS (MY HEART) HAS BEEN HIS KINGDOM."

Through the kindness of L. B. Balliett, M. D., we furnish our readers with this touching incident:

A boy dying of his wounds in one of our hospitals during the rebellion was asked by the lady nurse, "Are you ready to meet your God, my dear boy?" The large dark eyes opened slowly, and a smile passed over the young soldier's face as he answered, "I am ready, dear lady, for this has been His kingdom," and as he spoke he placed his hand upon his heart. "Do you mean," questioned the lady gently, "that God rules and reigns in your heart?" "Yes," he whispered, then passed away. His hand still lay over his heart after it had ceased to beat.

## 073 -- "I CANNOT BE PARDONED; IT IS TOO LATE! TOO LATE!"

Miss -- was the name of an amiable young lady of my acquaintance who died at the age of sixteen. She was the daughter of respectable and pious parents in one of the New England States. On the cultivation of her mind considerable attention had been bestowed. . . . To what extent her mind had been imbued with religious truth in childhood, I have not been able fully to learn. It is certain that, from her earliest years, she had regarded religion with respect and had entertained the expectation of becoming a Christian before she died . . . One morning, especially, the first impression she had when she awoke was that she must embrace religion then; and that her soul was in imminent danger of being lost if she delayed. . . . She deliberated, she reasoned, she prayed, and finally made up her mind to the deliberate resolution that she would repent and accept the offer of salvation before the close of that day. She did not actually repent then, but resolved that she would do it that day. . . . But the day had its cares and pleasures; business and company filled up its hours, and the night found her as thoughtless, almost, as she had been for months.

The next morning her religious impressions were renewed and deepened. . . . The violated vows of the previous morning gave her some uneasiness; she felt not quite the same confidence in herself that she did before; but she had now formed her resolution so firmly, she was so fixed in her purpose, that she considered the issue could hardly be any longer doubtful; and the agony of her soul gave way to the soothing reflection that she should soon be a Christian. She had now taken, as she imagined, "one step" -- had formed a solemn purpose and had given a pledge to repent that day. She felt, as she expressed it, committed, and hardly had a doubt as to the accomplishment of her purpose. This day also passed as before. She did, indeed, several times during the day think of her resolution, but not with that overwhelming interest she had felt in the morning, and nothing decisive was done.

The next morning her impressions were again renewed, and she again renewed her resolution, and it was dissipated as before; and thus she went on resolving and breaking her resolutions, until at length her anxiety entirely subsided and she entirely relapsed into her former state of unconcern. She was not, however, absolutely indifferent; she still expected and resolved to be a Christian; but her resolutions now looked to a more distant period for their accomplishment, and she returned to the cares and pleasures of the world with the same interest as before.

About this time she went to reside in a neighboring village, and I did not see her again for about three months, when I was called at an early hour one morning to visit her on the bed of death. . . . About daybreak, on the morning of the day she died, she was informed that her symptoms had become alarming, and that her sickness would probably be fatal. The intelligence was awfully surprising. . . . At one time her distress became so intense and her energies so exhausted that she was forced to conclude her soul lost -- that nothing could now be done for it; and for a moment she seemed as if in a horrid struggle to adjust her mind to her anticipated doom. But oh that word Lost. Her whole frame shuddered at the thought.

It was now nearly noon. Most of the morning had been employed either in prayer at her bedside or in attempting to guide her to the Savior; but all seemed ineffectual; her strength was now nearly gone; vital action was no longer perceptible at the extremities, the cold death-sweat was gathering on her brow, and dread despair seemed ready to possess her soul. She saw, and we all saw, that the fatal moment was at hand, and her future prospect one of unmingled horror. She shrank from it. She turned her eyes to me, and called on all who stood around her to beseech once more the God of mercy in her behalf.

We all knelt again at her bedside, and having once more commended her to God, I tried again to direct her to the Savior, and was beginning to repeat some promises which I thought appropriate, when she interrupted me, saying with emphasis, "I can not be pardoned; it i8 too late, too late!" And again alluding to that fatal resolution, she begged of me to charge all the youth of my congregation not to neglect religion as she had done; not to stifle their conviction by a mere resolution to repent. "Warn them, warn them," she said, "by my case" -- and again she attempted to pray, and swooned again.

She continued thus alternately to struggle and faint, every succeeding effort becoming feebler, until the last convulsive struggle closed the scene, and her spirit took its everlasting flight. -- Rev. E. Phelps, D. D.

"Seek ye the Lord while He may be found, call ye upon Him while He is near." (Isa. 55:6.)

## 074 -- "HERE SHE IS, WITH TWO ANGELS WITH HER."

We quote the following experience from A Woman's Life Work, written by the sainted Laura S. Haviland, whose life was full of good works. She says:

I met on the street a sister White, who was much distressed about her son, who was almost gone with consumption, and yet was unwilling to see any minister or religious person, to say anything to him about a preparation for the change. "Do, please, go with me now to see my dying son Harvey. May be he'll listen to you."

I went to her house and found him too weak to talk much. The mother introduced me as her friend who had called on her. I took his emaciated hand and said, "I see you are very low and weak, and I do not wish to worry you with talking, but you have but little hope of being restored to health I should judge from your appearance."

He turned his head on his pillow as he said, "I can never be any better -- I can't live."

"Then your mind has been turned toward the future, and may the enlightening influence of the Holy Spirit lead you to the Great Physician of souls, who knows every desire of the heart, and is able to save to the uttermost, even at the eleventh hour." I saw the starting tear as he looked earnestly at me, while I was still holding his feverish hand in mine. "Will it be too much for you, in your weak condition, if I should read to you a few of the words of our Lord and Savior?"

"O no, I'd like to hear you."

I opened to the fourteenth of John, and upon reading a few verses I saw that the impression made was deepening, and asked if it would worry him too much if l should spend a few moments in prayer. "O no, I'd like to hear you pray."

Placing my hand on his forehead, I implored divine aid in leading this precious soul to the cleansing fountain, and that his faith might increase, and in its exercise be enabled to secure the pearl of great price.

As I arose from his bedside, he reached out both hands for mine and said, "I want you to come tomorrow." He wept freely; and I left with the burden of that precious soul upon my heart.

The mother and sister, who were both professors of religion, stood near the door weeping for joy over the consent of the dear son and brother to listen to the few words of reading and prayer.

The day following I met the sick man again, and as soon as I entered his mother's room she said, "Oh, how thankful to God we are for this visit to my poor boy! He seems in almost constant prayer for mercy. Early this morning he spoke of your coming today."

As I entered his room he threw up both hands, saying, "God will have mercy on poor me, won't He?"

"Most certainly," I responded; "His word is nigh thee, even in thy heart, and in thy mouth."

"Do pray for me," he requested.

I read a few words from the Bible, and followed with prayer, in which he joined with a few ejaculations. I left him much more hopeful than on the previous day.

The next morning his sister came for me in great haste, saying, "Brother Harvey wants to see you, quick."

It was not yet sunrise; but I hastened to obey the message, as I supposed he was dying. Not a word passed between us until we reached her brother's room. Upon opening his door he exclaimed, "Glory, glory to God, Mrs. Haviland! Come to me quick, I want to kiss you; for God brought me out of darkness this morning about the break of day. O hallelujah! Glory to Jesus! He shed His blood for poor me; and I shouted louder than I could talk for a good many days. O, how I wish f had strength to tell everybody that I am happier in one minute than I ever was in all my life put together!"

He became quite exhausted in shouting and talking and I advised him to rest now in the arms of the beloved Savior.

"Yes, I am in His arms. Glory to His name for what He has done for me! I want you to see my cousin George; he is sick and not able to come to see me today."

I told him I would within a few days, and left him, with his cup of salvation overflowing.

About two hours before he died he looked at his mother, smiling, and said, "There's Mary; don't you see her, standing at the foot of my bed?"

"No, my son, mother don't see her."

"O, how beautiful she looks! It seems as if you must see her," and he looked very earnestly at the object. "There, she's gone now." Fifteen minutes before he breathed his last, he said, "Here she is again, and so beautiful! Mother, can't you see her?" "No, son, I can't see her."

"Beautiful, beautiful she is. There, she's gone again." Just as the soul took its flight, he upraised both hands, with a smile, and said, "Here she is, with two angels with her. They've come for me"; and the hands dropped as the breath left him, with the smile retained on his countenance.

The sister Mary, that died a number of years previously, was about four years old; and his mother told me she had not heard her name mentioned in the family for months before Harvey's death.

## 075 -- O MA, THE LORD IS HERE AND I HAVE THE VICTORY."

Beulah Blackman was a girl of unusual loveliness of person and character. As a school teacher, she held up the light of a pure and holy life, often bringing persecution upon herself by her unyielding adherence to the principles of Christianity and righteousness. The writer has seen her while under the pressure of severe criticism with tears streaming down her face as with a smile she said, "This is good for me!" Her aim in living was to do good, to "rescue the perishing" and uplift the downcast.

She was married in the summer of 1897 to Lewis Leonard, but on the following Easter Sunday -- the resurrection day -- her pure spirit took its flight to be forever with the Lord.

For months before she died, she was unable to get to the house of God, but she had her "Dethel"; her little red Bible was always near her, and the young girls who aided her in her housework received advice and admonitions which they will remember while life lasts.

We were called to her home on Saturday evening, and as we entered the room she held up her hands for loving greeting as she said, "O, ma, the Lord is here and I have the victory." As the Spirit came upon her, she laughed and cried as we praised God together.

Upon the arrival of the doctor, she told him that a greater Physician than he had been there and encouraged her so much. As he was not a Christian, she said to him, "You don't understand it."

All through the long night she manifested such patient endurance, with now and then a word for Jesus, in Whom we all knew she trusted. As her strength failed, she said again, "I am so glad I have the Lord."

As morning broke bright and beautiful, she welcomed her infant son into the world, "with only time for one long kiss and then to leave him motherless."

Her heart, naturally weak, failed, and she appeared to be paralyzed. An effort was made to arouse her so that she could look again at her babe, but she could neither move nor speak. Her husband begged of her to speak once more, and failing to do that, he asked her to smile if she still knew him, which she did, and as he kissed the dear pale lips they parted in an effort to return the demonstration of love. Then, like a weary child going to sleep in its mother's arms, she leaned her head on Jesus' breast and breathed her life out sweetly there.

While we wept she lifted her eyes upward and gazed an instant as if surprised, then smile after smile illuminated her face, showing plainly that fullness of joy was certain. A holy influence filled the room. There was no terror there. There seemed to be angelic visitors waiting to conduct her home. Tears were dried. It seemed as if the gates of heaven were ajar and a glimpse of the glory which awaits the faithful was given to mortals. A moment more and all was over. A look of peaceful victory rested on the lovely features. Truly God is our Father. He is love. -- Written For this work by Mrs. Anna M. Leonard, Manton, Mich..

## *076 -- "MURDER I MURDER I MURDER!"*

When Mr. R___, from Baltimore, was seized with cholera, he sent for me to come and see him, and said to me when I entered his room, "My wife, who is a Christian woman, has been writing me ever since I came here to make your acquaintance and attend your church, but I have not done it; and what is worse, I am about to leave the world without a preparation to meet God." He was as noble-looking a man as could be found in a thousand, and knowing' many of his friends in Baltimore I felt the greatest possible sympathy for him; my soul loved him, and I determined, if possible, to contest the devil's claim on him to the last moment of his life. But he was in despair, and after laboring with him about an hour, in urging him to try to fix his mind on some precious promise of the Bible, he said:

"There is but one passage in the Bible that I can call to mind, and that haunts me. I can think of nothing else, for it exactly suits my case: 'He that, being often reproved, hardeneth his heart; shall suddenly be destroyed, and that without remedy.' Mr. Taylor," continued he, "it's no use to talk to me, or to try to do anything further; I am that man, and my doom is fixed."

The next day when I entered his room he said to a couple of young men present, "Go out, boys, I want to talk to Mr. Taylor." Then he said, "I have no hope, my doom is fixed; but, for the warning of others, I want to tell you something that occurred a few months ago. I was then in health, and doing a good business, and a man said to me, 'Dick, how would you like to have a clerkship?' and I replied, 'I wouldn't have a clerkship under Jesus Christ.' Now, sir, that is the way I treated Christ when I thought I did not need Him; and now when I'm dying, and can do no better for this life, it's presumption to offer myself to Him. It is no use; He won't have me."

Nothing that I could say seemed to have any effect toward changing his mind. A few hours afterward, when he felt the icy grasp of death upon his heart, he cried, "Boys, help me out of this place!"

"O no, Dick, you're too sick; we cannot help you up."

"O do help me up; I can't lie here."

"O Dick, don't exert yourself so; you'll hasten your death."

"Boys," said the poor fellow, "if you don't help me up, I'll cry Murder!" and with that he cried at the top of his voice, which was yet strong and clear, "Murder: murder! murder!" till life's tide ebbed out, and his voice was hushed in death. How dreadful the hazard of postponing the business of life, the great object for which life is given, to the hour when heart and flesh are failing! -- California Life Illustrated.

### 077 -- "MY HEAVEN! HEAVEN -- GLORY!"

Mrs. Dorcas Eskridge, of Blue Grove, Texas, writes us as follows:

My father, Willison Foster, who was a licensed exhorter in the M. E. Church South, died near Chico, Texas, April 2, 1887, aged seventy-one years. He was one of the purest Christians I ever knew, was often made happy in a Savior's love and died shouting. His last words were, "My heaven! Heaven! Glory!" I had often heard him remark that he did not believe that the dying saints ever saw departed spirits, while dying. I believed they did. To satisfy myself on this subject, I made the request during his sickness that if he came to die and should see spirits near him, that he would raise his hand in token that he saw them, if he was unable to speak. Sure enough, just before consciousness left him, he raised his right hand and pointed upward. I do praise the Lord for the dying testimony of one in whom I had so much confidence. Dear, precious one! My mother also went home shouting.

### 078 -- FRANCES RIDLEY HAVERGAL -- "THERE NOW, IT IS ALL OVER! BLESSED REST."

This holy woman of God was born at Astley, England, Dec. 14, 1836. She was the youngest daughter of Rev. Wm. II. and Jane Havergal. Her father was a distinguished minister of the Episcopal Church. She was baptized in Astley Church by Rev. John Cawood, Jan. 25, 1837. She bore the name of Ridley in memory of the godly and learned Bishop Ridley, who was one of the noble army of martyrs. Many have been greatly helped by her writings in prose and verse.

She was translated to heaven from Caswell Bay, England, June 3, 1879. A short time before her death she spoke to her sister Ellen and said, "I should have liked my death to be like Samson's, doing more for God's glory than by my life; but He wills it otherwise."

Ellen replied, "St. Paul said, 'The will of the Lord be done,' and, 'Let Christ be magnified, whether by my life or by my death.'"

I think it was then my beloved sister whispered, "Let my own text, 'The blood of Jesus Christ, His Son, cleanseth us from all sin,' be on my tomb; all the verse if there is room."

She said to her sister, "I do not know what God means by it, but no new thoughts for poems or books come to me now." At another time she said, "Spite the breakers, Marie, I am so happy; God's promises are so true. Not a fear." When the doctor bid her good-bye and told her that he really thought she was going, she said, "Beautiful, too good to be true! Splendid to be so near the gate of heaven! So beautiful to go!"

The Vicar of Swansea said to her, "You have talked and written a good deal about the King, and you will soon see Him in His beauty. Is Jesus with you now?"

"Of course," she replied; "it is splendid! I thought He would have left me here a long while; but He is so good to take me now." At another time she said, "Oh, I want all of you to speak bright, bright words about Jesus, Oh, do, do! It is all perfect peace, I am only waiting for Jesus to take me in."

Afterward she sang the following stanza:

*"Jesus, I will trust Thee,*
*Trust Thee with my soul"*
*Guilty, lost and helpless,*
*Thou hast made me whole --*
*There is none in heaven,*
*Or on earth like Thee:*
*Thou hast died for sinners,*
*Thou hast died for me,"*

The parting scene is graphically described as follows:

"There came a terrible rush of convulsive sickness; it ceased, the nurse gently assisting her. She nestled down in the pillows, folded her hands on her breast, saying, 'There, now it's all over. Blessed rest!'

"And now she looked up steadfastly as if she saw the Lord; and, surely, nothing less heavenly could have reflected such a glorious radiance upon her face. For ten minutes we watched that almost visible meeting with her King, and her countenance was so glad, as if she were already talking to Him. Then she tried to sing; but after one sweet, high note, 'He--," her voice failed; and, as her brother commended her soul into her Redeemer's hand, she passed away. Our precious sister was gone -- satisfied -- glorified -- within the palace of her King! -- Life of Frances R. Havergal.

## 079 -- AN INFIDEL'S LIFE SPARED A FEW DAYS

"During the summer of 1862, I became acquainted with a Mr. A___, who professed infidelity, and who was, I think, as near an atheist as any I ever met. I held several conversations with him on the subject of religion, but could not seem to make any impression on his mind, and when a point was pressed strongly he would become angry.

"In the fall he was taken ill and seemed to go into a rapid decline. I, with others, sought kindly and prayerfully to turn his mind to his need of a Savior, but only met with rebuffs. As I saw that his end was drawing near, one day I pressed the importance of preparing to meet God, when he became angry and said I need not trouble myself any more about his soul, as there was no God, the Bible was a fable, and when we die that is the last of us, and was unwilling that I should pray with him. I left him, feeling very sad.

"Some four weeks after, on New Year's morning, I awoke with the impression that I should go and see Mr. A___, and I could not get rid of that impression; so, about nine o'clock, I went to see him, and as I approached the house I saw the two doctors, who had been holding a consultation, leaving. When I rang the bell, his sister-in-law opened the door for me, and exclaimed, 'Oh! I am so glad you have come; John is dying. The doctors say he cannot possibly live above two hours, and probably not one.' When I went up to his room, he sat bolstered up in a chair, and appeared to have fallen into a doze. I sat down about five feet from him, and when in about two minutes he opened his eyes and saw me, he started up, with agony pictured on his face and in the tones of his voice, and exclaimed, 'O! Mr. P___, I am not prepared to die; there is a God; the Bible is true! O, pray for me! pray God to spare me a few days till I shall know I am saved!'

"These words were uttered with the intensest emotion, while his whole physical frame quivered through the intense agony of his soul. I replied in effect that Jesus was a great Savior, able and willing to save all who would come unto Him, even at the eleventh hour, as He did the thief on the cross.

"When I was about to pray with him, he again entreated me to pray especially that God would spare him a few days, till he might have the evidences of his salvation. In prayer I seemed to have great assurance of his salvation and asked God to give us the evidence of his salvation by granting him a few more days in this world. Several others joined in praying God to spare him a few days, till he should give evidence of being saved.

"I called again in the evening; he seemed even stronger than in the morning, and his mind was seeking the truth. The next day as I entered, his face expressed the fact that peace and joy had taken the place of fear and anxiety. He was spared some five days, giving very clear evidence that he had passed from death to life. His ease was a great mystery to the doctors. They could not understand how he lived so long; but his friends, who had been praying for him, all believed it was in direct answer to prayer." -- Wonders of Prayer.

## 080 -- "YOU WILL LET ME DIE AND GO TO HELL BEFORE YOU WILL SUFFER A NEGRO TO PRAY FOR ME."

A Mr. H___, a wealthy planter in South Carolina about forty years since, came to the dying hour. He had made this world his god, and used his influence and money against the religion of the Bible. When the last hour came, he felt that he was a ruined man and requested his wife, who was as sinful as he, to pray for him. Her reply was, "I can't do it. I don't know how. I never prayed in my life."

"Well," said he, "send for one who is a Christian to pray for me."

She replied, "For whom shall I send?"

"Send at once," said he, "for Harry, the coachman; he is a man of God."

"No," she replied, "I'll never do that. It would be an everlasting disgrace to have a Negro pray for you in your house."

"Then you will let me die and go to hell before you will suffer a Negro to pray for me!" And she did. -- Written for this book by Rev. E. G. Murrah.

What a multitude are kept from coming to God by their pride and by the pride of other friends! "Pride goeth before destruction, and a haughty spirit before a fall." (Prov. 16: 18.)

## 081 -- "MOTHER, I'M GOING TO JESUS, AND HE'S HERE IN THIS ROOM, ALL AROUND ME."

The noted evangelist, Rev. E. P. Hammond, sends us this touching experience:

A lady from Brooklyn, New York, has just sent me a most touching story about a little cousin of hers, only nine years old. I could scarcely keep the tears from my eyes while reading it.

This little boy's praying mother had been called to part with five of her children. This, her youngest, she dearly loved, and when he showed signs of having learned to trust and love the dear Jesus, she loved him all the more.

I will let you read a part of this kind lady's letter, just as it was read to me:

"One Sunday evening, last spring, he was left alone with his sister, whose husband had died a few weeks before. After endeavoring to comfort her in various ways, he suddenly said, 'Sister, have you heard me tell a lie for a long time? I used to tell a great many, but I don't think I have now for six months, and

I don't think God will let me tell any more; I don't want ever to do another wrong thing.' When he went to bed that night, she heard him pray that God would soon make him fit for those mansions that eye had not seen, nor ear heard about.

"On Thursday of that week he went with two little boys to get some fireworks, that he might 'amuse sister' on the fourth of July. The railway train was going very slowly up a long hill, and for amusement the boys stepped off the back platform and on to the front one, when Charley slipped, and the wheel of the carriage passed directly over his hip, crushing the bone to powder. He uttered one scream, and then never complained again; but when a policeman was lifting him from his dreadful position, he opened his eyes and said, 'Don't blame anybody; it was my fault. But tell my mother I'm going right to my Savior.'

"The rough policeman in telling of this said, 'We all felt that there must be some reality in that boy's religion.' He gave his name and residence while they were carrying him to the hospital. The sad news was told to his mother by two little street children, who expressed it in these terms: 'Does Charley H___ live here? Well, he's smashed.' She followed the children and literally tracked her child by his blood to the hospital. When she entered the room where he lay, he opened his eyes and said, 'Mother, I'm going to Jesus, and He's here in this room, all around me. Oh, I love Him so much! Don't let them cut off my leg; but, if they do, never mind -- it won't hurt me as much as Jesus was hurt.' When his father arrived, he looked up and said, 'Papa, I am going to my Savior; tell my brother Eddy if he feels lonely now, because he has no brother, to learn to love Jesus, and He will be his brother, and love him so much.' These were the last words he said, for in about two hours he bled to death. The hospital nurse said, as she closed his eyes, 'He has gone to that Savior he talked so much about, and I will try to love Him too.' When his mother returned to her home, her only words were, 'The Lord has taken my Charley though He slay me, yet will I trust in Him.'"

Little Charley was very fond of the sweet hymns he had learned. Though he was but nine years old, he loved the Sunday school, where he heard so much about how Jesus died on the cross that our sins might all be washed away, and we be taken home to heaven to live with Him for ever.

## 082 -- "I AM READY! I AM COMING!"

The noted evangelist, Rev. E. P. Hammond, sends us this touching experience:

At a time when a great many little children were seeking the precious Savior, the following lines were handed to me. I am sure they will interest every little reader.

I must tell you the story about this dear "child angel." She lived near Barnet, where I think she learned to love the Savior. She used to learn little hymns about

Jesus. Before she was five years old, she grew very sick. But though she could hardly speak, she was often heard lisping sweet hymns about Jesus. Only an hour before she died, she rose up and asked for her best clothes; "for," she said, "I am going a long journey." She then walked up and down the floor of her room repeating the hymn, "Gentle Jesus." She soon grew very weak and had to be put into bed. After lying there awhile, she raised herself a little and turning to the wall lifted up her hands, as if she saw some one in the distance, and repeated, again and again, "I am ready! I am coming!" till her sweet voice was hushed in the silence of death, and she was led by Him who carries the lambs in His bosom, to the mansions above.

## *083 -- "I HAVE GIVEN MY IMMORTALITY FOR GOLD."*

About fifty years since, there died in Middle, Georgia, a Mr. F___. He began in his early manhood to lay up riches upon earth, and having labored to this end for forty years, came to the dying hour.

Just before his final departure he called his wife to his bedside and said, "I would rather lie on that bed of coals (pointing to the grate) and broil for one million years than go into eternity with the eternal horrors that hang over my soul! I have given my immortality for gold! I have enough of the sordid stuff to make you a horse block upon which to mount your horse, and its weight sinks me into an endless, hopeless, helpless hell!"

In those days horse-back riding was very common and to enable people to mount with ease they had what was called horse-blocks, made of the body of a forest tree, about two feet high, with a step on one side midway between the bottom and top. To this the dying man alluded. -- Written for this work by Rev. E. G. Murrah.

"And He said unto them, Take heed, and beware of covetousness: for a man's life consisteth not in the abundance of the things which he possesseth. And He spake a parable unto them, saying, The ground of a certain rich man brought forth plentifully: and he thought within himself, saying, What shall I do, because I have no room where to bestow my fruits? And he said, This will I do: I will pull down my barns, and build greater; and there will I bestow all my fruits and my goods. And I will say to my soul, Soul, thou hast much goods laid up for many years; take thine ease, eat, drink and be merry. But God said unto him, Thou fool! this night thy soul shall be required of thee: then whose shall those things be, which thou hast provided? So is he that layeth up treasure for himself, and is not rich toward God." (Luke 12: 15-21.)

## 084 -- BISHOP HAVEN'S LAST WORDS -- "THERE IS NO RIVER HERE. IT IS ALL BEAUTIFUL!"

This sainted bishop of the Methodist Church entered his episcopal office in 1872. One of his biographers says, "He was the most intense man of his generation." He could not rest night or day unless he saw the work of God prospering. His rest was in the Lord's work. "There remaineth therefore a rest to the people of God. For he that is entered into his rest, he also hath ceased from his own works, as God did from His." He was a very affectionate man. We read "that he mourned the death of his wife so intensely that he would spend whole nights at her grave in tears and groans." "I will lay my head in her lap for a thousand years in heaven and rest it," said he in a time of longing and accusation. In the end of 1879 a medical man of Cincinnati pronounced him suddenly worn out, and he hastened to his family home at Melden, Mass., to die. Crowds of friends came and his last days were a continual levee. He died in glorious peace, Jan. 3, 1880. In his last moments he said to his physician, "Good night, doctor: When we meet again it will be good morning!" His last words were, "There is no river here! All is beautiful."

## 085 -- AN INFIDELS LAST WORDS -- "HELL AND DAMNATION."

An aged and rebellious infidel died in Freedom, a few years ago. Whilst he lay sick he refused any Christian the privilege of talking with him on religious subjects. Shortly before he died he started suddenly up in his bed, screaming, "The devils are come, the devils are come, keep them off me!" and then fell into a swoon. Just before he died he seemed to summon all his strength, rose up in his bed, shouted "Hell and damnation, hell and damnation!" fell back, choked, strangled and died. -- Rev. Thos. Graham.

## 086 -- LAST WORDS OF DR. WAKELEY -- "I SHALL NOT BE A STRANGER IN HEAVEN."

The death-scene was in harmony with his life experience. Taken suddenly and violently ill, he was composed amid his acute sufferings, and without alarm as to the issue. When his physicians informed him they had no hope of his recovery, he received the information without agitation and continued tranquil and happy. I have seen many Christians die happily, but I never witnessed such perfect naturalness. He conversed and acted in the same manner, with the same tone of voice, the same pleasant countenance, and the same cheerful spirit which characterized him in health. In his sickness, from first to last, everything he said and did was perfectly Wakeleyan. It really did not seem like a death-scene. It appeared more like the breaking of morning and the advancing of day than the approach of evening and the gathering of the night shadows.

At my first interview with him he said, "The doctors tell me there is no hope of my recovery; but I can say with Paul, 'I am now ready to be offered, and the time of my departure is at hand; I have fought good fight; I have (almost) finished my course; I have kept the faith.' I see my crown and mansion and inheritance." I said to him, "Yes, but you must die to possess them."

He instantly responded:

*"By death I shall escape from death,
And life eternal gain."*

At another time he said, "I have fought long, fought honorably, fought heroically, fought successfully, fought for God, fought for Jesus, fought for Methodism, fought for Christianity. I have not gained all I wished; but, through Christ, I have taken great spoils."

He quoted, "I am the resurrection and the life. He that believeth in Me, though he were dead, yet shall he live; and whosoever liveth and believeth in Me shall never die." Looking at me very earnestly, he said, "Believest thou this?" I said, "With all my heart." He responded, with much emotion, "So do I." Lifting up his hand, he said,

*"The Head that once was crowned with thorns
Is crowned with glory now;
A royal diadem adorns
The mighty Conqueror's brow."*

"The spiritual kingdom of Christ in the earth is a mighty one. It must be set up in all the earth. It will over all prevail."

A few hours before his exit I said to him, "What shall I say to your brethren in the ministry from you?"

"Preach the Word; be instant in season, out of season; reprove, rebuke, exhort, with all long-suffering and doctrine"; repeating the words "with all long-suffering" three times. After a few moment's rest, he added, "Tell them what Peter says, 'If any man speak, let him speak as the oracles of God; if any man minister, let him do it as of the ability which God giveth, that God in all things may be glorified, through Jesus Christ, to Whom be praise and dominion for ever and ever. Amen.'"

After a moment's rest, while panting for breath, he added, "Tell them to preach the old gospel; we want no new one. The old gospel is to save the world; it can't be improved. One might as well attempt to improve a ray of sunshine while vivifying a flower. The grand old gospel forever!" After a short pause, to take breath, he said, "Tell them to go where they are sent."

Speaking of his whole case, all the interests involved in his demise, he said, "I leave all with God. I want it distinctly understood, I do so without any fear, without any cowardice, without any alarm; I do it with the boldness of an old soldier, and with the calmness of a saint."

He said, "They will inquire in the morning, 'Is Brother Wakeley dead?' Dead? No! Tell them he is better, and alive for evermore."

I said, "Yes, and a higher and nobler life."

He replied, "Wonderfully enlarged! Oh, wonderfully enlarged!"

"Let me have a little plot in the quiet cemetery, and let me sleep there until the great rising day."

"I know the old ship. The Pilot knows me well. He will take me safe into port. Heavenly breezes already fan my cheeks."

"I shall not be a stranger in heaven. I am well known up there."

"Like Bunyan, I see a great multitude with white robes, and I long to be with them. To depart and be with Christ is far better."

"When you go to the grave, don't go weeping. Death hath no sting. The grave hath no terror.

Eternity hath no darkness. Sing at my funeral,
'Rejoice for a brother deceased
Our loss is his gain.'

For many years neither death nor the grave had any terrors for me."

"Hark! hark! hear ye not the song? Victory is ours. There is great rejoicing in heaven. Roll open, ye golden gates, and let my car go through! I must wait until the death-angel descends" Soon the death-angel came. The silver cord was loosed, the golden bowl was broken, and his freed spirit ascended to glory and to God. -- Bishop Janes.

## 087 -- HE CLINCHED HIS TEETH WHILE HE CRIED "HELL, HELL, HELL!"

Near L___ lived P___ K___, talented and wealthy, but a hater of God, of the Lord Jesus Christ and of the Holy Bible. He talked, lectured and published books and tracts against the Savior and the sacred scriptures, circulating them freely wherever he could. His influence for evil had been very great in all that country for years.

From a near neighbor and from members of his household the following facts are learned concerning his death:

His death-bed beggared description. He clinched his teeth, and blood spurted from his nostrils while he cried "Hell! Hell!! Hell!!!" with a terror that no pen can describe. A neighbor declared that he heard him a quarter of a mile away. His family could not endure the agony of that death-bed scene. They fled to an adjoining wood across the road, and there remained among the trees until all became quiet at home. One by one they ventured back, to find the husband and father cold in death. He literally had been left to die alone, abandoned of God and of man. -- Written for this work by Milburn Merrill, Denver, Colorado.

## 088 -- THE LAST WORDS OF A MOTHER AND CHILD

Through the kindness of L. B. Balliett, M. D., of Allentown, Penn., we furnish our readers with this touching incident:

Little Mary was an attendant of an industrial school in New York City. In her last moments she sang, "Come to Jesus," when the angels carried her to heaven.

Two years after the mother died. As death drew near she exclaimed, "Don't you hear my child singing? She is singing the same sweet song, 'Come to Jesus,' that she learned at school."

## 089 -- DYING TESTIMONY OF CARDINAL WOLSEY

Thomas Wolsey, a distinguished person in the reign of Henry VIII., was born in the year 1471; and it is said he was the son of a butcher at Ipswich. Being made chaplain to the king, he had great opportunities of gaining his favor; to obtain which he practiced all the arts of obsequiousness. Having gradually acquired an entire ascendency over the mind of Henry, he successively obtained several bishoprics, and at length was made archbishop of York, lord high chancellor of England and prime minister, and was for several years the arbiter of Europe. The emperor, Charles the fifth, and the French king, Francis the first, courted his interest and loaded him with favors. As his revenues were immense and his influence unbounded, his pride and ostentation were carried to the greatest height. He had eight hundred servants, amongst whom were nine or ten lords, fifteen knights and forty esquires.

From this great height of power and splendor he was suddenly precipitated into ruin. His ambition to be pope, his pride, his exactions and his opposition to Henry's divorce occasioned his disgrace. This sad reverse so affected his mind as to bring on a severe illness, which soon put a period to his days. A short time before he left the world, the review of his life and a consciousness of the misapplication of his time and talents drew from him this sorrowful declaration: "Had I but served God as diligently as I have served the king, He would not have given me over in my gray hairs. But this is the just reward that I must receive for my incessant pains and study, not regarding my service to God, but only to my prince." -- Power of Religion.

## *090 -- "THE ANGELS SAY THERE IS PLENTY OF ROOM UP THERE."*

Sister Kate H. Booth, of Buffalo, N. Y., sends us the account of her sister's happy death. She says:

My sister was a devoted Christian. To show the depth of her piety, we quote from her diary:

"Friday, Aug. 22, 1879 -- I consecrated myself anew to follow God. The fire came down and consumed the sacrifice. All was put on the altar and remains there.

Tuesday, Aug. 26 -- I received such a baptism as I never received before, and today I say,

'Anyway, Jesus, only glorify Thyself.'
Give joy or grief, give ease or pain,
Take life or friends away,
But let me find them all again.
In that eternal day.'
Sudden death would be sudden glory."

She was constantly praising the Lord for His mercy and grace. She was thankful for every kindness shown. Some of her expressions were: "It's all right, it is all clear, death has lost its sting, almost there."

One evening while the sun was setting and the autumn leaves were tinged with a golden hue, she said, "Yea, though I walk through the valley of the shadow of death I will fear no evil, for Thou art with me. Thy rod and Thy staff, they comfort me."

She had a vision of the unseen world. While her face was radiant with a divine halo, and it seemed as though she was about to leave us, I called, "Oh, Jennie, what are your last words?" She revived and said, "Be true; but what made you call me back?" I said, "What did you see?" She replied, "It's all right there," and waved her hand in token of victory.

During her illness she would express the desire that she might retain her consciousness to the last, and she requested the members of her family to pray that her wish might be fulfilled. She did not want them to give up praying till the answer came.

Her desire was granted. In full possession of her faculties she came to the river brink. She would say.

"Labor is rest, and pain is sweet,
If Thou, my God, art here."

She asked me to read the hymn commencing, "How blest the righteous when he dies."

She thought it was so beautiful that she requested it to be sung at her funeral. On Tuesday night she said, "It is a hard struggle tonight, but a glorious victory tomorrow." Wednesday was her last day on earth; a bright and glorious one, for she felt she was soon to enter into the presence of her Lord. It was the first of October and her father's birthday. In the evening, an hour or two before her departure, the doctor came in and she looked up at him with a smile and said, "Doctor, how am I?" The tears were coursing down his cheeks, when she said, "The angels say there is plenty of room up there." Thus she neared the crossing.

## 091 -- THOMAS PAINE'S DYING WORDS -- "MY GOD, MY GOD, WHY HAST THOU FORSAKEN ME?"

Thomas Paine was born at Thedford, England, in 1737. He is widely known by his connection with the American and French revolutions and by his infidel writings.

In 1791 he published his work, entitled, The Rights of Man. In 1793, while in a French prison, he wrote his famous work, The Age of Reason, against atheism and against Christianity and in favor of deism. In 1802 he returned to the United States, where he died in 1809. We take the following from Farrar's Critical History of Free Thought:

"In Paine, who wrote in France in the midst of the French convention, we meet a reproduction of the spirit of early English deism, animated by the political exasperation which had characterized the French. His doctrines come from English deism; his bitterness from Voltaire; his politics from Rousseau. To Paine are due the socialistic schemes of Owen, which in some respects seem to be derived by direct lineage from him, also the expression of unbelief in the poetry of Byron and Shelley.... During the session of the French Convention, Paine composed his infidel work, Age of Reason, by which his name has gained an unenviable notoriety; and after the alteration of political circumstances in France he returned to America and there dragged out a miserable existence, indebted in his last illness for acts of charity to disciples of the very religion that he had opposed."

Again we quote from McIllvaine's Evidences:

"Paine's first wife is said to have died by ill usage. His second was rendered so miserable by neglect and unkindness that they separated by mutual agreement. His third companion, not his wife, was the victim of his seduction while he lived upon the hospitality of her husband. Holding a place in the excise of England, Paine was dismissed for irregularity; restored and dismissed again for fraud without recovery. Unable to get employment where he was known, he came to this country, commenced as a politician, and pretended to some faith in Christianity. Congress gave him an office, from which, being soon found guilty of a breach of trust, he resigned in disgrace. The French revolution allured him to France. Habits of intoxication made him a disagreeable inmate in the American minister's house, where out of compassion he had been received as a guest. During all this time, his life was a compound of ingratitude and perfidy of hypocrisy and avarice, of lewdness and adultery. In June, 1809, the. poor creature died in this country."

The Roman Catholic bishop Fenwick says: "A short time before Paine died I was sent for by him. He was prompted to do this by a poor Catholic woman who went to see him in his sickness and who told him if anybody could do him any good it was a Catholic priest. I was accompanied by F. Kohlmann, an intimate friend. We found him at a house in Greenwich (now Greenwich street, New York), where he lodged. A decent-looking elderly woman came to the door and inquired whether we were the Catholic priests, 'for,' said she, 'Mr. Paine has been so much annoyed of late by other denominations calling upon him that he has left express orders to admit no one but the clergymen of the Catholic Church.' Upon informing her who we were, she opened the door and showed us into the parlor... 'Gentlemen,' said the lady, 'I really wish you may succeed with Mr. Paine, for he is laboring under great distress of mind ever since he was told by his physician that he cannot possibly live and must die shortly. He is truly to be pitied. His cries when left alone are heart rending. "O Lord, help me!" he will exclaim during his paroxysms of distress; "God, help me! Jesus Christ, help me!" -- repeating these expressions in a tone of voice that would alarm the house.

Sometimes he will say, "O God! what have I done to suffer so much?" Then shortly after, "But there is no God"; and then again, "Yet if there should be, what would become of me hereafter?" Thus he will continue for some time, when, on a sudden, he will scream as if in terror and agony, and call for me by my name. On one occasion I inquired what he wanted. "Stay with me," he replied, "for God's sake! for I cannot bear to be left alone." I told him I could not always be in the room. "Then," said he, "send even a child to stay with me, for it is a hell to be alone." 'I never saw,' she continued, 'a more unhappy, a more forsaken man. It seems he cannot reconcile himself to die.' Such was the conversation of the woman, who was a Protestant, and who seemed very desirous that we should afford him some relief in a state bordering on complete despair. Having remained some time in the parlor, we at length heard a noise in the adjoining room. We proposed to enter, which was assented to by the woman, who opened the door for us.

A more wretched being in appearance I never beheld. He was lying in a bed sufficiently decent in itself, but at present besmeared with filth; his look was that of a man greatly tortured in mind, his eyes haggard, his countenance forbidding, and his whole appearance that of one whose better days had been but one continued scene of debauch. His only nourishment was milk punch, in which he indulged to the full extent of his weak state. He had partaken very recently of it, as the sides and corners of his mouth exhibited very unequivocal traces of it, as well as of blood which had also followed in the track and left its mark on the pillow. Upon their making known the object of their visit, Paine interrupted the speaker by saying, 'That's enough, sir, that's enough. I see what you would be about. I wish to hear no more from you, sir; my mind is made up on that subject. I look upon the whole of the Christian scheme to be a tissue of lies, and Jesus Christ to be nothing more than a cunning knave and impostor. Away with you, and your God, tool leave the room instantly! All that you have uttered are lies, filthy lies, and if I had a little more time I would prove it, as I did about your impostor, Jesus Christ.' Among the last utterances that fell upon the ears of the attendants of this dying infidel, and which have been recorded in history, were the words, 'My God, my God, why hast thou forsaken me?'"

### 092 -- "LOOK AT THE LITTLE CHILDREN; O MA, I MUST GO!"

Through the kindness of Mrs. T. W. Roberts, of East Nashville, Tenn., we furnish our readers with the following:

My little sister, Minnie Chatham, was born in 1861 and died in the spring of 1873, aged twelve years.

During her sickness, which lasted for two weeks, she was a great sufferer, Our father and mother were with her constantly night and day during her illness.

Minnie was always of a sweet, gentle and religious nature. She dearly loved her Sabbath school and teachers and was always present when her health would permit. Her constant prayer was, "O God, give me a new heart." Sometimes her older friends would say to her, "Why, Minnie, you are a good little girl, you don't need to pray for a new heart"; and she would reply, "Yes I do, there is none good, we are all sinners."

One day during her illness, with the consent of her parents, she managed to get out of her little bed and kneel down at the foot-board on the floor. With her hands clasped and eyes lifted toward heaven, she prayed the most earnest prayer that [ have ever heard. Her petitions were, "O Lord, give me a new heart," after which she repeated the Lord's Prayer through. She then arose, clapped her hands and said, "Oh, I am so happy!" Returning to her bed, she lay down and was as peaceful and quiet as though she had never experienced any pain. Her mother had told her that Jesus could ease her pain, so often when she was suffering you might have seen her little hands clasped in prayer. Sometimes she would sing a verse or two of her Sunday school songs that she loved so well. She called for her Testament and Sunday school papers, which she placed under her pillow and kept there until she died. Shortly before she breathed her last she sat up in her bed and said, "The angels have come for me, I must go! They are at the door waiting for me. Do, ma, let me go! Why do you want to keep me here in this wicked world? I would not want to stay here for anything." And then she looked up toward heaven and continued, "Look at the little children! O ma, I must go! I would not want to do anything to displease my dear Savior." After this she called her father to her bedside, requested him to be good and meet her in heaven and then added, "I want you all to be good."

The next morning she said to her mother, "Now, ma, if you had let me go, I would have been with the angels this morning." The day before she died, she sang her favorite Sunday school song:

*"There is no name so sweet on earth,*
*No name so sweet in heaven,*
*The name, before His wondrous birth,*
*To Christ, the Savior, given.*

Chorus

*We love to sing around our King.*
*And hail Him blessed Jesus,*
*For there's no word ear ever heard*
*So dear, so sweet as Jesus."*

Not long after this she closed her eyes and breathed her last as peacefully as though she had just fallen asleep. Her public school teacher came to see her the day after she died and as she gazed at the little silent face in the coffin she wept as though her heart would break. She said Minnie was the brightest and sweetest child she had ever met and was a perfect example for all her classes.

## 093 -- "THEN I AM DAMNED TO ALL ETERNITY."

Rev. Thomas Graham, the well-known evangelist, is authority for the following:

When I was holding a protracted meeting in Middlesex, Mercer county, Pa., December, 1843, a man named Edwards died under the following circumstances: He had killed his hog and was preparing the sausages. He took of the ground pepper and introduced it into the nostrils of several persons to make them sneeze. One of the company succeeded in doing so to him, which made him sneeze twice, He broke a blood vessel. The doctor was sent for, but to no beneficial purpose. The rupture was so far up in the head that nothing could be done for him. When he was told that he must die, he shrieked so that he could be heard almost a mile, crying "Then I am damned to all eternity!" and continued this fearful exclamation until he died -- being an awful warning to others not to defer the time of their return to God.

## 094 -- TRIUMPHANT DEATH OF MARTIN LUTHER

This great German reformer was born at Eisleben (a town in Saxony not far from Wittenberg), November 10, 1483. Died at the same place. February 18. 1546. We take the following from Schaff's encyclopedia.

Luther stands forth as the great national hero of the German people, and the ideal of German life. Perhaps no other cultivated nation has a hero who so completely expresses the national ideal. King Arthur comes, perhaps, nearest to Luther among the English-speaking race. He was great in his private life as well as in his public career. His home is the ideal of cheerfulness and song. He was great in thought and great in action. He was a severe student and yet skilled in the knowledge of men. He was humble in the recollection of the power and designs of a personal Satan, yet bold and defiant in the midst of all perils. He could beard the Papacy and imperial councils, yet he fell trustingly before the cross. He was never weary, and there seemed to be no limit to his creative energy. Thus Luther stands before the German people as the type of German character. Goethe, Frederick the Great, and all others, in this regard, pale before the German reformer. He embodies in his single person the boldness of the battle-field, the song of the musician, the joy and care of the parent, the skill of the writer, the force of the orator and the sincerity of rugged manhood with the humility of the Christian.

His last words were, "O my Heavenly Father, my eternal and everlasting God! Thou hast revealed to me Thy Son, our Lord Jesus Christ! I have preached Him! I have confessed Him! I love Him and I worship Him as my dearest Savior and Redeemer! Into Thy hands I commit my spirit."

## 095 -- LAST WORDS OF MRS. JEWETT -- "GOOD-BYE FOR A LITTLE WHILE."

Mrs. Jewett suffered with cancer in her throat, and starved to death. I called to see her. Upon hearing my voice she said, "Come to me." She threw her arms around my neck, saying as she did so, "Kindred spirit, I wanted so much to see you. I am sanctified. I have kept the faith. I am starving to death, but in a little while I shall pluck the fruit of the tree of life." She reached out her hand as if already doing so, saying, "Sweet, O, how sweet!" Then dipping her hand she said, "And I will drink of the water of life even now; good-bye for a little while," and died victoriously. -- Written for this work by Mrs. H. A. Coon, Marengo, Ill.

## 096 -- "I HAVE NEGLECTED THE SALVATION OF MY SOUL."

About twenty years ago, while we were doing some evangelistic work at L___, early one morning a little boy with a very sad heart called at our room, saying that his mother was dying and wished to see us. We hurried to Mrs. B___'s home, and as we opened the door we beheld a sorrowful sight -- a woman in despair. The expression on her face and the sad look in her eyes told of great agony. We were at a loss to know just what to say or do. Our heart was full. We said to her, "You are in great pain." With a wild look she replied, "Yes, I am in great pain; but that is nothing compared with the thought of going to meet God unprepared. What is this physical suffering compared to the remorse of conscience and the dark future before me? Then she cried out in agony, "All is vanity, all is vanity! 1 have lived for self and tried to find pleasure at the dance and other places of amusement. I have neglected the salvation of my soul! I am unprepared to meet God! Pray for me, oh, pray for me!" While we prayed she responded, "Amen, amen! God help me! What shall I do? Is there any hope for a poor sinner like me?" and many other similar expressions. Her ungodly husband cried bitterly while she told of their past sinful life. Her heart was hardened with sin, her ears were dull of hearing and her eyes too blind to see the light of God.

Her friends were coming in from the village and surrounding country to see her die. As they entered the room, she would take each one of them by the hand and plead with them not to follow her example, not to live as she had lived. Holding an uncle by the hand, a man deep in sin and who seemed to be far from God, she said, "Uncle, prepare to meet your God. Don't wait until you come to your dying day, as I have done. When you plow your ground, pray. When you plant your corn, pray. When you cultivate the same, pray. Whatever you do, pray! (She died in the month of May, the season for corn planting.) Many of her friends wept and promised to live better lives. Her mental agony was so far beyond her physical pain that she seemed to be unconscious of her intense bodily suffering. Her sins seemed to loom up before her as a great mountain, hiding from her the presence and love of God. As long as she was able to speak, she prayed and requested others to do so. In a few hours the voice, that had been pleading so pitifully for mercy, and warning others by the example of her ungodly life was hushed in the silence of death,

The pastor of the Methodist Church, whom we were helping, preached at her funeral. As e listened to his words of warning, we resolved as never before to further our efforts in warning lost humanity to flee from the wrath to come.

Soon after her death we called on her husband and reminded him of his wife's dying testimony and urged him to attend the revival meetings that we were holding in the town, but he seemed to be full of prejudice against Christianity and gave us no encouragement, and still continued to walk in the same sinful path as heretofore.

We trust that our readers will take warning by the sad experience related in this sketch. God help us all to redeem the time as we see eternity drawing near. Amen. -- Editor.

## 097 -- "DEAR MOTHER, YOU MUST NOT GRIEVE FOR ME; I AM GOING TO JESUS."

Through the kindness of L. B. Balliett, M. D., of Allentown, Penn., we furnish our readers with this touching incident:

Some years ago a steamer was sinking with hundreds of persons on board. Only one boat-load was saved. As a man was leaping into the tossing boat a young girl who could not be taken into the boat handed him a note, saying, "Give this to my mother." The man was saved. The girl, with hundreds of others, was drowned.

The mother got the note. These were the words written: "Dear mother, you must not grieve for me; I am going to Jesus."

## 098 -- HAPPY DEATH OF GERTRUDE BELLE BUTTERFIELD

This loved friend's last day of time was May 24, 1898, and then she passed on to that fairer country whose inhabitants count not the days nor the years.

Only twenty-four years of the earth-life were given her; but, "How long we live, not years, but actions tell."

In early girlhood she learned the beauty of a life in God's service, and became so willing "to spend and be spent for Him." A part of her service for Him was evangelistic work, and only the last great garnering time will tell how many soul-sheaves ripened from seeds of her sowing. And when she saw the field of labor widening, she consecrated her life to mission work in foreign lands, should God lead the way.

Upon graduating from the Evansville (Wis.) Seminary, a little less than a year before her death, she returned to her home near Reedsburg, Wis. She was weary and worn from work and study, but was so certain rest was all that was needful. She felt that life was before her and that she was just ready to live.

Love from one worthy -- life's richest gift -- had come to her, and her heart was satisfied.

But it was not long ere she knew that the weariness was consumption, and that life's plans must be put aside. In a letter written in January she says, "Oh, it would be easy to go, so easy, if it were not for my life-work all undone. I cannot but feel that it would please Him to let me live and work for souls who know not my Jesus." But later, that unfinished work was given up to Him, and all was at rest. Dreams of heaven came to her, and she was ready, yes, glad to go.

The last months of her life were very full of suffering, but there was no complaint.

"Everyone is so kind," often fell from her lips at some attention from those who tenderly ministered to her wants.

Very precious is the memory of some days spent with her, three weeks before her death. She was so pure, so gentle, so thoughtful of others, so like Him who had put upon her "The beauty of the Lord."

As the end approached, her sufferings became intense. The Sunday night before she went home, all thought the death-angel very near. She asked her friends to sing the beautiful hymn,

"Fade, fade each earthly joy,
Jesus is mine!"

For days she had scarcely spoken above a whisper but now the Spirit of the Lord came upon her in blessing, and as she raised her hands she repeated, in a voice clear and strong, "O death, where is thy sting? O grave, where is thy victory?"

"Yea, though I walk through the valley of the shadow of death, I will fear no evil; for Thou art with me; Thy rod and Thy staff they comfort me."

She was so eager for the release, asking those near her if they thought it the last, and saying, "Oh, I hope I won't be disappointed." But not until Tuesday afternoon did the end come, when the soul escaped as u bird from its prison of pain.

And we, who await this "dawning light" that so thrilled her soul, treasure the memory of one "faithful unto death," our sainted Gertrude. -- Written for this work by Cora A. Niles.

## 099 -- A DYING WELSH SOLDIER'S DESPAIR

A Christian worker observed: I once went to visit a soldier who had bought himself from the army. He was dying, but did not know it. I sat down by his side and said, "I will read a bit of the Bible for you." "Oh, you need not trouble; I am not so ill as all that," he replied. Poor fellow, he thought that he must be very ill before any one need offer to read a part of the Bible for him. Next morning when I called I found him much worse. I learned that he was a Welshman, and his mother was a Christian. Suddenly he threw himself back in bed, and wringing his hands he cried, "Oh, what shall I do, what shall I do! I am as a dead man; the mark of death is upon me, and I am not saved." There is a time when Christ may be found, but there is also a time when He may not be found. It is one of the saddest sights that one can look upon to see a soul seeking for Christ but unable to find Him. And this young dying soldier sought and sought for Christ, but it was all in vain; Jesus had passed by. He became delirious and died in agony. "Seek the Lord while He may be found; call ye upon Him while He is near." -- Crown of Glory.

## 100 -- "I AM HAPPY, I AM HAPPY! GLORY TO GOD!"

The death of Lovic Pearce Thompson, as related for this book by his brother, Rev. S. M. Thompson, of the M. E. Church, South, Tenaha, Texas:

Lovic was what you would call a bad boy. It was his very nature to be bad. He was rough-spoken, grum and snappish when he was mad. When in a good humor he was kind and affectionate. As long as everything went his way, there was peace; when it did not, there was war. If ever a seventeen-year-old boy was dominated by Satan, it was Lovic. His mother would oftimes remonstrate with him about his wicked ways, and often went to God in earnest prayer in his behalf. Yet Lovic, despite the loving words of a mother's counsel, and the fervent petitions of a mother's heart, remained in the "gall of bitterness and in the bond of iniquity." It seemed that he was incorrigible. But who knows the destiny of men? One thing is certain, God will not damn a man until he has given him a fair chance be saved, and that man willfully refuses all offers of mercy.

Old Forest Academy camp ground was a favorite place of resort for the old and young alike. Thither hundreds went in the summer; some in quest of pleasure only, while scores of others went in search of spiritual blessings.

In August, 1887, Lovic attended this camp of the saints. Faithful ministers proclaimed the gospel of peace and earnestly exhorted all sinners to "flee from the wrath to come." It was a Methodist meeting, and all Methodist meetings are provided with an "altar," commonly called a "mourner's bench." On Sunday night, after an earnest, pathetic sermon, sinners were invited to come to the "altar," seek Christ and be saved. Many came, among the number being Lovic. He tarried there, but no peace received. Again and again during the meeting he went to the altar, but no blessing did he receive. The last night of the meeting came. The benediction was pronounced, but poor Lovic went home unsaved.

But there had been an impression made. Verily,

*"There is a time, we know not when,*
*A place, we know not where,*
*That shapes the destinies of men*
*For glory or despair."*

Such was the case with Lovic. At that camp-meeting, at that altar, at some lonely hour, he drank the dregs from the cup of repentance, renounced his sins and vowed allegiance to the Savior of men. And being of strong determination, he went home that lonely night with no other thought than to keep the vow which he so faithfully at the altar made. Ever afterward, during his short stay on earth, his life was a complete transformation. He was not the same boy. He had lost all his roughness. He was not snappish as he used to be, and his temper had been subdued. The rough ashlar had become the perfect ashlar. A polishing had taken place, but by whom, or when, or how he did not seem to know.

On Friday night, October 5, he had a presentiment that he was going to die, and so informed his mother on the following morning, though he showed no signs of being sick. His mother remonstrated with him, but to no avail. He still said, "I'm going to die."

His father was a farmer, and the farm made a gradual slope from the house to the back side of the field. Saturday evening Lovic was picking cotton down in the valley; and as he was a great singer, just as the shadows of the western trees were stretching out across the farm, with a strong, mellow voice he began to sing, "Shall we meet beyond the river," the chorus being, "Yes, we'll meet," etc. He sang the song through, and as he would say, "Yes, we'll meet," away in the distance the echo answered, "Yes, we'll meet." He came home that night, ate a hearty supper, went to bed, slept soundly, got up in the morning; but took to his bed that evening, from which he never rose till strong hands carried his lifeless form to the hearse that bore his body to the "silent city of the dead."

What about his death? Well, listen. He had been sick for several days, most of the time unconscious. But a few hours before he died he seemed to be in great agony, throwing his hands about as if trying to fight off something. He seemed to be struggling with some powerful giant. At times you could see despair written on his face, at other times he seemed to be overcoming. But when spoken to, not a word would he utter. At last, after frightful gesticulations, he suddenly awoke from his unconscious sleep and began shouting, "I have whipped him. I have whipped him. See the devil; he tried to take me, but I have whipped him. I am happy, I am happy! Glory to God!" He then exhorted all in the room to meet him in heaven, asking all to promise him by giving him their hand. An infidel came into the room, and he exhorted him to be religious, assuring him that there was devil, a hell and a heaven. After a few hours of perfect peace he closed his eyes in death, leaving a smile on his face, which was, no doubt, a sign that he had vanquished the enemy and passed out into the spirit world bearing the laurels of victory.

### *101 -- "I SEE THE HEAVENS OPENED AND MILLIONS OF BRIGHT ANGELS READY TO RECEIVE US."*

Baudicon Oguier was a martyr burned at the stake with his father, mother and brother in the year of our Lord 1556. When chained to the stake, he turned his eyes toward the father and said, "Be of good courage, father, the worst will be passed by-and-by. Behold, I see the heavens opened and millions of bright angels ready to receive us, and rejoicing to see us thus witnessing to the truth in view of the world. Father, let us be glad and rejoice, for the joys of heaven are opened to us. Jesus Christ, Thou Son of God, into Thy hands we commend our spirits."

### *102 -- "OH GOD! I AM DAMNED, I AM DAMNED!"*

During the time of a protracted meeting one of the ministers' wives insisted on her son yielding to these better influences and seeking his salvation He replied to his mother, with a look of fiend-like hatred, that he would rather be damned than yield. He fell forward on the hearth. His mother picked him up whilst he exclaimed with his last breath, "Oh, God! I am damned, I am damned!" with his head resting in his mother's lap. He had gone to that hell he preferred to religion.
-- Rev. Thos. Graham.

## 103 -- THE END OF A GOOD MAN

Rev. John B. McFerrin was an old and honored minister of the M. E. Church, South, having filled many important positions in that denomination. He was at one time missionary secretary, and was book agent of the Publishing House at the time of his death. He belonged to the old style of Methodist preachers, and was a man of deep, solid piety. He took no stock in the modern innovations on old-time religion and was strong advocate of experimental godliness. The time came for him to lay down his work, and to those who knew him it was no surprise when this man of God failed to make his daily visits to the Publishing House. He soon realized that his race was run, but the serenity of his mind was not in the least disturbed. He declared his perfect resignation to the will of God, inclining to a desire to depart and be with Christ.

"Hitherto in my sickness," said he, "I have not felt that I was going to die, nor have I desired to go. But now I feel differently. My work is done. My eyesight and hearing are nearly gone; my temporal affairs are all arranged; my family is all provided for; the Publishing House is safe. My way is clear and I am ready to go."

There was one day during his last illness a slight depression of spirits, but after a visit from Bishop Fitzgerald, who read the scriptures (part of the eighth chapter of Romans), when his faith rallied, the cloud lifted, and he rejoiced in the God of his salvation. In a little while his nephew, Rev. J. P. McFerrin, came in and sang the hymn,

*"And let this feeble body fall,
And let it droop and die,"*

And the old soldier joined in with faltering accents, his face beaming with joy that filled his soul.

As he grew weaker, his son, John, who was an itinerant preacher, was constantly at his bedside, save when he had to go back to his charge to fill his appointments. The son had been with his dying father all the week until Saturday morning. "My son," said the old pilgrim, his heart still beating with loyalty to God and his church, "you had better return and fill your appointment tomorrow. If while you are away, John, I should happen to step off, you know where to find me." Thus on May 10, 1887, a little while after midnight, the soul of this old saint took its departure for the eternal kingdom. -- Life of Rev. J. B. McFerrin, by Bishop O. P. Fitzgerald.

## 104 -- GOVERNOR DUNCAN'S TRIUMPHANT DEATH

Joseph Duncan was born in Kentucky about 1790. He served in the war of 1812, after which he removed to Illinois. As a member of the Senate of Illinois, he originated a law establishing common schools. He was chosen member of Congress in 1827, and Governor of Illinois in 1834. He died January 15, 1844. We take the following from The Higher Christian Life, by Rev. W. E. Boardman

For many years the Governor was distinguished as a Christian -- a consistent member of his church. A rare and shining mark, both for the jests of ungodly politicians and for the happy references of all lovers of Jesus.

It is a very lovely thing, and only too remarkable, to see one occupying the highest position of honor in a State, himself honoring the King of kings. Happy is the people who exalt such a ruler to the places of power, and happy such a ruler in his exaltation; more, however, in the humility with which he bows to Jesus than in the homage which the people pay to him.

His conversion was clear and satisfactory, and he renounced all merit of his own as the ground of his acceptance with God. The blood of Jesus, the Lamb of Calvary, was all his hope. He was firmly grounded in the atonement of Christ. And all went well until death and the judgment drew near.
About three weeks before the hour of his departure he was seized with an illness which he himself felt would end in his death. And with the premonition of death came the question of fitness for heaven. He was troubled. His unfitness was only too apparent for his peace. The fever of his mind was higher than the fever in his veins -- and, alas, he had not yet learned that Jesus is the physician of unfailing skill, to cure every ill that the spirit is heir to. He saw plainly enough how he could be justified from the law, that it should not condemn him; for its penalty had been borne already by the Savior himself, and its claims on the score of justice were all satisfied. But he did not see that the same hands which had been nailed to the cross would also break off the manacles of sin, wash out its stains and adjust the spotless robe of Christ's perfect righteousness upon him, and invest him with every heavenly grace.

His perplexity was great. The night thickened upon him, his soul was in agony, and his struggles utterly vain.

The point of despair is sure to be reached, sooner or later, by the struggling soul, and the point of despair to him who abandons all to Jesus is also the point of hope. The Governor at last gave over and gave up, saying in his heart, "Ah! well. I see it is of no use. Die I must. Fit myself for heaven I cannot. O, Lord Jesus, I must throw myself upon Thy mercy, and die as I am."

This hopeless abandonment was the beginning of rest to his soul. Indeed, it was the victory that overcometh. Soon the loveliness of Jesus began to be unfolded to him, and he saw that the way of salvation from sin was by faith in the Savior. The fire in his veins burned on, steadily and surely consuming the vital forces of his manly frame, but the fever of his spirit was all allayed by the copious and cooling draughts given him from the gushing fountain of the waters of life flowing from the smitten Rock, and his joy was unbounded.

As his stricken and sorrowing family gathered around his bed for the last words of the noble man, he told them, with a face radiant with joy, that he had just found what was worth more to him than riches, or honors, or office, or anything else upon earth, "the way of salvation by faith in the Lord Jesus Christ," and he charged them as his dying mandate, by the love they bore him, not to rest until they too -- whether already Christians as he himself long had been or note -- had found the same blessed treasure.

They asked him what legacy he wished to leave for an absent relative whom they knew it was his intention to have remembered in the division of his estate.

"That is all arranged in my will," said he. "But tell her from me that I have found the way of salvation by faith in the Lord Jesus Christ, and if she too will find that, she will find infinitely more than I could bestow upon her, if I should give her all I am worth in the world."

They mentioned the name of a distinguished fellow officer and special friend of the governor's, living in a distant part of the state, and asked if he had any message for him.

"Tell him that I have found the way of salvation by faith in the Lord Jesus Christ, and if he will also find it for himself it will be better than the highest offices and honors in the reach of man upon earth." So he died. "Oh had he only known this before," you say. Yes, that was just what he himself said. "O, had I only known this when I first engaged in the service of God, how happy I should have been! And how much good I could have done!"

## 105 -- ETERNAL DEATH THE RESULT OF DELAY

A young man by the name of Smith was seen standing looking on with interest during the exercises of a prayer-meeting at camp-meeting in Rootstown, Ohio. One of the ministers observing him addressed him on the subject of religion. His eyes filled with tears and he seemed inclined to seek religion. One of his wicked companions perceiving it, stepped up and, looking him in the face, remarked, "Smith, I would not be a fool." Poor Smith could not resist such influences, and dashing the tears from his eyes turned on his heel and went away. He lingered about the camp ground until the meeting closed for the evening, and went off with his company. They bantered him on the subject of his feelings. To show to them that he had. not the feelings they supposed, he commenced cursing and blaspheming in a most awful manner and making all imaginable sport of religious things, when a large limb from a tree fell on him, and he, with a curse on his tongue, was forced into the presence of God, whom he had thus been blaspheming, without one moment's warning. -- Rev. Thos. Graham

## 106 -- "HE DIED AT HIS POST"

Away back in the 40's, a hymn with this title was very popular among Methodists and was often sung with the Spirit and with marked effect. It had its origin in the last words and triumphant death of a preacher in one of the conferences.

Rev. Thomas Drummond was born in Manchester, England, in 1806, came to this country in early life, and after his conversion joined the Methodist Church He soon was licensed to preach, and was admitted into the Pittsburgh Conference In 1835 he was transferred to the Missouri Conference and stationed in St. Louis.

On Sunday, June 14, of that year, he had preached with his usual power, expressing with pathos the feelings which animate the strong Christian faith in anticipation of heaven. The same evening he was attacked with cholera, and died the next day.

Though suffering great pain he was in his senses and died in triumph, saying among many other cheering things, "Tell my brethren of the Pittsburgh Conference that I died at my post."

Rev. William Hunter, on hearing the particulars of the death of this good man, composed the hymn, "He Died at His Post." -- .Life of Rev. J. B. McFerrin, by Bishop O. P. Fitzgerald.

## 107 -- "I CAN NOW DIE HAPPY. SOUL, TAKE THY FLIGHT."

Miss Addie Asbury was dying. She called her friends around her bedside and one by one bade them good-bye and asked them to meet her in heaven. The doctor had said that she could not live but a very short time, not longer than ten minutes. All at once she opened her eyes and said, "I want to see Tom." She was told that he was not there, but she insisted that she had a message for him, whereupon she was assured that Tom would be sent for. As it was well known that she had but a short time to live and that Tom lived at quite a distance, her friends doubted whether he could arrive before she died. Seeming to read their thoughts, she said, "The God that I have loved and served all of these years can keep me here until he comes. I have a message for him, so please send at once." She had been engaged to marry Tom for several years, but would not because he was not a Christian and drank. Now that she was dying she desired to speak a farewell word to him.

We went for him, and fully an hour had elapsed before we returned with him, but she still lived when he came in. She took him by the hand and said, "Tom, I want you to be a Christian. I am going to leave you and I want to know before I go that you are a child of God."

"Why, Addie," said he, "I can't say I am a Christian when I am not." I would like to be, but I can't." She then took her Bible and showed him from the Word of God that he could be if he would repent and believe on the Lord Jesus Christ, who could forgive his sins. He accepted God's word and became an heir of salvation.

Then, after bidding all good-bye once more, she closed her eyes and said, "I can now die happy. Soul, take the flight," and soon her soul took its departure.

A few years after, we saw Tom ordained a deacon in the Presbyterian Church, not far from the place where his betrothed had died, He is now one of the pillars of the church and is a faithful defender of the cause of Jesus Christ. -- Written for this book by Rev. G. P. Pledger, Chicago, Ill.

## 108 -- "I AM DYING AND GOING TO HELL."

A fashionable lady attended revival meetings at the Morgan Street Church, Chicago. Deep conviction settled on her soul She wept and said she would like to find peace, but was not ready to give up the pleasures of the world. To drown her convictions, she absented herself from the house of God. Time hurried on and soon she was on her death bed. Realizing her condition, she sent for a friend who had attended the meetings with her and who had listened to the spiritual pleadings and found the joy of pardoning love. This friend hurried to the bedside of the dying one. As she entered the room the dying woman looked at her with eyes of terror, and grasping her hand she exclaimed, "Oh, stay with me till I am gone! I am dying and going to hell! Tell Bro. C___ (the minister) to preach hell as he has never preached it before, for I am going to hell!" Then, pointing to the wardrobe, she said, "Go there and you will see what has ruined my soul." She opened the door and saw the rich, fashionable clothing and turned again to the side of the dying woman, who raised herself up and sang the hymn she had so often heard at the meeting:

"*Parting to meet again at the Judgment,*
*Parting to meet no more here below;*
*Oh, how sad the thought to thee,*
*Traveler to eternity,*
*Parting to meet again at the Judgment.*

As the last word fell from her lips she fell back on the pillow and her soul passed into eternity to meet the God whose mercy she had trifled with and turned away for the gaudy toys of this earth.

Dear reader, take warning from this sad death. Turn away from the vanities of earth and give God your heart and life's service, and eternal happiness shall be yours. -- Pentecost Herald.

## 109 -- "DO YOU NOT HEAR THEM SAY, 'PEACE ON EARTH; GOOD WILL TOWARD MEN'?"

Miss Mollie J. Herring, of Clear Run, N. C., writes us: I have a dying testimony of a sweet, cultured, Christian young lady, whose death occurred in my own home in 1884, when I was very young.

Miss Orphie B. Schaeffer, daughter of Rev. G. F. Schaeffer, a Lutheran minister, who at that time was President of the North Carolina Lutheran College, had been visiting at our home for some time past. We soon became warm friends and were closely attached to each other. A short time after she had come to our home she was taken ill, her sickness developing into a serious case of typhus fever which resulted in her death two weeks later.

She loved her Savior and put her utmost confidence in God. Often she would say, "It is so sweet to love Jesus. I have always loved him."

During her illness she would often speak of her loved ones, far away from her in Easton, Pennsylvania. We had not wired them of her illness, as we did not realize that it was of such a serious nature until the end drew near.

As I stood at her bedside as she was dying, she called me to come closer to her and said, "Mollie, I hear the sweetest music."

I asked her from whence the sound of the music came, and she replied, "Oh, just over the hill. Do you not hear them say, 'Peace on earth, good will toward men?'"

Again her wan features lighted up with the very light of heaven and she said, "Oh, can't you hear them singing? Do listen."

I strained my eager ears to catch the sound to which I knew she was listening, but I could hear nothing save her labored breathing.

Soon after she said, "Good-bye, mamma! Good-bye Florence! Good-bye, papa!" and just then she was seized with a hemorrhage, which caused her to grow weaker and weaker, and once more we heard her say, "I am so glad that I have always loved Jesus."

## 110 -- "DEVILS ARE IN THE ROOM, READY TO DRAG MY SOUL DOWN TO HELL."

Mrs. J___ B___, the subject of this sketch, came under the personal observation of the writer in 1886. I had often urged her to give her heart to God while she was in health, but she refused.

I called to see her during her last sickness and found her in a most distressing state of mind.

She recognized me when I came in, and was loath to let me leave long enough to bring my wife, who was only three-quarters of a mile away; saying, "Devils are in my room, ready to drag my soul down to hell."

She would begin in a low, measured tone to say, "It must be done! It must be done!" continuing to repeat the same with increasing force and higher pitch of voice, until she would end with a piercing scream, "It must be done!"

Her husband asked her, "Josie, what must be done?"

She answered, "Our hearts must be made right!" And again she would entreat me to take her away, affirming she could see devils all around her.

She would say, "See them laugh!" This would throw her into a paroxysm of fear and dread, causing her to start from her bed; but when I tried to get her to look to Jesus for help she said, "It is no use; it is too late!"

I trust I shall never be called upon again to witness such a heart-rending deathbed scene as hers. There was more that transpired, but I have tried to make this sketch as brief as possible. -- Written for this work by B. F. Closson, Bloomington, Neb.

## 111 -- LAST WORDS OF BISHOP GLOSSBRENNER

"Say ye to the righteous, that it shall be well with him." So it was with the devout Bishop Glossbrenner when he had reached the end of his earthly pilgrimage, January 7, 1887. Mr. John Dodds, of Dayton, Ohio, a warm personal friend of the bishop, spent a day or two with him shortly before his death, and found him in a most blessed frame of mind. When the subject of preaching was referred to, he said, "If I could preach again just once more, I would preach Jesus. I would preach from His words to the disciples on the Sea of Galilee, 'It is I, be not afraid.'" As Mr.

Dodds was leaving, he looked back when a few paces from the house, and to his surprise the bishop had gotten out of his bed unassisted and was standing by the door. He was visible affected, and with hand uplifted and tears running down his cheeks, said, "Tell my brethren it is all right; my home is over there." To another he said, '!My title is clear, but not because I have preached the gospel, but alone by the love and mercy and grace of our Lord Jesus Christ. Rely on nothing but Jesus Christ and an experimental knowledge of acceptance with God through the merits of Jesus."

In view of his rapidly approaching end, he said to his pastor, "I shall not be here much longer." When asked about the future his reply was, "Everything is as bright as it can be. What a blessing it is to have a Savior at a time like this." His last whispered words were, "My Savior." -- From Life to Life.

## *112 -- THE GLORIOUS TRANSLATION OF HELEN CARPENTER*

Helen A. Carpenter was born in Hamlin, N. Y. When but a child she was deeply conscientious, and one of the things she constantly practiced was every Saturday evening to go about the house and gather up all the secular work and reading matter and put it away until Monday, so that the Sabbath might be kept holy. She gave her heart to God at the age of seventeen years, and her entire after life was characterized by unswerving devotion to His cause.

When nineteen, while engaged in teaching school, she took a severe cold, which speedily developed into consumption and terminated her earthly career at the age of twenty years. During her illness she rapidly ripened for heaven, and her young friends who called upon her would afterwards say, "One would not think Helen was going to die; she speaks as if she were going on a most delightful journey!"

About a week before her death her mother, sitting by her couch, became suddenly conscious of a most heavenly influence pervading the entire room, and so powerful was it that she could scarcely refrain from shouting aloud. She wondered if Helen, on whose countenance rested a pleased expression, felt it too.

The next day Helen said, "Ma, you thought I was asleep yesterday while you were sitting by me. I was not; but two angels came into the room, the wails did not hinder their coming.

*'My spirit loudly sings,
The holy ones -- behold they come,
I hear the noise of wings.'
It was all true, only I did not hear any noise."*

A few evenings later her mother, observing her to be unusually restless, placed her hand upon her brow and found it damp with the dew of death. She said to her daughter, "Helen, I think you are very near home. Have you any fear?" "Not a bit," Helen replied; "call the family, that I may bid them good-bye."

As they gathered about her she bade each one a loving farewell, telling them she was going to heaven through the blood of the Lamb, enjoining them to meet her there. She then said, "I have been thinking of this verse: 'He that spared not His own Son' " -- and as her voice began to falter when she got this far her mother repeated it for her. Upon being asked if she would like to have them sing for her she replied, "Sing until I die; sing my soul away!" For some time her sister sang to her the sweet songs of Zion; then, while standing near her, Helen said, "The time seems long, don't it!"

Her sister, Augusta, referring to an absent sister, said, "O, I wish L were here. What shall I tell her for you?" "Tell her to trust in the Lord," was her reply.

As her eyes closed in death her sister, Mary, bent over her to catch the last expression, when Helen gave a start of delightful surprise, as though she saw something glorious beyond conception, and then her happy spirit went to be forever with the Lord, but the look of inexpressible delight remained on her lovely countenance.

She was by nature so gentle and retiring that her friends feared that when she came to the "swellings of Jordan" she might have some fear, but the grace of her Heavenly Father enabled her to pass joyously in holy triumph to the skies.

Her sister, Mary E. Carpenter, who afterward went to Monrovia, Africa, as a missionary and died there, said while dying, "Living or dying, it's all right," thus submitting her will to the will of her Heavenly Father, whose wisdom saw it better for her to come to beaver than to labor in Africa. -- Written .for this work by L. M. F. Baird, of Alabama,. New York.

## 113 -- "O MARTHA, MARTHA, YOU HAVE SEALED MY EVERLASTING DAMNATION!"

Rev. Thomas Graham, the noted revivalist preacher of the Erie Conference of the Methodist Episcopal Church, relates the following sad experience:

A man who lived in Westmoreland county, Pa., had strong religious feelings and had commenced a religious life. About this time he married a woman who was decidedly irreligious and who opposed him. She forced him to omit family worship; she forced him from his closet and followed him with her opposition until he finally, discouraged, gave it up. The Spirit of God left him. He told Rev.

Mr. Potter, a Presbyterian minister that he was lost forever and that he knew the very time and place the Spirit took its final departure; that he was going to hell but cared nothing about it. He lived some ten years after this and then died in the most awful agonies. He asked his wife to give him a glass of water for he would obtain none where he was going. He drank it greedily; then, looking his wife in the face, exclaimed, "O Martha, Martha, you have sealed my everlasting damnation!" and died.

## 114 -- LUCY G. THURSTON, THE YOUNG MISSIONARY OF THE HAWAIIAN ISLANDS

Lucy Goodale Thurston died on the 24th of Feb., 1841, in the city of New York, at the house of Mr. A. P. Cumings, one of the editors of the New York Observer. Her age was seventeen years and ten months.

She was born at Honolulu, April, 1823. Her father and mother were devoted missionaries. Their daughter was taken to heaven a few days after the arrival of the mother and children in this country for a rest. This was the first time the young missionary had ever been in a civilized country.

The night but one before her death, during an interval of comparative ease, she conversed with freedom and composure upon the probable result of her illness. After speaking of the ardent desire she had cherished of being fitted to return to her beloved home, to engage in the instruction of the natives, she said there was but one other trial to her in the thought of dying in her present circumstances. It was that she should not see her father. "But," she added, "in saying this I do not wish to be understood as expressing any opposition to the will of God concerning me." A friend

repeated the hymn commencing, "It is the Lord," which appeared to give her great comfort, and she soon after said, "It is all right -- all right."

When told that the hour of her departure yeas approaching, the struggle with her tender affections was evidently great. But it was short. "Mother, do you think I am going to die now?" said she. "Yes, my dear." said her mother, "I think you are going soon."

"Oh, I loved you all too well, too well -- I loved him too well." It was thought she alluded to her absent father. "But you love your Savior, too, Lucy." "Yes, mother, I do -- I do love Him." "Whom do you love, my dear?" "Jesus Christ. I love Him with all my heart, with all my soul and with all my strength. Mother, I know I love Him -- I do -- I do." -- The Missionary's Daughter,

## 115 -- "GOOD-BY, GOOD-BY. NOW I AM READY, JESUS."

Through the kindness of Rev. W. N. Hall, of Chicago, we insert this:

About three years ago, while serving as pastor of an Iowa church, there came under my observation a death that was most remarkable as an instance of divine grace, and faith of a true believer.

Mrs. M - was a young married woman, a member of the Baptist church, but without a pastor at the time. Being the pastor of her husband's family, she requested my ministries in her illness. In my frequent visits I was in every case deeply impressed with her faith, which enabled her to be in the state of religious triumph constantly. Her disease, consumption, and the rapidity of its advance, gave no hope of life beyond a few weeks. Yet death had no terrors for her, viewed from afar or near.

Quite frequently she had smothering spells, from which her friends would fear she would not be able to rally. To allay their fears, in each instance, as soon as possible she would say, "Don't be alarmed; my time to go has not come yet." On a beautiful Sabbath day the friends who inquired as to her condition were all told, "Hattie is much better to-day; she is unusually strong and free from any pain." The sun had just reached the meridian, and the family felt pleased with the bettered condition of their loved one. She requested all of them to come into her room. None could guess the reason. Looking upon the circle about her bed she said, "Are you all ready?" The answer was, "Yes, Hattie, we are all ready." Then she nodded to each, saying, "Good-bye, good-bye." Then with a voice clear and strong said, "Now I am ready, Jesus," and was gone instantly, there being no struggle or other sign of death. It was a case of believing in Jesus and not seeing death; of finding no valley between earth and heaven.

## 116 -- "I HAVE NO FEELING; THE SPIRIT OF GOD HAS LEFT ME."

A number of years ago, in the midst of a powerful revival, the preacher observed a young lady under deep conviction. He was moved by the Spirit of God to urge her to give her heart to God at once. He plead with her and urged her not to grieve the Holy Spirit, but she replied, "Not tonight." As she started for home, the man of God followed her to the door of the church, and urged her again not to leave the church without salvation. Again she replied, "Not tonight." He had a strange feeling in regard to the destiny of this young lady and was strangely moved to follow her out on the street and plead with her not to go home without giving her heart to God, but she again replied, "Some other time, not now." She went home under deep conviction and told her parents what a feeling she had, and how she had been halting between two opinions -- that she had never felt such concern for her soul before and had never realized her danger of being lost at any period during her life so much as she had realized it that night. Her father and mother were unsaved people. Their minds were planted in sin and unbelief and they had no sympathy with their daughter's interest in religion. She asked their opinion about becoming a Christian and uniting with the church. In reply they said, "You are young, and will have plenty of time when you settle down in life to think about your preparation for eternity. Why not enjoy life while you are young and not cut yourself off from society and other young people." With a sad heart she listened to their advice, and the enemy of her soul whispered, "Some other time will do just as well; you will have plenty of time to seek religion when your surroundings are more favorable."

She yielded to the advice of her ungodly parents and the devil and decided to wait awhile. A great struggle had been going on in her mind -- Satan struggling with her and showing her the pleasures of sin on one side, and the Spirit of God revealing the Kingdom of Heaven and everlasting life on the other. How sad that she should turn away from the Spirit of God and her prospects of heaven in order to please her ungodly parents and to enjoy the pleasures of sin for a season.

The revival meetings closed and her interest in religion was soon gone. In a short time she was taken very sick. After every effort to restore her to health had failed, and she continued to grow worse, and all human effort and hope were at an end, her parents realized that they could only have her with them for a few hours longer, they went to the bedside of their dying daughter and informed her that she had but a short time to live. They told her that if she wished to be a Christian they were willing, in fact they advised her that it was time now to make preparations for eternity. She looked up at her parents in surprise, her eyes stared and her face was the very picture of despair. She said, "Father and mother, you remember that during the recent revival I was greatly interested in the salvation of my soul. The Spirit of God was striving with me, and I felt my need of God as I had never felt it before. I asked your advice and you discouraged me. You advised me to wait until some other opportunity. I listened to your counsel, and now it is too late. My heart is as hard as stone. I have no feeling. The Spirit of God has left me." Her parents urged her, and to please them she consented to have them send for the minister. He came at once and plead with her and tried to show her that God was a merciful God, but her mind was full of unbelief, and she insisted that she could not repent before she died. She was in great distress of mind and body, and as a last resort she requested that her coffin be sent for. It was brought and placed by the side of her bed. With her own hands she rapped upon the coffin and cried, "Oh, for feeling! Oh, for feeling!" but no feeling came. Then she sent for her shroud, and as she looked upon it and held it up before her she said, as only a dying person could say, "Oh, for feeling! Oh, for feeling!" But her cry was in vain. The presence of a coffin and a shroud could not awaken her slumbering conscience or bring back the Holy Spirit, and she died in despair.

We pray that our readers may take warning by this sad experience, for God says, "My Spirit shall not always strive wish man." Therefore, "Seek ye the Lord while

He may be found, call ye upon Him while He is near. Let the wicked forsake his way and the unrighteous man his thoughts; and let him return unto the Lord, and He will have mercy upon him; and to our God, for He will abundantly pardon." -- Editor.

## 117 -- "MARK THE PERFECT MAN, AND BEHOLD THE UPRIGHT: FOR THE END OF THAT MALL IS PEACE."

Not long since I stood by the bedside of my class leader, who shortly afterward passed away from earth to receive the reward of the just, and truly his path was like a shining light; and it shone more and more until he crossed the line of worlds. He told us that he had no changes to make, for there was not a thing between him and God. He exhorted us to be faithful, and prayed for an unsaved stranger who was dying with consumption. Although too weak to rise or turn himself he would break forth in song and with joyful countenance join in praises to God and the Lamb.

He made all the arrangements for his funeral, which caused his friends sorrow, but he said, "If I live, well; and if I die it is meet that I should set my house in order."

A few hours before his death his shouts of joy were heard by the neighbors on the outskirts of the small village where he lived, and the unsaved, wondering at his exceeding joy, beheld the triumph of his soul in the hour of sorest need and the power of God through our Lord Jesus Christ to keep a soul to the end, according to the promise in Mat. 28: 20. -- Contributed for this book by E. C. Yerks, of Grand Ledge, Mich.

## 118 -- "NOT THE SHADOW OF A DOUBT; I HAVE CHRIST WITHIN, THE HOPE OF GLORY."

John P. Finley, my brother, was born in North Carolina, June, 1783. He was in the ministry about fifteen years. He was ordained deacon by Bishop Asbury on the 17th of September, 1815. He received ordination as elder at the hands of Bishop Roberts, July 2, 1820. At the time of his death he was a member of the Kentucky Annual Conference, actively dividing his time and energies between the business of collegiate instruction and the labor of the pulpit. . . .

As a minister, in the pulpit he was able, impressive, and overwhelming. The cross of his redemption was his theme; and in life and death it became to him the "emphasis of every joy." In all these relations I knew him well, and can, therefore, speak from the confidence of personal knowledge and accredited information. . . .

He died on the 8th of May, 1825, in the forty-second year of his age, and sixteenth of his ministry; and at the same time that this bereaved family wept upon his grave, the sadness of the church told that she had lost one of her brightest ornaments. Just before his triumphant spirit rose to sink and sigh no more, he was asked how he felt, and what were his prospects upon entering the dark valley and shadow of death. He replied, in language worthy of immortality, "Not the shadow of a doubt; I have Christ within, the hope of glory. That comprehends all!" and then, with the proto-martyr, he "fell asleep." -- Autobiography of Rev. James B. Finley.

## 119 -- LAST WORDS OF EDWARD GIBBON, THE NOTED INFIDEL -- "ALL IS DARK AND DOUBTFUL."

Edward Gibbon, the noted historian and infidel writer was born at Putney, England, 1787. He was expelled from Oxford on account of his having abjured Protestantism. To effect hit cure from popery he was sent to Lausanne, in Switzerland, to board in the house of M. Pavilliard, a Calvinist minister, who had the satisfaction of seeing him reconverted to Protestantism, in witness of which he received the sacrament in the church of Lausanne on Christmas, 1754, his belief in popery having lasted not quite eighteen months. -- Schaff's Encyclopedia of Religious Knowledge.

Bishop J. F. Hurst, in his History of Rationalism, says: Gibbon was even more of a Frenchman than Hume. Sundering his relation to Oxford, in his seventeenth year, he embarked upon a course of living and thinking which, whatever advantage it might afford to his purse, was not likely to aid his faith. By a sudden caprice he became a Roman Catholic, and afterwards as unceremoniously denied his adopted creed.... In due time he found himself in Paris publishing a book in the French language. He there fell in with the fashionable infidelity, and so far yielded to the flattery of Helvetius and all the frequenters of Holbach's house that he jested at Christianity and assailed its divine character. He has left less on record against Christianity than Hume, but they must be ranked together as the last of the family of English deists.

D. W. Clark, in Death Bed Scenes, says: Gibbon, the author of the Decline and Fall of the Roman Empire, is well known to have been what is termed a philosopher and an infidel.... In his memoirs, Gibbon has undesignedly presented a striking view of the cheerless nature of infidelity. Having no hope for eternity, he was eager for the continuation of his present existence.

During his short illness, Gibbon never gave the least intimation of a future state of existence.

Rev. E. P. Goodwin, in Christianity, and Infidelity, says: Gibbon is one of the fairest as he is one of the ablest of infidels; and he has given us an autobiographical account, wherein, amid all the polish and splendor of the rhetoric of which he is such a master, there is not a line or a word that suggests reverence for God; not a word of regard for the welfare of the human race; nothing but the most sordid selfishness, vain glory, desire for admiration, adulation of the great and wealthy, contempt for the poor and supreme devotedness to his own gratification.

He died in London in 1794. His last words were, "All is now lost; finally, irrecoverably lost. All is dark and doubtful."

## 120 -- "HALLELUJAH, HE HAS COME; I AM GOING TO TELL ALL MY FRIENDS GOOD-BYE."

Mrs. H. A. Coon, of Marengo, Ill., sends us the following:

My mother died ten years ago, aged eighty-eight years, and had been a Christian since quite young. She was sick only two weeks towards the inst. After suffering intensely for ten days, she held tip her hands, with the nails showing death marks, and said, "See here, I am going now, glory to God! Yes, Jesus is coming for me. I shall soon be on the other side." ] said to her, "Ma, are you sure the way is all clear? Is everything under the blood?" She immediately replied, "Yes, darling, you will find me in the City of Light as sure as you live." She asked me to read her precious Bible to her, repeating, "In my Father's house are many mansions," etc., and sang,

"I know I am nearing the holy ranks,
Of friends and kindred dear;
For I Brush the dew on Jordan's banks,
The crossing must be near."

Then raising both hands above her head she clapped them together shouting, "Hallelujah, He has come. I am going to tell all my friends good-bye." She slept about two hours and was gone.

# Part Three – Testimonies 121 to 236

### 121 -- THE LAST HOURS OF JOHN THORNTON, THE NOTED ENGLISH SAINT AND PHILANTHROPIST

This man of God went to heaven in the month of November, 1790.

Mr. Thornton was noted both for his piety and his liberality. We are told that he gave away in acts of love and mercy more than one-half million dollars. At his death he was not worth much more than this amount.

Rev. Henry Venn, his life long friend, says: "I have very sensibly felt the loss of my old affectionate friend, John Thornton, after an intimacy of thirty-six years, from his first receiving Christ till he took his departure with a convoy of angels to see Him who so long had been all his salvation and all his desire. Few of the followers of the Lamb, it may be very truly said, have ever done more to feed the hungry, clothe the naked and help all that suffer adversity and to spread the savor of the knowledge of Christ crucified!"

On visiting the children of Mr. Thornton, he says: "I rejoice I am come to see the children of my dear departed friend, John Thornton, and to hear of his life, acts of love, and death; many particulars of which I could not have heard at home. Some of these I send you now, which I received from the nurse who attended him. She said, 'To see the sons, the day before he died, weeping tears of grief and love, and to hear the dying saint affectionately exhort and press each to hold fast the faith and to lead. the life of a Christian, was to the last degree affecting. They asked him whether he was now happy. "Yes," said he, "happy in Jesus; all things are as well as they can be!" And the last words he was able to articulate were, "Precious, precious -- " Jesus would have been added, but his breath failed.'"

### 122 -- "O GLORY! O GLORY!! O GLORY!!!"

"Precious in the sight of the Lord is the death of His saints!"

Mrs. Susan C. Kirtland, my mother's sister, first saw the light of this world in Gilbert's Mills, Oswego Co., New York, May 18,1822. She gave her heart to God at an early age, during a revival held in the Free Will Baptist Church near her home, and though her life was one of much privation and disappointment, in the midst of its trials she lived a cheerful, devoted Christian, well described by the motto she so often expressed in words, "It is better to suffer wrong than to do wrong."

She was translated "from glory to glory," April 3, 1864, while visiting at our home in Burr Oak, Michigan, after a very painful illness of only one week.

Even upon that sick-bed she found opportunities to work and speak for Jesus. Though at that time I was less than four years old, I distinctly remember how, while lying upon that bed of suffering, she taught me that beautiful verse, "I love them that love Me; and they that seek Me early shall find Me," carefully explaining the meaning of the words and lovingly pressing home the lesson to my heart.

And we have often heard mother speak of her heavenly conversation during those days when neither of them knew that her death was near.

As soon as it was known that she was dangerously ill, her brother, an able physician, was summoned from a distance, but too late for human power to save. A few hours before her death she knew from mother's manner that something troubled her and asked what was the matter. With much feeling mother said to her, "Susan, we fear your stay with us is very short." Calmly she replied, "Well, if it be so, I don't know when I could have had a better time to leave this stage of action!"

Two of her four children were with her. While they stood weeping by her bedside, she tenderly and earnestly exhorted them to live for God and meet her in heaven, and by them sent loving messages to the absent ones. Then she bade good-bye to all the friends who were present. No other preparation was needed. She was ready to go. Nor was she left to journey alone. There was to her no dark valley -- no gloom. As the circle of those who loved her so dearly watched around her bed, her face suddenly lighted up with indescribable joy. She had evidently caught sight of things hidden from their eyes. Still looking upward and eagerly raising both hands, she exclaimed in a voice of holy triumph which no words can describe., "O glory: O glory!! O glory!!!" and was gone, having entered upon the "inheritance incorruptible, undefiled, and that fadeth not away!" -- Mrs. Etta E. Sadler Shaw.

## *123 -- CARDINAL BORGIA -- "I AM TO DIE, ALTHOUGH ENTIRELY UNPREPARED."*

Czsar Borgia, a natural son of Pope Alexander VI., was a man of such conduct and character that Machiavel has thought fit to propose him, in his famous book called The Prince, as an original and pattern to all princes who would act the part of wise and politic tyrants. He was made a cardinal, but as this office imposed some restraints upon him, he soon determined to resign it that he might have the greater scope for practicing the excesses to which his natural ambition and cruelty prompted him, for cruel, as well as ambitious, he was in the highest degree. After this he was made Duke of Valentinois by Louis XII. of France. He experienced a variety of fortune, but displayed on every occasion the most consummate dexterity and finesse and seemed prepared for all events. The reflections he made a short time before his death (which happened in the year 1507) show, however, that his policy was confined to the concerns of this life and that he had not acted upon that wise and enlarged view of things which becomes a being destined for immortality. "I had provided," said he, "in the course of my life, for every thing except death, and now, alas! I am to die, although entirely unprepared." -- Power of Religion.

## 124 -- LAST WORDS OF REV. WILLIAM WATTS -- "ALL IS WELL; ALL IS WELL."

Rev. E. Ray, of Fredericktown, Missouri, writes as follows:

I was called last Sunday to preach the funeral services of this brother and received this testimony from his wife.

Bro. Watts had preached the gospel for forty-five years as a Methodist preacher in good standing in his church, and died in the faith, April 30, 1898. He was reared in Bollinger county, and at the time of his death was nearly seventy years old, and therefore one of the pioneers in preaching the gospel here in our great state.

I have proclaimed the gospel for nearly thirty years, and during that time have preached many a funeral sermon, but remember none where I have seen such joy as on this occasion. There were many of his friends present to hear the sermon to his memory. As on the Day of Pentecost, the power fell on all of the people present, melting all hearts.

Bro. Watts suffered greatly during the first of his illness, but during his last days on earth, while the outward man grew weaker and perished, the inward man grew stronger day by day. The last day seemed a golden sunset indeed, or rather the Sun of Righteousness arose with healing in His wings, and he passed away in a flood of glory, with peace on earth and good will toward men.

He said to his wife frequently, "I am in a revival of religion." Sister Watts told me that the last day he lived on earth he sang, alone,

" How firm a foundation, ye saints of the Lord!

Is laid for your faith in His excellent word."

He died at three o'clock in the morning, and shortly before he passed away he said, "All is well, all is well."

As Sister Watts felt very keenly her loss, she said to him, "I want to go with you." "No," he replied, you must wait." And thus sweetly passed the life away, calm as a May morning, his feet placed firmly on the Rock of Ages. "How firm a foundation."

## 125 -- "O, I CAN SEE THE ANGELS ALL IN THE ROOM; CAN'T YOU SEE THEM?"

We are thankful for this glorious experience sent us by Mrs. Anna Crowson, of China Spring, Texas. She says:

My sainted mother's death was one of triumph and great victory. She was a great worker in the vineyard of the Lord. She was a woman of great faith and made the Bible her constant study. Some years before her death she found that she could be established in the faith, and went to God in earnest prayer, making an entire consecration, and by faith was enabled to take Christ as a complete Savior. She knew the blood of Jesus cleansed her from all sin. From that time she lived in an ocean of God's love and was kept from all sin by the power of God through faith.

It was mother's custom to always attend church, and one Sabbath morning while preparing for the same she took a chill and was obliged to go to bed. She said from that time on until her death that she knew she was going to die. She remarked to her eldest daughter, "I have been looking for something to happen for a long time to bring father back to Jesus, but thought He was going to take Samuel" (their eldest boy). It seemed that the Lord had revealed to her that she must die, as it was the only means that would cause father to come back to the fold.

Among others, she exhorted my father to give his heart to God and said, "I am going to heaven, meet me there." He had great faith in her prayers, and he begged her to pray for God to spare her life, saying, "I cannot live without you and raise the children alone!" But with a heavenly smile upon her face and with faith unwavering she said, "God will take care of you and my children; weep not for me, I am going to glory! Husband, never touch liquor any more!" He promised her he would not. She exhorted us all to meet her in heaven. Then she shouted aloud and praised God and said, "Oh, I can see the angels all in the room. Can't you see them?" Then, at her request, we sang, "I saw a wayworn traveler," and, "Oh come, angel band," and she joined with us, and while singing the last song her spirit went home to God.

From the time of mother's death our father kept his vow. He erected a family altar and taught, us six children, by example and precept, to trust in our mother's God and meet her in heaven. He was a devoted Christian from that time on. Every night and morning he would take us to God in prayer around the family altar, and five years after mother's death he too died in the triumphs of faith and went to heaven.

## 126 -- THE ATHEIST, HOBBES -- I AM ABOUT TO TAKE A LEAP IN THE DARK."

Thomas Hobbes was born at Malmesbury, in Wiltshire, England, April 5, 1588; died at Hardwick. Hall, in Devonshire, December 4, 1679. He was educated at Magdalen Hall, Oxford, and spent the first part of his life, up to 1637, as tutor in various noble families, often traveling on the Continent with his pupils, and the last, after 1637, in a comprehensive and vigorous literary activity, first in Paris (1641-52), then in London, or in the country with the Hardwick family.... The philosophical standpoint of Hobbes may be described as an application to the study of man of the method and principles of the study of nature; and the results of this process were a psychology and a morals utterly antagonistic, not only to Christianity, but to religion in general. On account of the merely preliminary stage which the science of nature had reached in the time of Hobbes, his conception is premature; but he carried it out with great vigor; and it happens, not infrequently, that the materialistic psychology and utilitarian morals of to-day return to his writings and adopt some modification of his paradoxes. -- Encyclopedia Britannica.

We take the following from Guide to the Oracles: When the atheist, Hobbes, drew near to death, he declared, "I am about to take a leap in the dark," and the last sensible words that he uttered were, "I shall be glad to find a hole to creep out of the world ate"

## 127 -- "OH! SEEK TO SERVE GOD AND TO FIND THE GATE OF HEAVEN."

A mother who denied Christ and sneered at religion came to her dying bed. Looking up from her restless pillow on the group of weeping sons and daughters gathered at her bedside, she said, "My children, I have been leading you on the wrong road all of your lives. I now find the broad road leads on to destruction; I did not believe it before. Oh! seek to serve God and to find the gate of heaven, though you may never meet your mother there." So, in clouds and darkness, set her sun of life. -- Sent us by Dr. L. B. Balliett, of Allentown, Penn.

## 128 -- "WHY, HEAVEN HAS COME DOWN TO EARTH. SEE THE ANGELS. THEY ARE FLYING THROUGH THE HOUSE."

"Precious in the sight of the Lord is the death of His saints." Co-worker with Dr. Redfield and the glorious little band of early Free Methodists, was the Rev. William Kendall. The closing scenes of his life were so blessed that we give them a place here:

He revived on Sabbath, and was very happy, his face radiant with glory. He said, "This is the most blessed Sabbath I ever knew." The next day he had a severe conflict with Satan, but gained a glorious victory. He said, "Jesus, the mighty Conqueror, reigns!" The next day he exclaimed, "Why, heaven has come down to earth. I see the angels. They are flying through the house!" After a little sleep, on waking, he exclaimed, "I have seen the King in his beauty -- King of glory; have slept in His palace! I was intimate with the angels -- O so intimate with the angels!" For a while he was delirious. Again he had a conflict with the powers of darkness, but quickly triumphed, and exclaimed with a smile, "I can grapple with the grim monster, death." On the Sabbath he was thought to be dying. His wife had her ear to his lips, as he lay gazing upward and waving his arms, as though fluttering to be gone, and heard him breathe, "Hail! hail! all hail!" "What do you see?" He replied, "I see light! light! light! I see -- " and, pausing in silence a while, he suddenly broke out in a clear, though somewhat faltering tone: "Hallelujah to the Lamb who hath purchased our pardon! We'll praise Him again when we pass over Jordan."

One asked, "Is all well?" He replied, with ineffable sweetness, three times, "All is Well!"

The chill of death came on soon, and pointed to his speedy relief. Once more he revived and sang very sweetly:

"O how happy are they, who their Savior obey."

Then-

*"My soul's full of glory,
Inspiring my tongue;
Could I meet with the angels,
I'd sing them a song," etc.*

A few more struggles of nature, and the silver cord loosened, and the warrior fell to rise immortal, February 1, 1858. -- Wayside Sketches.

## 129 -- "I AM GOING TO HELL!"

A preacher in the west sends us the sad account of his grandfather's death. He says:

"The last words of my grandfather, Mr. S . He had been sick for a long time and had always been an unsaved man. He spent three years on the plains with the noted Indian scout, Kit Karson.

"During the last three months of his life, he would often send for me to talk with him on the subject of religion, but when pressed to seek the Lord at once, he would say, 'I have got along so long, I think I will wait a while longer.'

"He died July 3, 1883. Almost (if not) the last words he uttered were these: 'I am going to hell.'

Awfully sad. Fearfully true."

How sad that many put off the most important duty of this life until it is too late, forever too late.

## 130 -- HUGH LATIMER'S LAST WORDS WERE: "O FATHER OF HEAVEN, RECEIVE MY SOUL."

Hugh Latimer, one of the most influential preachers, heroic martyrs and foremost leaders of the English reformation, was born at Thurcaston, Leicestershire, in 1490 or 1491, died at the stake in Oxford, October 16, 1555. We take the following from Life Stories of Remarkable Preachers:

Under the reign of Mary, Latimer, was committed to the Tower as a "seditious fellow." To the Tower Ridley and Cranmer were also sent; and in March of that year all three were brought before the Queen's commissioners at Oxford, condemned for heresy, and sent back into confinement. Eighteen months later Latimer and Ridley were brought down to Oxford to be burned. When stripped for execution Latimer had on a new long shroud. They embraced each other at the stake and knelt and prayed and kissed the stake. There stood this withered old man, quite erect and perfectly happy, with a bag of powder tied around his neck. Just as the fire to consume them was lighted, Latimer addressed his fellow-sufferer in the memorable words, "Be of good comfort, Brother Ridley, and play the man; we shall light such a candle in England to-day as will never go out!" As the flames leaped up he cried vehemently, "O Father of heaven, receive my soul!" He seemed to embrace the flames. Having stroked his face, he bathed his hands in the fire and quickly died.

The amount paid by Queen Mary for lighting that fire was 1 pound 5s. 2d. To popery that fire was the costliest ever kindled. To England, thank God, it was the light of religious liberty, the candle of the reformation, which popes, priests and devils have never been able to blow out, and never will.

## *131 -- "I AM LOST. I HAVE SOLD MY SOUL TO THE DEVIL FOR DRESS."*

Through the kindness of L. B. Balliett, M, D., of Allentown, Penn., we furnish our readers with this sad experience:

A missionary of New York City relates the sad experience of a dying woman, the wife of a wealthy man, who, when told by her physician that she could not live an hour longer, exclaimed with great consternation, "If I cannot live an hour longer I am lost. I have sold my soul to the devil for dress! Pray for me, oh pray for me! All who can pray, do pray!" Uttering these words the damp of death came over her and her voice was silenced forever.

"And be not conformed to this world; but be ye transformed by the renewing of your mind, that ye may prove what is that good, and acceptable, and perfect will of God." (Rom. 12:2.)

## *132 -- "COME ON, I AM READY TO GO."*

In the year 1847, during a powerful revival, my sister, Filura Clark, then nineteen years of age, and myself, two years younger, were saved and found great peace with God. What happy times we had together, living for the Lord, while other young people went after the things of the world! Her loving instruction and devotion to God were not fully comprehended until after she was gone.

My dear sister was taken very ill and only lived a few days. O, how hard it was to part with her! It seemed as though my heart would break, the blow was so great; but; oh! what a blessed, happy death was hers. It was not death to her; she did not think of death, but heaven and eternal life with Jesus was all her theme as the moments sped along.

She called us one by one to her bedside, took our hands and bade us good-bye, and begged us all to meet her in heaven.

After she had bidden her relatives farewell, she said to her physician, "Now, doctor, you come." And she bade him good-bye and requested him to meet her in heaven. He was overcome by the affecting scene.

As we stood by her bedside weeping she said to us, "Don't weep for me. Jesus is with me, I will not have to go alone!" After she had finished speaking, she looked up as though she saw someone waiting for her, and said, "Come on, I am ready to go." She wanted to go; her work on earth was done.

Her death had a wonderful influence in the community, especially upon the young people. Many turned to the Lord and said, "Let me die such a death as hers." And what a blessing her death has been to me in my past life! How it has strengthened me and helped me to live according to the blessed truths of the Bible! When trials and temptations have arisen, her dying testimony has been the means of bringing my soul nearer to the Lord than it ever had been before. Praise the Lord! -- Written for this book by Mrs. Wealthy L. Harter, Fort Wayne, Ind.

## 133 -- "O, IT IS TOO LATE NOW; THERE IS NO HOPE FOR ME!"

Some years ago I was laboring as an evangelist in the town of M___, and during the meetings there was much conviction by the power of the Holy Ghost. Among others that were wrought upon was a young girl of about seventeen years. All through the meetings the Holy Ghost strove with her, and I talked with her at different times, but she resisted. The last evening of the services I went to her side. Again she stood weeping and trembling. I urged her to seek God. She said, "O, I cannot, I cannot!" I replied, "Yes, leave your young friends and come." She still said, "O, I cannot, I cannot!" Afterward she said that the young people would have laughed at her had she gone. She left the house in this condition, went to her boarding place (she was boarding and attending school) and made the remark that she did not come to get religion, she came to get an education. She could attend to religion afterward at any time.

She retired for the night, but was taken violently ill and continued to grow worse for one week, and then passed into eternity. She said to those of her young associates who came to see her, "Oh! I ought to have sought the Lord in that meeting." I was with her the last day and before she died I tried to point her to the Lamb of God, but her agonizing reply again and again was (calling me by name), "It is too late now. O, it is too late now! There is no help for me!" and so passed into eternity. -- Written for this book by Julia E. Strait, Portlandville, N. Y.

## 134 -- CARDINAL MAZARINE -- OH! MY POOR SOUL! WHAT WILL BECOME OF THEE? WHITHER WILT THOU GO?"

Julius Mazarine, a famous cardinal, and prime minister of France, was born in the kingdom of Naples in the year 1602. The greatness of his abilities was conspicuous, even in his early years; and he had the advantage of being instructed by a very able tutor. He studied the interests of the various states in Italy, and of the kingdoms of France and Spain, and became profoundly skilled in politics. It was through the influence of Cardinal Richelieu that he was introduced into the French cabinet. That cardinal made him one of the executors of his will, and during the minority of Louis XIV. he had the charge of public affairs. His high station and great abilities excited the envy of the nobility of France, and this occasioned a civil war that continued several years. Mazarine was at last forced to retire; a price was set on his head, and even his fine library was sold. But this disgrace did not long continue. Mazarine returned to the court with more honor than he had ever enjoyed, and conducted the affairs of the kingdom with so much ability and success that he obtained the French king's most unreserved confidence. He possessed, in an eminent degree, the power of discovering the dispositions and views of men, and of assuming a character adapted to circumstances.

He was a man of great ambition, and pursued with ardor the chase of worldly honors. But, a short time before his death, he perceived the vanity of his pursuit, and lamented the misapplication of his time and talents. He was greatly affected with the prospect of his dissolution and the uncertainty of his future condition. This made him cry out, "Oh, my poor soul! what will become of thee? Whither wilt thou go?"

To the queen dowager of France, who came to visit him in his illness, and who had been his friend at court, he expressed himself in these terms: "Madam, your favors have undone me. Were I to live again I would be a capuchin rather than a courtier." -- Power of Religion

## 135 -- "WHEN THE ROLL IS CALLED UP YONDER, I'LL BE THERE; YES, AND BROTHER, TOO."

While Mrs. Anna Rounds lay on her death-bed (as was supposed) in Indianapolis, Indiana, she was greatly burdened for the conversion of her brother, John W. Jenkins, who lived at Gano, Illinois. He had been the subject of her prayers for many years, and she could not die without seeing him saved. The doctor gave her no hope of her recovery, but she prayed fervently to God to spare her life, so that she might go and see her brother and deliver her last message before she died. She began at once to improve, and was soon on her way to her brother's house. As soon as she reached the place she sent for us, as pastor of the Methodist Church, to call at her room. We hurried to the place and found her on her dying bed. She told us of her desire to see her brother converted, and how God had answered her prayer in enabling her to come to him. After prayer with her we went into the next room and spoke a few words to her brother, and urged him to take the advice of his dying sister and meet her in heaven. He was overcome with emotion, and got down on his knees and plead with God for mercy. He soon found deliverance. He was made a new. creature in Christ. With a joyful heart he went to the room where his sister was dying, and said, "God bless you, sister Anna, your prayers have been answered. I am a child of God. You are now going away from me and I will meet you in heaven." Then kneeling by the side of his sister, he thanked God for all of His mercies, and prayed for the departing loved one. Death had laid his cold hand upon her, and she was rapidly passing away. Her face was lit up with a heavenly brightness, and she joined with her brother and friends and sang:

"When the roll Is called up yonder, I'll he there."

Adding, as they sang, "Yes, and brother, too will be there." The burden of her heart had rolled away -- she felt that her work was done, and, looking into the face of God a few moments after, she was translated to heaven. -- Written for this book by Rev. Clifton P. Pledger, Chicago, Ill.

A few weeks ago we preached for Bro. Pledger at Kensington M. E. Church, where Bro. Jenkins has been an active member for some time. We referred to the above touching incident, and mentioned how Bro. Jenkins had been saved through the influence of his dying sister. His heart was melted, and when we gave the invitation to come to the altar for the fullness of God, he, among others, came forward, and wrestled with God until he was baptized with the Holy Ghost, and shouted for joy. -- Editor.

### 136 -- "JESUS, HAVE MERCY ON FATHER," WAS LITTLE MARY'S DYING PRAYER.

In a shanty on First Avenue, New York City, little Mary B___ lay dying. Suddenly she turned toward her mother and said, "Mother, I am dying, but I am not afraid." "Not afraid to die?" said her unchristian mother. "Oh, it is awful to die!" Little Mary replied, "Not when you have Jesus with you, mother. O mother, you must love my Savior!" plead this little angel.

At the bedside, on bended knees, was the drunken father. On his head rested the hand of his little daughter, as she repeated three times, at intervals, "Jesus, have mercy on father."

Shortly afterwards she was numbered with the angel choir in heaven, and three months after her death both of her parents were converted, and from that time led Christian lives. -- Written for this book by Rev. L. B. Balliett, M.D., of Allentown, Penn.

### 137 -- "MY GOD, MY GOD, MY DOOM IS SEALED! I AM LOST, LOST, LOST!"

Through the kindness of Rev. N. L. Stambaugh, of Fort Wayne, Indiana, we furnish our readers with the following sad experience:

In the year 1886, while the writer was at Crawfordsville, Indiana, working in revival meetings, there was a certain young man present at the meetings who was under deep conviction. He would sit in his seat and tremble, while tears would roll down his cheeks. I plead with him night after night, but he would not yield One evening (the last night that he was there) I plead with him more earnestly than on previous occasions, for somehow I was impressed with the feeling that some thing would happen to this young man if he did not re pent that evening; but still he would not yield to my entreaties. I went home with the solemnity of death resting upon me.

Next morning at about three o'clock there was a loud rap at my door. I went to the door, and there stood a young man before me, who requested me to go over to such a street and such a number as quickly as possible, as there was a young man there dying who wanted to see me.

I hastened as quickly as possible to the address given, and there I found the same young man that I had plead with the evening before, dying.

He looked at me, and said, "Oh, if I had just settled it last evening. Oh, if I would only have yielded -- if only I would have got saved." I said to him, "There may be hope for you yet." He began to shake his head and say, "No, no; I am suffering too much pain now to pray." I tried to point him to the Savior, but it was of no avail. In a few minutes he began to cry out, "My God, my God, my doom is sealed! I am lost, lost, lost!! I am going to hell!!!" and then drew his last breath. That awful scene I can never forget.

## *138 -- JOHN OXTOBY'S WONDERFUL REVELATION AND UNSPEAKABLE JOY AT DEATH.*

This holy and powerful man of God was born in Yorkshire, England, in 1762 He was soundly converted to God in 1804 after having spent many years of his life in sin. He soon commenced to preach the gospel as a Methodist preacher and wherever he went the revival flame was kindled, and thousands of precious souls were converted to God.

His biographer, Harvey Leigh, thus depicts the character of this holy man:

"His most usual theme in the pulpit was faith. He had such a faculty of accommodating and reducing his expressions, relative to this important grace, to the apprehension of the lowest capacity, that every one was enabled to profit considerably under him if at all attentive to him.

"But that which gave lasting effect to all his labors in the Lord's vineyard was the uncommon power of the Spirit which attended his word. Seldom or never did he open his mouth either in preaching, praying or personal conversation, but such an unction attended his words that those addressed by him usually felt its force. Not infrequently have numbers fallen under his preaching and prayers, and apparently under the most striking apprehensions of their sin and danger, they have cried out for mercy. Others who have with great difficulty escaped home have been obliged to send for him or others to pray for them before they dared attempt to sleep; and, strange as it may seem, some have fallen down on their way home, and others at their work, from the effects of his preaching and prayers.

"Thus, while he had no superior mental capabilities for the pulpit, he was attended with the most powerful influences of the Holy Spirit; and this made him, in the absence of other qualifications, an able minister of the New Testament. But, while he did not shine in the things to Which we have referred, he did excel in the strength and constancy of his faith, which was singularly strong. Perhaps in this he was second to none. He was a genuine son of Abraham; for he did not stagger at the promises, but credited them with a confidence unshaken, and which gave glory to God.

"John Oxtoby is now regarded as one of the great men of Methodism. During the whole of the affliction which hastened his death he had the most glorious displays of the divine favor; he received such a baptism of the Holy Ghost that his soul was filled with peace and joy unutterable. Amidst the sinkings of mortality, the sorrowing of his friends and his near approach to eternity, he possessed the most steady and serene confidence, and approached the vale of death as if

" *Prayer was all his business.*
*And all his pleasure, praise."*

A little while before his departure he mentioned the names of several persons with whom he had been familiarly acquainted and said, "Tell them that strong as my faith has been, and great as have been my comforts while among them during the years of my life, yet all the former manifestations which I have had are nothing compared with those which I now feel."

To his sister he said, "O, what have I beheld! Such a sight as I cannot possibly describe. There were three shining forms stood beside me, whose garments were so bright, and whose countenances were so glorious, that I never saw anything to compare with them before." His dying prayer was, "Lord, save souls; do not let them perish." Shortly after, he shouted in holy triumph, "Glory, glory, glory!" and immediately soared on high, November 29, 1829. -- Shining Lights.

## 139 -- NO HAPPINESS IN THE MOHAMMEDAN RELIGION; CALIPH ABD-ER-RHAMAN IS WITNESS

This great caliph, the third of his name, who was distinguished for his patronage of learning and the arts, and who raised the Moslem empire in Spain to its highest point, was born in 888 and died in 961.

The testimony of this ungodly successor of Mohammed at the end of his career shows how neither the possessions of earth nor the teachings of the Mohammedan religion had power to satisfy a human soul. His words were: "Fifty years have passed since first I was caliph. Riches, honors, pleasures, I have enjoyed all. In this long period of seeming happiness I have numbered the days on which I have been happy. They amount to fourteen."

## 140 -- "OH, HE IS COMING, HE IS COMING! JESUS, COME AND TAKE ME NOW!"

Sister Nannie Belle Gilkey was born in Pennsylvania, Sept. 21, 1877. and died at Harvey, Illinois, July 18, 1897. She was one of God's own afflicted children, who suffered for some time with that dread disease, consumption. During the intense suffering which she passed through toward the close of her life she manifested a sweet spirit of patience. Her circumstances being so adverse, much grace was needed, and she proved the truthfulness of the promise, "As the day, so shalt thy strength be."

When Jesus came for Nannie he found her waiting and willing to go with Him. For three days before her death she knew that her time in this world was short. During the day that she died she was very happy, singing several times in the afternoon,

*"Anywhere with Jesus I can safely go."*

and

*"I am so happy in Jesus,*
*From sin and from sorrow so free."*

Once she said, "Jesus is so near. Do you not feel that He is near, mamma?" At times her suffering was intense. She said, "O, what shall I do!" and when told to look to Jesus, He was the only one who could help her, she looked up and said, "Yes, Lord!" And Jesus came so near that she exclaimed, "O, He is coming, He is coming! O, Jesus, come and take me now -- I am ready." A few minutes before she left us she waved her hand and said, "Good-bye all," and she went to be forever with the Lord. -- Written for this work by Sadie A. Cryer, of Rockford, Ill.

## 141 -- LAST WORDS OF THE VENERABLE BEDE

This eminent saint of God was born in 674. He was noted as a theologian and historian. He furnished an early political and ecclesiastical history of England, of great value. In St. Paul's Church is to be seen, chair which belonged to him. He was buried there in the year of our Lord 735, in the sixty-first year of his age.

The evening of his death he spent in finishing the translation into the Saxon from the Latin, of the Gospel of St. John.

The last words he uttered before he expired were, "Glory be to the Father, to the Son, and to the Holy Ghost."

## 142 -- "I AM AS MUCH LOST AS THOUGH I WERE IN HELL."

Through the kindness of Mrs. H. A. Coon, we publish the following" Mother Hart and I were sent for to visit this neighbor. We found him in terrible distress of soul, pacing the floor and groaning. I said to him, "Mr. C___, we have come to help you, if that is your desire." He replied, "I know it; you are all right, but it is too late. I attended your meetings two years ago. The Spirit said to me, 'Hurry! Go to the altar! Plead with God for mercy!' I could scarcely sit on the seat. I had been a class leader in the east. I came to Marengo -- have been under deep conviction, but would not yield. The Spirit left me, and I am as much lost as though I were in hell already. I feel the fire is kindled here (striking upon his breast). It is too late; I am going to hell, and my sons with me." He lived two weeks. It was a place of darkness and devils until he died.

## 143 -- POINTING ABOVE, JERRY MCAULEY SAID, "IT IS ALL RIGHT!"

Many of our readers have no doubt heard of Jerry McAuley and his rescue mission work in the great city of New York. He was a brand plucked from the burning.

He was born in Ireland, and .came to New York when thirteen years old, where for a number of years he was by profession a "river thief," stealing goods from vessels by night; and plunging into sin of every form without restraint. He grew up to be a prize fighter and highway robber. In the midst of his crimes he was arrested, convicted, and sent to states prison, where after a few years he was powerfully converted to God, and commenced to preach Christianity to the other prisoners. Through his instrumentality many were converted. After serving out half of his time he was pardoned out of prison, and continued his work for God in the slums of New York. Thousands of criminals have been saved through his influence, and some have become evangelistic workers.

We are personally acquainted with his successor, Col. C. H. Haddley, now in charge of the great McAuley Mission in New York, where a successful work is being accomplished. Bro. Haddley was as low down in sin as McAuley, and is one of his converts.

McAuley died in New York, Sept. 18, 1884. Just before being transferred to heaven, arousing himself, he pointed above and said, "It is all right," then sank back and died.

## 144 -- "I HEAR THE ANGELS SINGING AROUND MY BED!"

Through the kindness of Julia E. Strait, of Portlandville, N. Y., we furnish our readers with the following:

In the spring of 1895, in the town of Worcester, N. Y., an aged lady left the shores of time. She had suffered much during a long illness, but she proved the grace of God sufficient, and was kept by the power of God from complaining.

During the last three days of her life, while suffering untold distress and pain, she exhorted those of her children and neighbors who came to her bedside to prepare to meet their God. When they wept, she said to them, "O do not weep, this suffering wilt soon be over! I hear the angels singing around my bed! This poor body will soon be at rest!" and so she passed into the rest that remains for the people of God.

## 145 -- BISHOP BEDELL'S LAST WORDS WERE -- "I HAVE KEPT THE FAITH."

History tells us that Bishop William Bedell was one of the best Prelates that ever adorned the English Church.

He was born at Black, Notley, Essex, in 1570. In 1604 he accompanied Sir Henry Walton as his chaplain to Venice. While residing here he translated the English book of Common Prayer into Italian.

In 1627 he was elected Provost of Trinity College, Dublin, and at the end of two years he was promoted to the united Bishoprics of Killmore and Ardagh. The translation of the old testament into Irish was accomplished under his direction. (The new had already been translated.)

When he came to die in 1642 he said, "I have finished my ministry and life together; I have kept the faith, 'and am persuaded that He is able to keep that which I have committed unto Him against that day.'"

## 146 -- "GO ON, ANGELS, I AM COMING. GO ON, ANGELS, I AM COMING."

Through the kindness of Rev. N. L. Stambaugh, of Fort Wayne, Indiana, we furnish our readers with this triumphant translation:

In the year 1895, while I was traveling a circuit at Elkhart, Ind., in September, Anthony Foster Herman, one of my members, also class leader, aged eighteen years, was taken ill with typhoid fever. His illness was of short duration, but his suffering during that time was untold. He was never heard to murmur nor complain. After one of his paroxysms of pain he exclaimed. "O God, Thou hast suffered more than this for me, I'll gladly suffer all for Thee."

The writer had the privilege of standing by his side the last night, and until his death. I said to him, "Bro. Foster, how is it with your soul?" He answered, "Bro. Stambaugh, there isn't a cloud or trial to mar my peace with God. All is well." As the end was drawing near he called for a glass of spring water, and after drinking it he said, "That is good, but I have better water than that -- the water of everlasting life is springing up in my soul."

A few minutes later his face lit up with glory; then he looked at me and said, "Bro. Stambaugh, do you know what I was thinking about? .... No. What is it, Bro. Foster?" He replied, "This house that I live in (at the same time raising up his hands and pointing to his body) is almost gone; it is just about ready to fail to pieces," then added, "but Glory to God, (with a voice with the ring of heaven in it) I see the new house, the mansion, and oh, how beautiful! Just see what a glorious mansion! Oh, I am so anxious to go. Yes, they are getting ready to come to me -- I am going shortly." A little later he threw up his hand, waved it, and said, "Go on angels, I am coming! Go on angels, I am coming!" and took the wings of the morning and flew away to be with Jesus.

## 147 -- JOHN DONNE, A FAMOUS BRITISH POET AND PREACHER

John Donne, D. D., a famous British poet and preacher, was born in 1573.

For several "years he was secretary to Sir Thomas Egerton, and in later years he was ordained as a preacher of the Gospel. Immediately after ordination he was appointed royal chaplain, and in 1620 Dean of St. Paul's. In 1630 he preached his last sermon, which was afterwards published under the title of Death's Duel.

He died March 31, 1631. Although he was the author of many books, and a great theologian, and noted for his piety, yet when he came to die he said, "I repent of all my life except that part of it which I have spent in communion with God, and in doing good."

## 148 -- CARDINAL BEAUFORT -- "WILL NOT MY RICHES SAVE ME?"

Henry Beaufort, Cardinal and Bishop of Winchester, was born about 1370. He was a half-brother to King Henry IV. He was educated in England and Germany, and in 1404 became Bishop of Winchester. He was present at the Council of Constance, and voted for the election of Pope Martin V., by whom he was subsequently made a cardinal. In 1431 Beaufort conducted the young king, Henry VI., to France, to be crowned in Paris as King of France and England. Here he also endeavored, but vainly, to reconcile the Duke of Bedford, Regent of France, with the offended Duke of Burgundy.

He died at Winchester in 1447. His memory is stained by his suspected participation in the murder of the Earl of Gloucester and of the Maid of Orleans.

His last words were: "And must I then die? Will not my riches save me? I could purchase the kingdom, if that would prolong my life. Alas! there is no bribing death!"

## 149 -- THE EARL OF ROCHESTER -- "I SHALL NOW DIE"

The Earl of Rochester (John Wilmot), a noted courtier and versifier, was born in 1647. His wit and love of pleasure made him the favorite of a dissolute court, but his nature before he died was greatly changed; he was born again, and made a new creature in Christ.

He died in 1680, only thirty-three years of age. As he neared the shores of eternity he said, "I shall now die, but O, what unspeakable glories do I see; what joy beyond thought or expression am I sensible of; I am assured of God's mercy to me through Jesus Christ; O, how I long to die and be with my Savior!"

## 150 -- AWFUL CALAMITY THAT BEFELL A YOUNG LADY WHO OFFERED A MOCK PRAYER.

Rev. Thomas Graham, the noted revivalist preacher of the Erie Conference of the Methodist Episcopal Church, relates the following sad experience:

When stationed in Fredonia, a girl who lived about three miles from that place, toward Sheridan, and had been awakened at a meeting held in the village by me, but who refused to seek religion, went to a ball on Wednesday, being the evening following, and, being bantered about her religious feelings, to prove to the contrary, took a cloak, and throwing it down in the middle of the floor called it her "mourner's bench," then, taking the hand of a young man, kneeled down by it and offered a mock prayer. That very moment she was struck crazy. Her friends got her into a sleigh and hurried home with her. A physician was sent for immediately, but it was of no use. She died, crazy, on Friday evening, about the same hour of the day. She had not one lucid moment until she died. It was emphatically her "mourner's bench." Her lifeless remains were carried to the grave the following Sunday in Fredonia, followed by her friends, who would not be comforted.

## 151 -- JEREMIAH EVERTS -- "O, WONDERFUL! WONDERFUL! GLORY! JESUS REIGNETH!"

This American author and editor was corresponding secretary of the American Board of Commissioners for foreign missions.

He was born in Vermont in 1781, and died in Charleston, South Carolina, in 1831, at the age of fifty years. In his last moments he exclaimed, "O, wonderful! wonderful! wonderful! Glory that cannot be comprehended! Wonderful glory! I will praise Him! I will praise Him! Wonderful glory! Jesus reigneth!"

## 152 -- "IF THIS IS DEATH, LET ME ALWAYS BE DYING."

Mrs. H. A. Coon, of Marengo, IlL, sends us the following:

Mrs. Eliza Lamphare, my eldest sister, died thirty-one years ago, leaving her baby girl to me. She suffered twenty-five years with rheumatic consumption. She was converted in our home fifteen years before her death. On the day of her death, before she passed away, she said to her family, "I am going to heaven!" She sent for her pastor and neighbors and told them of her joy at the thought of so soon seeing Jesus. She said, "If this is death, let me always be dying." And, although she had not had her voice for six weeks, sweetly sang,

"'What's this that steals, that steals upon my frame.
Is it death -- is it death?"
And, coming to the verse,
"Bright angels are from glory come,
They're round my bed, they're in my room;
They wait to waft my spirit home,
All is well!"

She exhorted all to be faithful and meet her in heaven. She sent messages of love to me, committing her little one to my trust. With her face lighted up with a heavenly radiance, she waved her hands and shouted, "Victory, and glory," until her spirit had departed.

## 153 -- "JESUS HEARS ME! WHY, THE ANGELS ARE AROUND ME!"

A great many readers have but very little conception of true prayer. They excuse themselves when invited to pray in public by saying, "I am not gifted in that way; I am not educated." They regard the opinions of men and the face of clay more than they do the will of God. They fail to realize that true prayer is the desire of the heart, uttered or unexpressed.

We have a beautiful example in a dying young man: He was so concerned about his relation to God that he lost sight of his surroundings and the people who stood by him. "I cannot make a very smooth prayer," he said, "but Jesus hears me. Why, the angels are around me; if you could see them as I do you would be glad, too. Jesus hears me." When God lends a listening ear and regards our cry, every voice should be hushed and every excuse banished. Nothing should interrupt or hinder our communion with God; and if we abandon ourselves to His will, He will see that our fellowship and prayer is unhindered, for "the effectual, fervent prayer of a righteous man availeth much."

## 154 -- REV. DAVID NELSON -- "MY MASTER CALLS, I AM GOING HOME; IT IS WELL."

This noted Presbyterian clergyman was born near Jonesborough, Tennessee, Sept. 24, 1793.

In 1810 he graduated at Washington College, Virginia, and for some years practiced medicine, and was surgeon in the United States army, during which time he became an infidel; but in the providence of God he was brought under conviction and saved from a refuge of lies. He was made a new creature in Christ, and licensed to preach in the spring of 1825.

After working for the Lord for five years in Tennessee and Kentucky, he went to Missouri and established Marion College, and was its first president, filling that position for six years.

In 1836 he opened a training school for missionaries, and wrote that widely circulated book, Cause and Cure of Infidelity.

He died in 1844. His last words were, "My Master calls, I am going home. It is well."

## 155 -- "MY PEACE IS MADE WITH GOD! I AM FILLED WITH LOVE!"

My dear father, William H. Whitford, was taken with a severe hemorrhage of the lungs on April 9, 1898, from which he gradually failed in strength, and died a few days after. He was a devoted Christian, and as long as he was able to speak he would say, "Praise the Lord! Praise the Lord!"

Father suffered from a complication of diseases which often caused him severe pain, and when suffering he would often go to God in prayer and secure relief and get richly blessed in his soul. One morning his face was lit up with a holy light as he shouted, "Hallelujah! Glory to God!" Sister Palmer, who was in the next room, said that she, too, felt the power of the Holy Spirit and shouted. Oh, how the Spirit would come upon us. Indeed it was a heavenly place. The gloom was all taken away. It did not seem like dying.

Although father was in his eighty-second year when he died, his mind was very clear all the time, and he would think of everything needful to be done. His only desire to live was to help me, as we lived alone. He gave that to the Lord. He talked about his funeral very calmly, and selected the text, Psalms 87:37, and desired that the old hymns be sung, mentioning this one, "And must this body die." I asked him if he wanted flowers, to which he replied, "Oh, no. I want it very plain, clothed in righteousness." He sang with us a short time before he died, and oh, how his face lit up with joy while singing.

"Hallelujah! Glory to God!" he shouted, and then clapped his hands and said, "If I could only get up, I feel I could leap and shout for joy. Peace, peace; my peace is made with God. I am filled with His love. Jesus alone heaves in sight." It seemed as though he had a view of heaven. His last words were, "O, bless the Lord[ Praise the Lord!" and thus he went sweetly to sleep, safe in the arms of Jesus. -- Written for this book by his daughter, Mrs. A. Slade, of Portland, New York.

## 156 -- "OH GOD, IF THERE BE A GOD, SAVE MY SOUL, IF I HAVE A SOUL."

Bro. R. Thomas, of Orleans, Nebraska, sends us the following for our book:

When father moved to Iowa in 1863, it was our privilege to settle near a well-to-do family, the father of which was an infidel. There were several sons in the family, and all save one were irreligious. The one who professed religion was a Universalist preacher. In fact the family were surrounded by every influence that would make infidel belief satisfactory, if it could be so, but such was not the case. No doubt many reminiscences of interest could be given, but suffice it to say that the day-star of this intelligent, well-to-do farmer set in the dark, and his last words were this short prayer, "Oh God, if there be a God, save my soul, if I have a soul."

## 157 -- THOMAS HALYBURTON -- "MY PEACE HATH BEEN LIKE A RIVER!"

This noted Scotch Presbyterian minister was born in 1674. He studied at Rotterdam, then at Perth and Edinburgh, and in 1692 entered the University of St. Andrews. In 1700 he was ordained in the parish of Ceres, and in 1710 he was appointed to a Professorship of Theology in St. Andrews.

He was author of several works, including Natural Religion Insufficient and Revelation Necessary to Man's Happiness, The Great Concern of Salvation, and others. These works, especially the autobiographic memoir of the Holy Halyburton, were formerly very popular in Scotland, and still are greatly relished by persons of serious disposition.

He died in 1712. His last words were, "My peace hath been like a river." He had promised some friends that when he was so far gone that he could speak no more, he would give a sign of triumph, and accordingly, when the powers of speech were gone, he lifted and clapped his hands, then expired.

## 158 -- "MADGE IS DEAD AND DAVID IS CRAZY."

In the spring of 1891, while Rev. C. B. Ebey was holding a meeting at Colgrove, California, two young ladies and their brother, who had been regular attendants at the meeting, were brought under deep conviction, but would not yield to the Spirit. The youngest was a bright, healthy young girl of fourteen years, named Madge.

One day Bro. Ebey said to her, "Madge, I believe this meeting is being held for you." She felt that she ought to give her heart to God, and decided to do so, but was persuaded by her brother David not to for awhile longer. Her brother dearly loved her, and knew if she got saved that it would end their worldly pleasures together, so he persuaded her to wait a few years, and then they would both get saved. The meeting closed, and they had both said to the Spirit, ' 'Wait until a more convenient season." A few weeks afterwards Bro. Ebey received word that Madge was dead, and was asked to come to her home immediately. He went as quickly as he could. The mother met him at the door, and said, "Bro. Ebey, you have come to a sad home. Madge is dead, and David is crazy." When the doctor had said that Madge could not live, David went in by her bedside, knelt down, and commenced to pray as only a sinner could pray, for God to save his sister. He urged Madge to pray, but she was too sick to make any effort, and she died without leaving any evidence of salvation. The strain was so much for the young man when he realized that his sister was dying unsaved, and that he was the cause of it, that his reason gave way. -- Written for this work by Rev. F. A. Ames.

## 159 -- "I AM GOING HOME AS FAST AS I CAN."

An aged Christian, Mr. Mead, when crossing over to heaven, was asked how he did? He answered, "I am going home as fast as I can, as every honest man should do when his day's work is over, and I bless God that I have a home to go to."

## 160 -- HULDA A. REES -- "ALL BRIGHT AND GLORIOUS AHEAD."

This holy woman of God was a successful evangelist of the Society of Friends. She was born Oct. 15, 1855. She went to heaven June 3, 1898. Her devoted husband, Seth C. Rees, is also a successful minister in the same church, and author of that excellent book, The Ideal Pentecostal Church.

We take the following from her published biography, entitled Hulda, the Pentecostal Prophetess, written by her son. He says:

"We saw from a distance the end approaching, but we could not fully realize the truth. It did not seem like 'the valley of the shadow.' We had read of the triumph of the saints when approaching the River, but surely this excelled anything of which we had ever heard. Such sweet resignation to all God's will, such divine unction in prayer, such holy tenderness in exhortation and admonition, such victory and gladness in the furnace of pain and agony! -- these luminous beacons did much to dispel the gloom and lighten the shades of the nearing evening.

"Many visitors came to see her -- some from considerable distance -- and whenever her strength permitted it she always had them admitted to her room. Her words were ever full of cheer and eternal hope. On one occasion, when a minister called whom she had known for years, she said to him with the greatest exultation, "The glory holds!" Yes, thank God, it did hold. The gospel she had preached to so many thousands with emphasis and assurance was found true and unshakable in this time of earnest testing. One day her husband said to her:

" 'My dear, is it all true that we have preached?'

" 'Yes, yes; we have not put it strong enough! It is all true, and more!'

At another time she said: 'If the Lord takes me, it will be from the evil to come. Perhaps he sees something coming to me from which He wishes to protect me by taking me to Himself.'

"In one of her prayers she said: 'Thou hast put, O Lord, a great laugh in my heart. Glory! Glory be to Thy Name forever! No evil can come to me! All is turned to blessing!'...

"One afternoon the family were all gathered about her, when her face suddenly lighted up as if a candle were burning beneath the transparent skin. With the brightest, sweetest smile, and a far-away look as if she were gazing off In the distance, she said in a soft, reflective tone, 'I didn't know it was so beautiful.' After a moment or so she exclaimed rapturously, 'Can it be that the glory of the Lord is risen upon me?'

"Thus this daughter of the Most High drew near to her exit from this world. It was indeed to her, as she said, 'all bright and glorious ahead.'

"The night before she ascended she attempted to sing:

*'Fear not, I am with thee:*
*Oh, be not dismayed,*
*For I am thy God,*
*I will still give thee aid."*

But she could only whisper the words. Her husband read the entire hymn to her.

"In the evening of Friday, June 3, as the darkness was deepening about us, we watched her slip quietly away. There was no struggle. She passed away from us as calmly as a child falling asleep. We knew that she was with the Lord, both hers and ours."

## *161 -- JOSEPH ALLEIN, D. D. -- "O, HOW SWEET WILL HEAVEN BE."*

This famous English divine, author of Alarm to the Unconverted, was born in 16331 died in 1668. Although he died at the age of thirty-five, his influence for good was great. He lived a devoted life, and as the sun was setting, and he came to the end of life's journey, he exclaimed, "O, how sweet will heaven be! O, what a blessed day will the day of resurrection be! Methinks I see it by faith!"

## *162 -- "LORD, HAVE MERCY ON MY SOUL!"*

While laboring in Canada on my first charge, two young men attended the meeting. They were bent on breaking up the service. I was visiting a family where one of them boarded. He was sullen and morose. He did not kneel when we prayed, nor pay any attention to our questions in regard to his soul. It was not long after this when both the young men were engaged in the brick-yard. It was the first day with one. The brick-yard caved in, and the friend whom we had warned was instantly killed. His companion lived long enough to groan out, "Lord, have mercy upon my soul! Lord, have mercy upon my soul!" Without leaving any evidence behind of having obtained his request, he was called to stand before his Maker. I attended the double funeral; a sad occasion it was. One of the mothers, who had opposed her son joining the Salvation Army, thinking it would be a disgrace to her, threw herself upon the casket and said, "Lord, have mercy on his soul!" But her interest in his soul came too late. It is a warning to all mothers who oppose their children in obeying their convictions of duty. -- Written for this work by Kate H. Booth, of Buffalo, N. Y.

### 163 -- "NOTHING REMAINS BUT THE BRIDGE OF THE SAVIOR."

Byron Bunson, one of the most distinguished statesmen and scholars of Germany, was born in 1791 at Korbach, in the principality of Wualdeck. In 1841 he was sent on a special mission to London to negotiate for the erection of an Anglo-Prussian Bishopric in Jerusalem, and was shortly afterward appointed ambassador at the English court. He is known in literature by his Constitution of the Church of the Future, Christianity and Mankind, God in History, and many other works. He was a great statesman and philosopher.

He died at Bonn, in Germany, in 1860. On his deathbed he cried out, "All bridges that one builds through life fail at such a time as this, and nothing remains but the bridge of the Savior!"

### 164 -- "IT IS BRIGHT OVER THE RIVER, OH, SO BRIGHT OVER THERE."

Some years ago I was called to the bedside of an aged lady, familiarly known as Grandma Shears, to witness her departure from this life. We watched at her bedside all night, and sang many cheering songs to her, as

*"O, think of the home over there,"*

and others. As her mental powers gradually gave way, her children greatly feared that she would not be able to tell us of the rapture in passing over the River of Jordan, washed in the blood of the Lamb; but I said to them that God would clear her mental skies and let her tell us all about it; and He did. For an hour she lay calmly, saying "It is bright over the river; oh, so bright over there," and she passed sweetly to the land of flowers. -- Written for this work by Rev. E. Ray, of Fredericktown, Mo.

### 165 -- THE SAD DEATH OF ALL INFIDEL

Mary E. Jenks, of McBain, Michigan, sends us the following: The people of the village of M have been greatly shocked of late by the terrible death of one of its residents, a Mr. T___, an infidel.

This man had lived an ungodly life, making no preparation for the great beyond to which he was hastening. He did not attend the house of God, and cared for none of these things that could in any way lead him to a better life. But disease fastened upon him, and death's cold hand reached for him. Although near the valley of the shadow of death, he still continued to make calculations for the future, and once, when asked how he was, sneeringly said that God wouldn't let him die; he was too good to die. But as he grew worse he was made to feel that the end was drawing near. He could not lie down, but sat in his chair day and night, while his limbs were badly swollen.

He belonged to two secret orders, and one day sent for one of the brotherhood. He came, and Mr. T said to him, "Well, I am here yet, but I am going to die, and I want you to see to it that I am buried according to the ceremonies of the orders." The man responded, "That will be all right, but you had better be thinking about something else now." Mr. T went on with his directions, saying something about flowers, etc. How can anything in this world be more sad than to see a strong man dying without God, and with no heart to repent, but trying to comfort himself with how the last few rites will be performed over his lifeless remains.

Poor, wretched man; even this request was denied him. He would curse God while in the agonies of death.

Finally the end came, but instead of flowers, pomp and show over his body, he was gathered up in the blankets in which he sat, hurried into a box and carried to a Christless grave, while his soul went to meet the God he had so insulted. Who would not choose to die the death of the righteous?

## 166 -- "I AM LOST, LOST, LOST, LOST, LOST!"

Rev. J. B. Davis, of Davis Station, W. Va., sends us this sad experience, which we pray may be used of God as a warning to the living. He says:

Mrs. B___, of C___, W.Va., who had attended a revival meeting at Davis Creek Church (near my father's home), was besought by Christian friends to give her life to the Lord, but she refused. Shortly after this she was seized with a disease which soon brought her to death's door. Rev. J. D. Garrett, who had conducted the revival meeting at which she was present, was sent for, and, as he entered the home, the dying woman exclaimed, "I am lost, lost, lost, lost, lost!" The minister said to her, "My sister, Jesus loves you, and if you will trust Him He will save you." He then quoted some of God's promises to her.

"Oh, Bro. Garrett," she exclaimed, "if I had given Him my life when you were holding that meeting here, it would have been all right. He wanted to save me then, but it is too late now. I am lost, lost, lost!"

Bro. Garrett tried to get her to stop and reason with him, but she continued to cry, "Lost, lost," etc. The minister said that it seemed as though hell were near them that night, and was uncapped as the poor, dying woman wept over her lost condition.

Her son, who was away from home, was sent for, and, as he entered the room where his mother lay dying, she turned her face toward him and said, "Charley, is that you?" "Yes, mother," he replied, "how are you?" She exclaimed, "I am lost, lost!"

He went to her bedside, threw his arms about her, and told her of the Savior's love for sinners, but she cried, "It is too late for me, Charley; I am lost, lost," and she continued repeating this until her soul took its departure.

## 167 -- LITTLE HATTIE BUFORD'S LAST PRAYER

This little girl died in 1865, when only six years old. She was the child of Major-General John Buford. She was taught to repeat the Lord's prayer every night. As the child lay on her dying bed, and the hour of her departure was drawing near, she all of a sudden opened her soft blue eyes, and, looking confidently into her mother's face, said, "Mamma, I forgot to say my prayers!" Summoning what strength she had left, she clasped her little white hands together, and, like a little angel, prayed thus:

*"Now I lay me down to sleep.*
*I pray Thee, Lord, my soul to keep:*
*If I should die before I wake,*
*I pray Thee, Lord, my soul to take."*

The prayer finished, she never spoke again.

I wonder how many of our readers say their prayers every night before they go to sleep. Editor.

## 168 -- THE LAST WORDS OF JOSEPH BARKER, THE CONVERTED INFIDEL

No doubt many of our readers have heard of Rev. Joseph Barker. For the early part of his life he was a noted worker in the service of the devil, and preached his infidelity wherever he had an opportunity, but we are thankful to God that the last part of his life was spent in the service of the Lord. He was converted from infidelity, and became a preacher of righteousness.

He died at Omaha, Nebraska, in 1870, at the age of seventy-one years. A few days before his death he spoke as follows to his son and two friends who were present:

"I feel that I am approaching my end, and desire that you should receive my last words and be witness to them. I wish you to witness that I am in my right mind, and fully understand what I have just been doing; and dying, that I die in the full and firm belief in Jesus Christ. I am sorry for my past errors; but during the last years of my life I have striven to undo the harm I did, by doing all that I was able to do to serve God, by showing the beauty and religion of His Son, Jesus Christ. I wish you to write and witness this, my last confession of faith, that there may be no doubt about it."

## 169 -- "YOU GAVE ME NOTHING TO HOLD ON TO."

In a country village of Pennsylvania there lived an infidel physician, who by infidel books persuaded a young man to deny his Savior.

In about 1875 this man died, aged fifty years. The infidel teacher was his physician. When his end was approaching, the doctor told him to die as he had lived -- a rejecter of God and Christ. "Hold on to the end," urged the doctor. "Yes, doctor," said the dying man, "there is just my trouble; you gave me nothing to hold on to." The doctor did not reply.

## 170 -- "OH! THE DEVIL IS COMING TO DRAG MY SOUL DOWN TO HELL!"

N. M. Nelms, of Kopperl, Texas, sends us this very sad experience. He says: Miss A___, who lived at C___, in Georgia, was taken very sick, and was informed that she could not live. Realizing the way she had lived, surrounded by her ungodly associates, with whom she had indulged in the pleasures of sin, and how her parents had educated her to follow the fashions of the world, and decorated her in gay clothing, and turned her away from the truth of God, she called her ungodly father to her bedside and said, "Your heart is as black as hell. If you had taught me to live for God, rather than to have spent your time quarreling with mother, I might have been saved." Then, turning to others who stood by her dying bed, she plead with them, saying, "Do not follow my ungodly example; do not do as I have done; do not enjoy or indulge in the hellish pleasures of the world. Oh, if I had heeded the warnings of my friend who lived a holy and devoted life." Then she said, "Oh, the devil is coming to drag my soul down to hell! Don't live in pleasure and be found wanting, bat live in Christ complete and wanting nothing. I am lost, lost forever! Oh, lost, lost, lost!" -- then died.

## 171 -- DAVID BRAINERD -- "I AM ALMOST IN ETERNITY; I LONG TO BE THERE TO PRAISE AND GLORIFY GOD!"

This celebrated missionary to the Indians was born at Haddam, Connecticut, April 20, 1718. His parents were noted for their piety, and were closely related to high officials of the church and state.

In 1739 he entered Yale College, where he stood first in his class. He was greatly favored of God in being privileged to attend the great revival conducted by Whitefield, Jonathan Edwards and Tenent.

President Edwards says, in his memoir of Brainerd: "His great work was the priceless example of his piety, zeal and self devotion. Why, since the days of the apostles none have surpassed him. His uncommon intellectual gifts, his fine personal qualities, his melancholy and his early death, as well as his remarkable holiness and evangelistic labors, have conspired to invest his memory with a book halo, and the story of his life has been a potent force in the modern missionary era. It is related of Henry Martyn that, while perusing the life of David Brainerd, his soul was filled with a holy emulation of that extraordinary man, and after deep consideration and fervent prayer, he was at length fixed in a resolution to imitate his example."

Brainerd was a representative man, formed both by nature and grace to leave a lasting impression upon the piety of the church.

He died at Northampton, Oct. 9, 1747. The last words of this dying apostle were, "I am almost in eternity. I long to be there. My work is done. I have done with my friends; all the world is nothing to me. Oh, to be in heaven to praise and glorify God with His holy angels."

## 172 -- LAST WORDS OF SAMUEL RUTHERFORD -- "I SHALL SOON BE WHERE FEW OF YOU SHALL ENTER."

This eminent Scotch Presbyterian divine was born in 1600, and died in 1661. He was commissioner to the Westminster General Assembly in 1643, and was for some time principal of St. Andrews College. When on his death-bed he was summoned to appear before Parliament for trial, for having preached Liberty arid Religion. He sent word with the messenger to tell Parliament "That I have received a summons to a higher bar -- I must needs answer that first; and when the day you name shall come, I shall be where few of you shall eater."

## 173 -- REV. RICHARD WATSON -- "I SHALL SEE GOD! HOW SHALL I PRAISE HIM?"

The great reformer, Rev. Richard Watson, was one of God's most noted preachers and theologians. He was born in England, Feb. 22, 1781; died Jan. 8, 1833. He took an active part in the Anti-slavery movement, and lived to see the preparation for the emancipation of all slaves in British colonies.

He was the author of many books. In his dying hour he exclaimed, "I shall see God! -- I -- I individually. I, myself, a poor worm of the earth, shall see God! How shall I praise Him?"

## 174 -- THE AWFUL END OF AN INFIDEL SCOFFER

Rev. Fred. Scott, of Arkansas City, Kansas, sends us this sad experience. He says: In the year 1880, in company with a few other pilgrims, I held a little street meeting off Brightside Lane, Sheffield, England, our object being to extend an invitation to passers-by to come to the services at the little Primitive Methodist Chapel, which was close by.

We stopped on the street, close to the home of the subject of this sketch (whose name I do not remember), and commenced to sing and talk to the people. He came out of his house in great rage and excitement, saying that we were disturbers of the peace and ought to be prosecuted. He secured the attention of some of the people, and preached his infidelity to them, telling them that the Bible was a humbug, and Christianity a fraud; churches and ministers an imposition on the people, and that society should be rid of them all. We tried to reason with him, but all in vain.

The following week some of the Pilgrims called at his home, and offered to pray with him and give him tracts to read, but he scornfully refused all of their offers. He abused their good intentions, and in a boasting way talked to them of the narrowness of Christianity, and the great freedom of his infidelity. Several times after that he made it a rule to meet us on the street, and try and confuse the people and break up the meeting. His presence was such an annoyance to us, and so detrimental to the meetings, that we scarcely could hold them. The lust time I ever saw him come out of his house was on Sunday morning, when he came walking down the street, close to where we were singing, with a stick in one hand and an axe in the other, and when he came very close to us he began to chop the wood for the purpose of getting the attention of the people from us. The chips began to fly around, and we thought best to move on, which we did. From that time on we all began to offer special prayer for his conversion; but God did not answer our prayers in the way we thought he would.

The next Sunday we went to our street meeting, feeling that in some way God would give us a victory over him, but to our surprise we did not find him there. I inquired about him, and found that he was suddenly taken very ill. The following week I was called to his room, and found him in a very dangerous condition. He was much changed in his mind; was very mild, tender and teachable, but could not repent. Many of the pilgrims visited him and tried to lead him to Jesus, but their efforts were in vain. He said that he knew that he was lost and doomed forever. In a few days I called again, and found him very close to the crossing. I told him of God's boundless mercy, and how it had reached Nebuchadnezzar and Manasseh, and that God had given His Son even for him; but he insisted that it was too late now, as he had sinned against light and knowledge when he knew better.

The fact of having disturbed our meetings preyed upon his mind, and he told me to faithfully warn all such scoffers of their danger. He wept bitterly as we talked to him of his lost condition, and said that if he could only live his life over again he would live for God; but it was a vain hope -- it was past -- his last chance was gone. The awful distress of his mind "became worse and worse until the end came. He expired in great agony of soul.

To live without Christ is folly; to be without Him on a deathbed is distressing; to die without Him is awful But oh, the thought of an eternity without Christ! My scoffing friend, take warning! Stop in time -- stop now! "Because I have called, and ye refused; I have stretched out My hand, and no man regarded; but ye have set at nought all My counsel, and would none of My reproof; I also will laugh at your calamity; I will mock when your fear cometh." (Prov 1: 24-26.)

### 175 -- "HALLELUJAH TO GOD! I AM GOING HOME TO GLORY."

In Arkansas there was an aged lady, Mrs. Abbott, who had been suffering for some time. I was at her house just before she died She would sing and pray and exhort the people, especially the young folks, telling them to get ready to meet her in heaven, and to quit their sins and to give their hearts to God. The night that I visited her, I shook her emaciated hand, and as I looked into her wrinkled face she said to me, "I am ready to go! All that are ready to meet me in heaven, were they to die tonight, come and shake my hand. Hallelujah to God! I am going home to glory and be with my Jesus." A few hours afterwards she triumphantly passed away singing praises to God and praying for husband and seven children. Praise the Lord for ever and ever. -- Written for this work by N. M. Nelms of Kopperl, Texas.

### 176 -- HE CRIED, WITH AN AWFUL WAIL OF DESPAIR, "TOO LATE, TOO LATE, TOO LATE!"

Bro. J. Earnest, of Searcy, White Co., Arkansas, sends us this sad experience. He says:

When I lived in the town of H___, in West Tennessee, I was well acquainted with a noted infidel who neither feared God nor regarded man. He would consider it an insult to his dignity for anyone to speak to him on the subject of religion; in fact, he had been known to fight some who had dared to approach him about his soul's salvation. He was well favored with the earthly possessions of this life, but it seemed to me that he was the most unhappy man that I had ever seen. He was such a hard case that the Christian people were afraid of him.

When he was dying, his brother-in law, a whisky-drinking infidel, at the request of his weeping wife went for my uncle, Mr. B___, to come and pray with him. My uncle came and when he entered the room the dying infidel said to him, "I can now see and realize that I am doomed for hell. Pray for me!" Uncle prayed and sang, and put forth all the powers of his soul for the wretched man, but it did not seem to do any good. While uncle was praying and singing, I tried to keep his mind on the Lord by talking to him. He warned all present not to live as he had lived, and sink at last to a devil's hell. At last he turned his face towards the wall, and cried with an awful wail, "Too late, too late, too late!" and his soul went out into eternity.

## 177 -- A GREAT REPROOF TO PROFESSING CHRISTIANS

In the year 1877, in Newark, New Jersey, a young man was hung for murder. Just before the fatal hour, he said to the Christian people about him, "If I had received one-half the attention and care from the good people of this city in early life that has been shown me since this trial commenced, I should never have been a murderer."

What a reproof to professing Christians were the statements made by this young man. A few years ago we held a revival meeting in a certain town in Illinois, and where two men met their death on the scaffold just before our meetings commenced, and the excitement had not yet died away. We were informed that two of the most prominent pastors of the town manifested considerable interest in these young men before they were doomed to death. They visited them often, talked and prayed with them, and they professed to be saved One of the doomed men exhorted the people from the scaffold to take warning by his example, and urged them to seek the Lord before they became guilty of some sin which would cause them and their families disgrace.

If the interest of Christians had been brought to bear upon these criminals before their conviction and crime, they might have been saved in their youth. O, that God might wake up his people and help them to rescue the perishing before they become guilty of some great crime, is our prayer. -- Editor.

## 178 -- JOHN KNOX, SCOTLAND'S GREAT REFORMER

This great reformer was noted for his faith and prayer. The name of John Knox is widely known throughout Christendom. He lived in the days of Queen Mary of Scotland, and she once stated that she feared the prayers of Knox more than all the armies of Scotland.

The Roman Catholic Church, with all its corruption and degradation, had great power and influence in the British Isles. The Queen of England, and many of the high officials in church and state, were nothing but tools in the hands of the pope in persecuting and destroying the Protestants. In the jails and prisons, as well as at the stake, God's devoted children suffered beyond description. The whole land was a scene of desolation. Many were burned alive for their faith and devotion to the Protestant religion. The great heart of John Knox was deeply moved. Night and day he cried to God to save Scotland.

At one time Knox was so greatly burdened for Scotland that he retired for secret prayer, but was soon discovered by some of his friends, by his groans. They heard him groan out, "Give me Scotland or I die!" Then after a few moments they heard him repeat these same words, "Give me Scotland or I die!" They heard him breath out the longings of his soul until he found relief. God gave him Scotland.

He died in 1572, in the sixty-seventh year of his age. After commending the care of his church to Christ, he said, "I now commend my soul into Thy hands." A few moments after, he exclaimed, "Now it is come!" Who will doubt but what God sent a convoy of angels to carry him to Abraham's bosom?

The Earl of Morton pronounced at his grave, in the presence of many of the nobles of Scotland, these words, "There lies he who never feared the face of man."

## 179 -- "MAY GOD ALMIGHTY BLESS THEE, MY BELOVED SONS AND BROTHERS IN CHRIST."

Two brothers and their father were beheaded in the year 1524 for preaching the gospel in Germany.

On the scaffold one of the sons said, "Father, farewell, my beloved father. Henceforth thou art my father no longer, and I am no longer thy son, but we are brothers still in Christ our Lord, for whose sake we are doomed to suffer death. Fear nothing." "Amen!" answered the old man, "and may God Almighty bless thee, my beloved sons and brothers in Christ." And all three knelt down in Christ's name, and their heads were severed from their bodies,

## 180 -- "I SHALL SOON BE A DEAD MAN, AND MY SOUL WILL BE IN HELL."

A minister, while traveling one day, was overtaken by a thunderstorm and took refuge in what was called a tavern. His attention was soon directed towards a man who seemed to be trying to entertain himself and others by using profanity in its lowest degree. He claimed to be an atheist, and blasphemed the name of God with unusual recklessness.

Finally, while the storm was raging wildly, he said to those around him, "There is no God, and to prove to you that I am right about it, I will go out there on that little hill and dare Him to strike me with His lightning." To the horror of that little company he went, and looking up toward heaven, his lips moved, and he brought his fists together with the appearance of doing what he said he would, though his voice could not be heard above the roar of the storm. In a short time he came back, saying as he did so, "You can see for yourselves that there is no God. If there were, He would have killed me while daring Him to do so." But God moves in a mysterious way, and his awful sin did not go long unpunished.

He took a chair and was quiet for some time. He had uttered his last oath, and when he again spoke it was in subdued tones, as follows, "There is a God, and He is going to teach me that He can take my life with a smaller instrument than a shaft of lightning. Soon after I came in here, a little insect lit upon my hand and stung it. It commenced to pain me and soon affected my arm and is fast doing its fatal work. The pain is almost unendurable, and I shall soon be a dead man, and my soul will be in hell. Yes, there is a God."

And so he died, in awful agony of body and mind, and his soul passed into the great beyond.

"Surely the fool hath said in his heart, There is no God." -- Reported for this book by Mary E. Jenks, of McBain, Michigan

## 181 -- "THIS IS HELL ENOUGH! THE DEVILS ARE DRAGGING ME DOWN."

There was a young man in Georgia who was constantly warned by his parents and others to turn from his wickedness, profanity and gambling, but he would not taste their advice, and became a miserable wreck of humanity.

He was taken ill, and during his sickness he would exclaim, "Oh, drive these devils away with their chains, they will drag my soul down to hell before I die! Oh, brother and sister, take warning! Don't come to this hell. This is hell enough! The devils are dragging me down!" And as he cried mightily, "Don't come to this hell of woe, this hell, this hell!" his soul departed to everlasting ruin and perdition.

Young people, take warning from this awful experience and repent before it is too late. -- Written for this work by N. M. Nelms. of Kopperl, Texas.

## 182 -- THE SAINTED A. J. GORDON'S LAST WORD WAS, "VICTORY!"

One of the most noted and devoted Baptist preachers of this country was Rev. Adoniram Judson Gordon, for many years pastor of Clarendon Street Baptist Church, Boston He was a noted author as well as 'preacher. He went to heaven Feb. 2, 1895. "A short time before his death," says the memorial number of The Watchword, "he called his wife to his side and said, 'If anything should happen, do not have a quartet choir; I have selected four hymns I want to have sung. Write them down: "Abide With Me," "The Sands of Time are Sinking," "Lord if He Sleep He Shall do Well," "My Jesus I Love Thee." ' He was assured that his wishes should be regarded, and the subject was dropped.

"Friday morning such a decided change for the worse was evident that a consultation was called, with the result that, though the patient's condition was pronounced dangerous, it was not hopeless. With the utmost devotion did these two physicians watch every symptom during the day, visiting him four times together that they might mark and check a relapse, or hasten any signs of recovery. At 5 P. M. the doctor sat by him, and speaking with a cheery voice to rouse him said, 'Doctor, have you a good word for us tonight?' and with a clear, full voice he answered, 'Victory!' This was his last audible utterance. Between nine and ten in the evening the nurse motioned to his wife that she was wanted, and bending to listen, he whispered, 'Maria, pray;' and as she led in prayer, he followed in a whisper, sentence by sentence, and at the close tried to utter a petition for himself. But his strength was not sufficient to articulate.

"A tearful group of friends were tarrying in the parlors of Carey Home; and beloved deacons waited with the members of the family to watch the ebbing tide of mortal life.

"Five minutes after midnight on the morning of February 2 he fell asleep in Jesus. 'And while he blessed them he was parted from them and taken up into heaven.'"

## 183 -- "OH, DO YOU HEAR THE MUSIC?"

May Wilcox, of Marengo, Illinois, when twenty-one years of age, was taken from earth to heaven.

She was a worker in the vineyard of the Lord -- a self-sacrificing, devoted Christian. Shortly after her conversion she was called of God to work for souls. She gave her life "for others' sake," to gather jewels for her Master, and proved faithful in declaring the truths of God's Word; thorough in altar work, efficient in calling among the people, and a worthy example as a child of God.

*"While fighting in ardor in mid-day of life,*
*The Master in mercy then ended earth's strife;*
*She said, in much wonder, 'I've only begun;'*
*He smiled back in answer, 'Come, faithful, well done.'*
*She looked for white harvest, the sheaves yet unbound;*
*She reached forth to gather, He gave her the Crown."*

At the close of a series of meetings in Bradford, Illinois, she went to her home to recruit for the next battle, but it seemed that her battles were then to end.

Being taken with typhoid fever, she lingered in its heat and suffering a little over a month, then Jesus came and took her to Himself. Once during her sickness, when unconscious to those around her, her mother came in; but she failed to recognize anyone. Her mother said, "May, do you know Jesus?" She replied, "Jesus? O, yes, I know Jesus." The mentioning of His name brought consciousness to her. She well knew that name.

Shortly before she passed away she called all of her loved ones (who were then outside of the ark of safety) and tried to exhort them to prepare to meet their God; but, her tongue being swollen, she could not make them understand. But the Lord enabled her to tell of the glories that filled her soul in that wonderful hour. She threw up her arms -- the unsaved ones standing around her bed saw the light that came from heaven into that little room -- they felt its divine influence as May said, "Oh! do you hear the music?" Her soul then took its flight -- she continued to hear the music on the other side of the River. Thus ended the career of one triumphant in life and death. -- Written for this work, by Sadie A. Cryer, of Rockford, Ill.

## 184 -- TRIUMPHANT DEATH OF MARGARETTA KLOPPSTOCK

Kloppstock, the great German poet, author of the well-known epic poem, "The Messiah," was born in 1724, and died in 1803. His wife, Margaretta, was a devoted Christian. In her last moments, being told that God would help her, she replied, "Into heaven!" The last words she whispered were, "The blood of Jesus Christ cleanseth from all sin! O, sweet words of eternal life!"

## 185 -- "O, LORD, MY STRENGTH AND MY REDEEMER."

Mrs. Win. Barnes' conversion was brought about shortly after the death of her little girl. She lives in Buffalo, N. Y. Before her daughter died she was not a Christian, but since the death of her little girl, four years ago, she has been leading a godly life and traveling in the way to heaven.

The following is recorded as related by Mrs. Barnes: My little daughter May, when but eight years old, was taken ill with scarlet fever, and died four days later. During her short sickness she was such a patient little sufferer, and when asked if she was suffering, she would say there didn't anything hurt her, but she did not want to stay with us any longer -- she wanted to go to heaven, and kept repeating this all through the long night. Not long after this she repeated the Lord's prayer, and then thanked us for all that we had done for her, and told us not to worry about her. Then she looked up and said, "I thank Thee, dear Jesus. Dear Jesus, I thank Thee," and then sang some beautiful songs.

Just before she died she raised her eyes toward heaven and said, "O Lord, my strength and my Redeemer." Then, with a peaceful look on her face, she raised herself, and with a glad expression she said "Oh," and saw something which our eyes could not see, and thus passed away.

She had a Bible and three other books given her for constant attendance at her Sunday-school, where she had been a scholar for four years.

Dear reader, I think this message is for you just as much as it is for me. The Bible says, "A little child shall lead them." -- Written for this work by Kate H. Booth, of Buffalo, .N. Y.

## 186 -- MERRITT CALDWELL'S LAST WORDS -- "JESUS LIVES, I SHALL LIVE ALSO."

This great and good man, principal of Wesleyan Academy, Maine, and vice-president of Dickinson College, Pennsylvania, was a distinguished advocate of total abstinence and a gifted writer. He was born in 1806, died in 1848.

Shortly before his death he said to his wife, "You will not, I am sure, lie down upon your bed and weep when I am gone. You will not mourn for me when God has been so good to me. When you visit my grave, do not come in the shade of the evening, nor in the dark of night; these are no times to visit the grave of a Christian; but come in the morning, in the bright sunshine, and when the birds are singing." His last expressions were, "Glory to Jesus! He is my trust; He is my strength! Jesus lives; I shall live also!"

## 187 -- "GOOD-BY! WE WILL SOON MEET AGAIN; CHRIST LIGHTS THE WAY!"

Our readers have noticed the great contrast between the last words of the saved and the unsaved. We herewith give a striking example:

Edward Adams, the noted actor's last words were, "Good-bye Mary; good-bye forever." What a contrast with one of the martyrs who, while going to the stake, said to his wife, "Good-by, Mary, till morning." The next morning, while she was being put into a sack, to be thrown into a pond, she handed her babe to a kind neighbor and said, "Good-by, children; good-by, friends; I go to my husband. We will soon meet again. Christ lights the way." -- L. B. Balliett, M.D.

## 188 -- "HARK! HEAR THAT MUSIC! THEY DON'T HAVE SUCH MUSIC AS THAT ON EARTH."

Rev. Hiram Case, of Frankford, N. Y., was translated to heaven in the year 1878.

A few weeks before his death he said, "It seemed as if I were stepping into a very cold stream, which sent a shiver through my entire being, but which was gone in the twinkling of an eye, and the place was lit up with a glory that far outshone the noonday sun. What I saw and felt was unutterable. Tongue is too short and words too lame to express what I saw and felt of the presence of the Lord with me."

He had some relatives who were Advents, and he said he wished they could only know how he felt when he thought he was dying. They would never again think that their spirits would sleep in the grave until the resurrection, but would know beyond a doubt that immediately after the spirit had left the body it was with the redeemed host in a conscious existence in the presence of the Great Redeemer of men. He talked freely about dying, saying that, while it was hard to part with his wife and little ones, the Lord knew what was best, and would take him while he was ready. At another time he heard the heavenly music. He said, "Hark! Hear that music! They don't have such music as that on earth."

During these last days he desired that each of his children might have a Bible bought, and following are the texts of scripture he wrote with trembling hand, one for each child:

"My son, if sinners entice thee, consent thou not." "Remember now thy Creator in the days of thy youth, while the evil days come not, nor the years draw nigh, when thou shalt say, I find no pleasure in them." "For God so loved the world that He gave His only begotten Son, that whosoever believeth in Him should not perish, but have everlasting life."

The presence of the Lord was with him during all these trying days, and when the power of speech and sight was gone, by the pressure of the hand and the farewell kiss he gave us the token that "All is well-Written for this work by his wife, Mrs. Gertrude M. Case, of Clyde, N. Y.

## 189 -- JOHN RANDOLPH'S LAST WORDS -- "REMORSE! REMORSE! REMORSE!"

This great American statesman was born at Cawsons, Va., in 1773. He descended from a wealthy family, a lawyer by profession, and in 1799 was elected to Congress. He was the Democratic leader of the House of Representatives, but quarreled with Jefferson. In 1825 he was chosen United States Senator from Virginia, and in 1830 was appointed United States Minister to Russia.

He died at Philadelphia in 1833. As the doctor and servant were sitting by his bedside, the dying statesman turned toward them and exclaimed, "Remorse! remorse! remorse! -- you don't know what it means! But," Randolph added, "I cast myself on the Lord Jesus Christ for mercy."

## 190 -- "PRAISE HIM, YOU ALL PRAISE HIM."

Through the influence of room-mates and associates, while attending boarding school, Ethel had been influenced to believe that making a public confession of the Lord Jesus Christ, and receiving baptism by immersion was all the preparation needful to insure her soul endless joy when life on earth was over.

For years Ethel's Christian mother had endeavored to impress upon her daughter's mind the importance of being born, not of water, but of the Holy Spirit. With resolute tenacity Ethel clung to the doctrine of "Water Salvation," which she had so deeply imbibed from her companions while away at school. Notwithstanding all discouragements, Ethel's mother knew from past experience that God was faithful in his promises of divine truth, so by persistent faith and daily prayer she called upon Him at the Throne of Grace to show Ethel the error of resting upon ordinances for spiritual safety, when the blood of Christ, and a saving faith in its atoning merits alone, could secure to her soul eternal life and a home in heaven.

One day, after much earnest wrestling in prayer, her mother was comforted by receiving the assurance of the Holy Spirit that God would be gracious and eventually turn Ethel from the error of building on a foundation of sand.

Not long after this, although but twenty-two years of life had passed over her head, Ethel came to know that she stood with the billows of death rolling very near her feet. It was then that she began to realize the fact that water baptism would not avail to rescue her soul from the perils of sin and the coming judgment. "Man's extremity is ever God's opportunity," and now the Holy Spirit began to convince her that she had need, not only to repent and call upon the Lord, but to believe in Him as a personal Savior. The conflict of her soul with doubts and fears was short but severe. Faith at length triumphed.

Only five days before her departure from earth, after lying speechless for hours, in the throes of dissolution, her mother, who was near her couch, heard Ethel say, with great effort, "Whosoever -- will -- may come." Just then the saving power of the Holy Ghost fell upon her heart, and as a bright smile over-spread her beautiful face, she exclaimed, "Praise Him, you all praise Him." Those were Ethel's last words on earth. -- Written for this work by Mrs. V. E. Markin, of Litchfield, Ky.

## 191 -- REV. ROBERT HALL'S LAST WORDS -- "COME, LORD JESUS, COME."

Rev. Robert Hall, one of the most eloquent of modern preachers, was born in Arnsby, Leicestershire, England, May 2, 1764; died at Bristol, Feb. 21, 1831.

In 1790 he accepted a call to the Baptist church at Cambridge. Here he remained for fifteen years, increasing in influence and reputation, and was recognized as one of the foremost preachers of his day.

In 1806 he removed to Leicester, where he labored for twenty years, when, at the call of the Broad Street Baptist Church, he returned to Bristol to finish his ministry. He did much to liberalize the opinions of his generation. His fame, great while he lived, has become a cherished tradition among English-speaking Christians, and his works are among the classics of the modern pulpit.

When he came to die he was fully prepared. In his last moments he exclaimed, "It is death, it is death, it is death! O, the sufferings of this body!" His wife inquired whether he was comfortable in mind. "Very comfortable, very comfortable. Come, Lord Jesus, come!" were his last words.

## 192 -- "I AM GETTING IN SIGHT OF THE CITY. MY HOPE IS FULL."

Daniel Wilmot was born in Prospect, Conn.. Aug. 13, 1816, being eighty-two years old when he died; was married Jan. 7, 1839, and lived almost fifty-nine years with our now widowed sister....

Brother Wilmot did not grow old on the inside-always keeping in touch with domestic interests and public events, growing old gracefully. It was blessed to behold such joy and victory as he uniformly had. At one of the Thursday night meetings held in his home, which he invariably attended, and only four weeks ago, his cup of rejoicing overflowed. With beaming face and transfigured countenance he poured forth a glowing testimony, saying, among other things, "I am 'most home. Glory to God! I am getting in sight of the city My hope is full, oh, glorious hope of immortality! The Lord saves me -- saves me fully. No doubt, no fear disturbs my soul. Praise the Lord! oh, praise the Lord!" And after he resumed his seat he continued amid the tears of some and the shouts of others, to praise God. Had it been a conference love feast or camp-meeting scene the rejoicing in God could not have been greater. The benediction of that hour, the sight of that face and sound of that voice that night I shall carry with me as one of the richest experiences of my life. In his frequent paroxysms of pain, he was patient and unmurmuring. As his strength declined and his pain increased, he would pray and ask his companion to pray the Lord to take him home, the day before his departure....

Sister Thompson read from The Christian Witness, a paper he loved for its soul food Saying, "I am tired," and asking, "Is my bed ready?" he was helped to bed. But he was not to sleep in that bed again. Jesus was about to rest the tired saint within the tender pressure of his everlasting arms. Pain laid hold on him again, and for the last time, thank God! While remedies were being prepared to relieve him he grew faint from nausea, the heart began to slow its beating, he sank into unconsciousness and soon was "absent from the body and present with the Lord." Truly the saints die well. -- Geo. W. Anderson, in Christian Witness, of October 27, 1898.

## 193 -- "EMPTIED OF SELF; FILLED WITH CHRIST; CLOSE TO GOD; NO FEAR."

My dear brother, Charles G. Jones, was a very unselfish man. In whatever enterprise he embarked, it was not so much to benefit himself as to help others.

He early felt the power of religion, and I remember his saying to me, when I was speaking to him of its claims, "Yes, I believe man should be pure -- pure as water." He felt a deep sense of his responsibility to God, and would say, "I must give an account; I must give au account." His heart went out toward the needy, and a favorite maxim of his was, "Never turn away thy face from the poor man, and the Lord will not turn His face from thee."

For two years and upwards, before his death, he was a great sufferer. In his last letter to me he spoke of his faith in God for all things, and said, "Having therefore obtained help from God, we continue unto this day."

About four months later, on the sixth of January, 1898, at his residence, No. 8 Windsor avenue, Montreal, Canada, he passed from earth to heaven. His last words were, "Emptied of self; filled with Christ; close to God; no fear." -- Written for this work by W. D. Jones, of Chicago, Ill.

## 194 -- SIR JOHN MASON -- "WERE I TO LIVE AGAIN, I WOULD CHANGE THE WHOLE LIFE I HAVE LIVED."

A strong testimony to the importance of religion is given by Sir John Mason, who, though but sixty-three at his death, had flourished in the reigns of four sovereigns (Henry VIII., Edward VI., Mary, and Elizabeth), had been privy-counselor to them all, and an attentive observer of the various revolutions and vicissitudes of those times. Toward his latter end, being on his deathbed, he spoke thus to those about him: "I have lived to see five sovereigns, and have been privy-counselor to four of them. I have seen the most remarkable things in foreign parts, and have been present at most state transactions for the last thirty years; and I have learned from the experience of so many years that seriousness is the greatest wisdom, temperance the best physic, and a good conscience the best estate. And were I to live again, I would change the court for a cloister, my privy-counselor's bustle for hermit's retirement, and the whole life I have lived in the palace for an hour's enjoyment of God in the chapel. All things now forsake me, except my God, my duty and my prayers." ...

From the regret expressed by Sir John Mason, it appears that his error consisted, not in having served his king and country, in the eminent stations in which he had been placed; but in having suffered his mind to be so much occupied with business as to make him neglect, in some degree, the proper seasons of religious retirement, and the prime duties which he owed to his Creator. -- Power of Religion.

## 195 -- MRS. ETTA KATRINA YANKLE -- "PRAISE THE LORD!"

This saint of God went to heaven Dec. 9, 1887, in the fifty-third year of her age. We were well acquainted with Sister Yankle. The Lord greatly used her in a great revival we held near her home, New Haven, Michigan, in the winter of 1885. Several of her children, and more than one hundred of her neighbors, were soundly converted to God in that revival, and as many more were reclaimed from a backslidden state and filled with the Spirit of God during the meetings. Sister Yankle for many years lived a very devoted Christian life. She was not in words only, but in deed, a "mother in Israel." Many are the souls she has led to Christ, and larger still is the number whom she has helped and encouraged and cared for as a mother a child. Among all our acquaintance we know but few to whom so high praise could justly be given. As wife, and mother, and friend she filled nobly, grandly, the place God had given her. Soon after her death, her daughter, the wife of Rev. John Kirn, wrote us as follows: "I know that God doeth all things well. I am glad that my heart says, the Lord's will be done. Mother said after brother Freddie's death; 'The Lord never makes any mistakes.' I feel the same now. I cannot understand why the Lord took mother home, when it seems that we needed her so much; but He knows best. Her work is done. It would have done you good to have seen her in her sickness, she was so patient-never murmured nor complained, but was praising God all the time. When those who came in spoke of her being so sick, and suffering so much, she always replied that she was resting in Jesus' arms, and that she believed the Lord would heal her, but if not, she was ready to go; and would praise the Lord so that the unsaved could hardly bear it. She was not able to talk much. Her last words were, 'Praise the Lord!' She tried to say more, but could not. The funeral sermon was preached to a large congregation, in the power of the Spirit."

May God raise up more such devoted women, is our prayer. -- Editor.

## 196 -- VICTORIOUS DEATH OF JANE, THE PROTESTANT QUEEN OF NAVARRE

This excellent queen was the daughter of Henry II., King of Navarre, and of Margaret of Orleans, sister of Francis I., King of France. She was born in the year 1528.

From her childhood she was carefully educated in the Protestant religion, to which she steadfastly adhered all her days. Bishop Burnet says of her: "That she both received the Reformation, and brought her subjects to it; that she not only reformed her court, but the whole principality, to such a degree that the Golden Age seemed to have returned under her; or rather, Christianity appeared again with its primitive purity and luster."

This illustrious queen, being invited to attend the nuptials of her son and the King of France's sister, fell a victim to the cruel machinations of the French court against the Protestant religion. The religious fortitude and genuine piety with which she was endued did not, however, desert her in this great conflict, and at the approach of death.

To some what were about her, near the conclusion of her time, she said, "I receive all this as from the hand of God, my most merciful Father; nor have I, during my extremity, feared to die, much less murmured against God for inflicting this chastisement upon me; knowing that whatsoever He does with me, He so orders it that, in the end, it shall turn to my everlasting good."

When she saw her ladies and women weeping about her bed, she blamed them, saying, "Weep not for me, I pray you. God, by this sickness, calls me hence to enjoy a better life; and now I shall enter into the desired haven, toward which this frail vessel of mine has been a long time steering."

She expressed some concern for her children, as they would be deprived of her in their tender years, but added, "I doubt not that God Himself will be their father and protector, as He has ever been mine in my greatest afflictions. I therefore commit them wholly to His government and fatherly care. I believe that Christ is my only Mediator and Savior; and I look for salvation from no other. O my God! in Thy good time, deliver me from the troubles of this present life, that I may attain to the felicity which Thou hast promised to bestow upon me." -- Power of Religion.

## 197 -- "I'M GOING UP IN THE CHARIOT SO EARLY IN THE MORNING."

Mrs. Harriet McManamey went home on the 18th of February, 1887. Though suffering to the last, she passed away quietly to her home in the paradise of God. She had been converted twelve years before, and was a member of the Wesleyan Methodist Church and a devout Christian and an earnest worker both in the church and Sabbath school. About three years previous to her death she entered into the experience of perfect love through the instruction and labors of Bro. S, B. Shaw. As she listened to his radical teaching on holiness, conviction seized her heart anew. She believed it and entered in -- came through into the promised land shouting and praising God. Her class-meeting testimony was never complete without some allusion to her experience of heart purity. How and when she obtained it, she wanted all to know. She was a lover of singing, and the Spiritual Hymns was a favorite with her. Her breathing was very short, but on one occasion when all was silent she broke out and sang,
*"I'm going up in the chariot
So early in the morning."*

All through she clapped her hands as if in a campmeeting. The Holiness Record was a welcome visitor to her household. She read the January number all through and asked about the February number. Her family and friends do not weep as those who have no hope, but joyously await the call of the Master when the reunion will take place never to be broken. -- Mrs. L. G. Whitney, Hemlock, Mich.

## 198 -- SIR PHILIP SIDNEY -- "I WOULD NOT CHANGE MY JOY FOR THE EMPIRE OF THE WORLD."

Sir Philip Sidney was born in Kent, in the year 1554. He possessed shining talents, was well educated, and at the early age of twenty-one was sent by Queen Elizabeth, as her ambassador, to the Emperor of Germany. He is described by the writers of that age as the finest model of an accomplished gentleman that could be formed, even in imagination. An amiable disposition, elegant erudition, and polite conversation, rendered him the ornament and delight of the English court. Lord Brooks so highly valued his friendship, that he directed to be inserted as part of his epitaph, "Here lies Sir Philip Sidney's friend." His fame was so widely spread, that if he had chosen it, he might have obtained the crown of Poland.

But the glory of this Marcellus of the English nation was of short duration. He was wounded at the battle of Zutphen, and carried to Arnheim, where, after languishing about three weeks, he died, in the thirty-second year of his age... After he had received the fatal wound, and was brought into a tent, he piously raised his eyes towards heaven, and acknowledged the hand of God in this event. He confessed himself to be a sinner, and returned thanks to God that "He had not struck him with death at once, but gave him space to seek repentance and reconciliation."

Compared with his present views of religion, his former virtues seemed to be nothing. When it was observed to him that good men, in the time of great affliction, found comfort and support in the recollection of those parts of their lives in which they had glorified God, he humbly replied, "It is not so with me. I have no comfort that way. All things in my former life have been vain."

On being asked whether he did not desire life merely to have it in his power to glorify God, he answered, "I have vowed my life unto God, and if tie cut me off, and suffer me to live no longer, I shall glorify Him, and give up myself to his service."

The nearer death approached, the more his consolation and hopes increased. A short time before his dissolution, he lifted up his eyes and hands, and uttered these words, "I would not change my joy for the empire of the world." His advice and observations, on taking the last leave of his deeply afflicted brother, are worthy of remembrance. They appear to have been expressed with great seriousness and composure. "Love my memory; cherish my friends. Their fidelity to me may assure you that they are honest. But, above all, govern your will and affections, by the will and word of your Creator. In me behold the end of the world and all its vanities." -- Power of .Religion.

## 199 -- "I SEE ANGELS CLAPPING THEIR HANDS AROUND THE GREAT WHITE THRONE."

Eva Greening, who was nine years old, passed from the terrestrial to the celestial state at half past four o'clock January 4, 1887. She realized that she must die, about two o'clock on the day previous, without anyone telling her. She commenced clapping her hands and shouting praises to God. She sang several hymns; not remembering words to one or two, she made words so appropriate that I knew her mind was wonderfully illuminated by the Holy Ghost. She said she was so happy, and so glad papa and mamma had trained her to be a Christian. Mr. and Mrs. Steele and daughters (her grandparents and aunts) came in. She called them one at a time to her bedside and asked and plead with them to be true Christians and meet her in heaven. She asked Mr. Steele to send for her uncle, Willie Steele, who lives in Los Angeles. Willie came on the first train. She called him to her bedside and asked him to quit sinning and come to Jesus and be a good man and meet her in heaven. We sent for our little girl, who was at Mr. Butler's, and when she came Eva called her and told her she was almost home, to be a good girl, live a Christian and meet her in heaven. A lady whom Eva loved came in. She had on jewelry. Eva admonished her to put off her jewelry and put on white robes (meaning robes of righteousness) and prepare to meet her around the great white throne. We had taught Eva that wearing jewelry was positively forbidden in God's word, and that such personal adornment was an evidence of pride and vanity, and that money so expended ought to be used to spread the gospel and to relieve the poor. We sang several hymns for her, such as I knew she loved. We could not find one we wanted to sing, and although she was getting so weak she could hardly speak, she told us the words so that we could find it. While she was lying perfectly still and calm, she said, "I see stars." Mr. Steele asked her what they looked like. She said, "Bright lights, the stars of God. I see an angel." Mr. Steele asked how he looked. She said, "He has on white robes." She again said, "I see angels clapping their hands around the great white throne." A few minutes before she died, when she could not speak, I asked if she saw me. She shook her head. I asked if she saw Jesus. She nodded that she did. There were members of several different denominations, which are not in sympathy with holiness people, in the room, who expressed themselves as not doubting the soundness of Eva's mind and the truth of her statements. Eva had been a true Christian most of the time for more than two years. As she swept through the gates she left a stream of living light that will shine down through future ages with brilliancy and effect, to an extent that will never be known until the final harvest. For more than a year before, t our family devotions, morning and evening, after I lead in prayer, Eva would pray, and continued to pray aloud at our worship until the day before her death. In speaking of heaven when dying, she said, "Nothing but holiness can carry us through." I never before understood the comforting power of the Holy Ghost while passing through the shadow of death. Indeed, while Eva was dying, it was manifested to us that death was only a shadow that she was passing through. Although our home is left so desolate, and when I go home at noon and night I no longer receive the happy greeting I always received, yet the Holy Ghost comforts us. Myself and wife willingly submit to the wisdom of God, knowing that he knows best and that everything works together for good to them that love Him. -- By her father, E. G. Greening, Downey, Los Angeles, Cal.

## 200 – LAST WORDS OF EMPEROR CHARLES V

Charles V., Emperor of Germany, King of Spain, and Lord of the Netherlands, was born at Ghent in the year 1500.

He is said to have fought sixty battles, in most of which he was victorious; to have obtained six triumphs, conquered four kingdoms, and to have added eight principalities to his dominions -- an almost unparalleled instance of worldly prosperity, and the greatness of human glory.

But all these fruits of his ambition, and all the honors that attended him, could not yield true and solid satisfaction. Reflecting on the evils and miseries which he occasioned, and convinced of the emptiness of earthly magnificence, he became disgusted with all the splendor that surrounded him, and thought it his duty to withdraw from it, and spend the rest of his days in religious retirement. Accordingly, he voluntarily resigned all his dominions to his brother and son, and after taking an affectionate and last farewell of the latter, and of a numerous retinue of princes and nobility that respectfully attended him, he repaired to his chosen retreat. It was situated in Spain, in a vale of no great extent, watered by a small brook, and surrounded with rising grounds covered with lofty trees.

A deep sense of his frail condition and great imperfections, appears to have impressed his mind in this extraordinary resolution and through the remainder of his life. As soon as he landed in Spain, he fell prostrate on the ground, and considering himself now as dead to the world, he kissed the earth, and said, "Naked came I out of my mother's womb, and naked I now return to thee, thou common mother of mankind."

In this humble retreat he spent his time in religious exercises and innocent employments; and buried here, in solitude and silence, his grandeur, his ambition, together with all those vast projects which, for nearly half a century, had alarmed and agitated Europe, and filled every kingdom in it, by turns, with the terror of his arms, and the dread of being subjected to his power. Far from taking any part in the political transactions of the world, he restrained his curiosity even from any inquiry concerning them; and seemed to view the busy scene he had abandoned, with an elevation and indifference of mind which arose from a thorough experience of its vanity, as well as from the pleasing reflection of having disengaged himself from its cares and temptations.

Here he enjoyed more solid happiness than all his grandeur had ever yielded him, as a full proof of which he has left this short but comprehensive testimony: "I have tasted more satisfaction in my solitude in one day than in all the triumphs of my former reign. The sincere study, profession and practice of the Christian religion have in them such joys and sweetness as are seldom found in courts and grandeur." -- Power of Religion.

## 201 -- BISHOP HANBY -- "I AM IN THE MIDST OF GLORY!"

Bishop Hanby was a devoted preacher of the United Brethren Church. -- Editor.

Awhile before he died the bishop was observed, by his daughter who sat near his couch, to be weeping. "What is it father?" was the tender inquiry. "Oh, I am so happy," was the reply. "My long, toilsome journey is nearly ended; my life work is joyfully over; half of my children are already safe in heaven, and I am just as sure the rest will be. Half are safe at home, and all the rest are on the way. Mother is there (referring to his wife), and in a little while I shall be there, too. These lines are in my mind constantly:

'The Lord my Shepherd is,
I shall be well supplied;
Since He is mine, and I am His,
What can I want beside?'"

After he had descended into the river, he shouted back, "I'm in the midst of glory!" -- From Life to Life.

## 202 -- AN AWFUL JUDGMENT ON A YOUNG MAN

The following incident from the pen of Sister M. A. Sparling, Claremont, N. H., is an illustration of the words of Holy Writ, that "the wicked is ruined in the work of his own hands." She writes:
While reading Echo From the Border Land, something said, "You have an echo from the 'lower region.' " If it were Father's will, I'd love to stand up in your congregation and deliver the message I can now only write.

A few years ago I was at a camp-meeting in Rockingham, Vt., and a gang of rowdies got together to set a time to break up the whole meeting. They lived eight miles away. So on Thursday evening they came to the ground to accomplish their fiendish work and "have their fun," as they told some of their friends. Their plan was to lay trails of powder into every tent, and under the beds, and when the town clock struck twelve all were to touch fire to the powder and run to a distance and see the frightened women and children run and scream. At ten a distant thunder was heard, and while they were waiting for the horn" to start the fire God sent one of the most terrific thunder and hail storms I ever witnessed. It had been a hot day and these young men had no overcoats to put on, and as their last resort, after seeing their powder all wet and their plans defeated, they were compelled to ride back to their homes, eight miles, all drenched with rain and chilled through. The ringleader had to be carried into the house, benumbed. His mother tried for hours to get him warm. Then came a burning fever. And then he called his dear mother and told her what he had done, saying, "Mother, I've got to die! Do pray! Do pray! What shall I do? O, how can I die?" She said, "I never prayed." "Then call father," cried the dying man. He could not pray. Then he cried, "What shall I do? O, how can I die?" Then he would clutch his hands and ring them in agony, crying, "I can't die so! I can't die so! Mother, mother, do pray! do pray!"

The father went for a Baptist deacon, but before he arrived the young man was past help, and with distorted eyes, hands uplifted over his head, and writhing in agony, he died raving: and among his last words were: "I'm going to hell; I'm lost, lost, lost! I can't die so! I can't, I can't! Mother, 'tis awful to go to hell this way!" -- The Revivalist.

### 203 -- "HOW BEAUTIFUL EVERYTHING APPEARS."

Bro. Samuel G. Bingaman, of Williams, Oregon, sends us this touching experience. He says:

When I was a soldier in Memphis, Missouri, a comrade said to me, "I wish you would go over to that house yonder and stay with them to-night, for they are in a terrible condition there."

About dark I went over, and found things in a terrible state. The house was dilapidated -- almost ready to fall down, and the cellar was full of muddy water. I ascended an old pair of stairs on the outside of the house, and entered a small room -- the house of affliction, the drunkard's home. It contained no furniture, not even chairs or bedsteads, nothing but an old trunk, on which an elderly lady sat, and held in her arms a little child, almost dead, while on the floor lay another that had died but a few minutes before, and a third one was very low. The lady then pointed to an old pile of dirty bed quilts on the floor in one corner of the room, saying, "There lies the mother, and we don't think that she will live until morning; and worse than all this (we thought, What can be worse?), we are looking for the father to come home to-night, drunk."

About midnight he came; but that awful scene of the dead and dying did not affect the poor drunkard's heart. He drew out his bottle of whiskey and begged me to drink with him!

But there was one of that family who was deeply penitent, and earnestly desired to "flee from the wrath to come" -- it was the broken-hearted mother. At her request I often visited her, and talked to her of the Savior, and sang to her of heaven.

One day while calling to see her, I found her cold, and sinking fast. Death was folding her in his cold embrace. But just as those dark billows of death were rolling over her, they were suddenly turned to bright dashing waves of glory. She looked up and said, "How beautiful everything appears." A lady who was present at her dying bedside said to her, "I do not see anything beautiful." "No," replied the dying woman, "there is nothing in this house but dirt and rags, but I see things beautiful and lovely." Her face then lit up with a happy look, and with a smile upon her countenance, her spirit took its flight to bright mansions of bliss. As I stood and looked upon her lifeless form, with the peaceful expression on her face: I thought, surely death to the child of God is but the gate of heaven.

## 204 -- LAST WORDS OF JESSE APPLETON, D. D. -- "GLORY TO GOD IN THE HIGHEST!"

This saint of God was a prominent educator, and for some time president of Bowdoin College. Dr. Appleton was also a noted Congregationalist preacher and theologian. He was born in 1772 and died in 1819. His last words were: "Glory to God in the highest; the whole earth shall be filled with his glory."

## 205 -- REV. JESSE LEE -- "GLORY! GLORY! GLORY! HALLELUJAH! JESUS REIGNS!"

This apostle of New England Methodism was born in Virginia in 1758, and was powerfully converted and joined the church in 1773. He was a Holy Ghost preacher, and a great revivalist. Much of his time was spent in traveling and preaching from the year 1787 to 1800.

He was three times chaplain of the United States House of Representatives, and also wrote a history of American Methodism.

He died in 1816, in the fifty-eighth year of his age. As the time for his departure drew near, he suddenly, in a rapture, exclaimed, "Glory! Glory! Glory! Hallelujah! Jesus reigns!"

## 206 -- I HAVE BEEN IN SUCH A BEAUTIFUL PLACE, AND HAVE SEEN THE REDEEMED ONES."

Mrs. J. Ransom, of Lawrence, Michigan, with whom we are well acquainted, sends us this touching experience:

Hannah was the wife of a Methodist minister. She was much beloved by all who knew her. Her whole soul was engaged in the work of the Lord, but consumption laid its withering hand upon her, and she went home to die. She was very triumphant as she drew near to the river. Her spirit seemed to have taken its flight, and they were about to close her eyes, when she aroused with a heavenly light on her face and said, "I have been in such a beautiful place, and saw the redeemed ones." Her mother said, "Did you know them?" She replied, "Some I knew, and some [ did not." Her husband asked, "Did you see our baby?" (a little one who had died a short time before,) She said, "Yes, I saw my baby." And after talking for some time in the same rapturous strain, the glad spirit soared away to join the happy throng.

## 207 -- GIDEON OUSLEY -- THE SPIRIT OF GOD SUSTAINS ME."

The life of this remarkable Irish preacher, who spent most of his long life traveling through Ireland on horseback, and preaching to the humble poor from his saddle, was written by the Rev. William Arthur, author of The Tongue of Fire. The Lord saved Ousley from a life of sin and dissipation, and made him a power for good, and many were turned from the evil of their ways through his influence.

The village of Dunmore, in the County of Galway, in the province of Connaught, Ireland, was Gideon Ousley's birthplace. He was born on the 24th of February, 1762. We quote the following from Life Stories of Remarkable Preachers, by Rev. J. Vaughan:

In the latter part of his life Gideon Ousley did more good by his publications than by his preaching. No man was better qualified to grapple with the errors of popery than he, and this he did right manfully. His principal work, which was written in clear and popular style, was his Old Christianity, which did a vast amount of good. Some of his tracts, too, were scattered broad. cast over the country. This man of God, who, on account of his preaching so frequently from the saddle, was called by many a "Cavalry preacher," had faithfully served his God as a Mission rider and preacher on Irish soil for forty years, when on coming to Dublin at the close of his seventy-seventh, year, he became too weak to leave his lodgings. His faithful Harriet was soon at his bedside. It soon became evident that his work was done. Being asked what he thought of the gospel which he had preached for so many years, he replied, "Oh, it is light, and life, and peace." The last words he uttered were, "I have no fear of death -- the Spirit of God sustains me -- God's Spirit is my support." About mid-day on the 13th of May, 1839, he entered into that rest that remaineth for the people of God. Fourteen years afterwards his gentle and loving wife followed him to the land of life and glory.

## 208 -- DYING WITHOUT GOD

A youth at one of the large iron works in Sheffield was some time ago accidentally thrown on to a red hot armor plate. When he was rolled off by his fellow-workmen, it was doubtful if he could live, as nearly all one side of him was burned to the bone. His workmates cried, " Send for the doctor," but the poor suffering youth cried, " Never mind sending for the doctor; is there anyone here can tell me how to get saved? My soul has been neglected, and I'm dying without God. Who can help me?"

Although there were three hundred men around him, there was no one who could tell him the way of salvation. After twenty minutes of untold agony he died as he had lived.

The man who saw this accident, and heard the cries of the dying youth, was a wretched backslider, and when I asked him how he felt about the matter, he said, "I have heard his cries ever since, and wished I could have stooped down and pointed him to Jesus, but my life closed my lips."

Does your life tell sinners that you are saved, or does it close your lips, when those around hear your talk and witness your actions? -- William Baugh.

## 209 -- THE LORD GAVE HER STRENGTH TO PRAISE HIM TO THE LAST

While we were holding revival meetings at Miller's Landing, Missouri, over twenty years ago, a very sick woman living in the village desired to see us. We called at her home, and found her on her death-bed. She had heard of the revival meetings, and how God had opened the windows of heaven and poured out a great blessing on the community. A number had already been gloriously saved. The Lord used the influence of this revival' to awaken in her heart a great desire for a deeper and richer experience. We were greatly blessed in praying and singing with her, and we remember well how she shouted and praised the Lord and clapped her hands for joy while we sang,

"My heavenly home is bright and fair:
No pain, nor death can enter there:
Its glitt'rng towers the sun outshine:
That heav'nly mansion shall be mine."

She was so greatly blessed of God that she praised the Lord night and day. She died in a few days praising God with almost every breath. We preached her funeral sermon to a large congregation of sympathizing friends. We were impressed with the fact that she was unable to talk above a whisper on other subjects, yet while she was under the influence of the Holy Spirit she could shout and praise the Lord with a loud and strong voice. The Lord gave her strength to praise Him to the last, and she had a triumphant entrance into the courts of glory.

We are thankful for the privilege of witnessing such a triumphant death, and pray that our readers may so live that God can bless them in prosperity, in affliction, and under all circumstances and give them an abundant entrance into that city not made with hands, eternal in the heavens. -- Editor.

## 210 -- "HE IS COME! MY BELOVED IS MINE AND I AM HIS FOREVER!"

"The life of Thomas Walsh, says Dr. Southey, "might almost convince a Catholic that saints were to be found in other communions as well as in the Church of Rome." Walsh became a great biblical scholar; he was an Irishman. He mastered the native Irish that he might preach in it, but Latin, Greek and Hebrew became familiar to him, and of the Hebrew, especially, it is said that he studied so deeply that his mind was an entire concordance of the whole Bible. His soul was as a flame of fire, but it burnt out the body quickly. John Wesley says of him, "I do not remember ever to have known a man who, in so few years as he remained on earth, was the instrument of converting so many sinners." He became mighty in his influence over the Roman Catholics. The priests said that "Walsh had died some years ago, and that he who went about preaching on mountains and highways, in meadows, private houses, prisons and ships, was a devil who had assumed his shape." This was the only way in which they could account for the extraordinary influence he possessed. His labors were greatly divided between Ireland and London; but everywhere he bore down all before him by a kind of absorbed ecstasy of ardent faith But he died at the age of twenty-seven. While lying on his death-bed he was oppressed with a sense of despair, even of his salvation. The sufferings of his mind on this account were intense. At last he broke out in an exclamation, "He is come! He is come! My Beloved is mine, and I am His forever!" and so he fell back and died.

Thomas Walsh is a great name still in the records of the lay preachers of early Methodism. -- The Great Revival.

## 211 -- A MOTHER'S LAST WORDS -- "I AM GOING TO LEAVE YOU; I AM GOING TO HEAVEN NOW; GOOD-BYE."

Some of the experiences of this book are very touching, but the experience of my own precious, sainted mother, Joanna M. Shaw, is so closely related to my own that my heart is greatly moved whenever I think of her life and death. She was born in Ohio, Dec. 28, 1835; died in Lake Co., Indiana, near Crown Point, March 11, 1867.

Her father's family, including eight children, moved to Lake Co., Indiana, in the spring of 1845.

"During the winter of 1847 Rev. H. B. Ball, of the Methodist Church, held a revival meeting in the community in the new log church, when many were converted, and one night during this revival meeting," writes her brother, Rev. R. H. Sanders, of Laport, Indiana, "after listening to a sermon preached from the text, ' One sinner destroyeth much good' (Eccl. 9:8), and while they were singing,

'There is a spot to me more dear
Than native vale or mountain,
A spot for which affection's tear
Springs grateful from its fountain.
'Tis not where kindred souls abound.
Though that is almost heaven;
But where I first my Savior found,
And felt my sins forgiven!'

I knelt at the old-fashioned mourner's bench. Your mother knelt by my side, and together we sought and found the Savior. After that we often sang,

My brethren, I have found
A land that doth abound
With food as sweet as manna,' etc.

I feel she is still singing it above, and I below. While I write, her spirit seems very near me; and I can almost hear her as then, singing,

My soul doth long to go
Where it shall fully know
The beauties of my Savior,' etc.

Your mother's was a very clear conversion, as well as my own. I do not think she ever doubted it. Her life was a very exemplary one; she seemed to possess her soul in patience, having abiding faith in God, from whom she also received great consolation. Knowing her life as I did, I do not wonder that, though death came suddenly and apparently without warning, it found her ready. As nearly as I can remember, the circumstances as related by your father to me are about these:

"She had been suffering for a few days with a cold, but nothing serious was anticipated. She arose in the morning, but soon complained of dizziness and either fell, or was about to fall, when your father helped her to the bed, where for a few moments she remained unconscious, or apparently so. Then, reviving, she opened her eyes and said to him, "I am going to heaven. Bring up the children in the fear of the Lord, and meet me there. And now, good-by," when she again became unconscious, and her spirit fled to be with Jesus; and yet, as I verily believe, to linger near and woo us heavenward."

Uncle is a member of the Northwest Indiana Conference of the M. E. Church, and has preached the gospel for nearly forty years. A great many have been saved through his influence. He was in his fourteenth year, and mother in her twelfth, when they were made new creatures in Christ.

She was married when quite young, and I was the first-born of her five children. My earliest recollection of my mother was when she knelt by my little trundle bed at night, and taught me to say,

*"Now I lay me down to sleep,
I pray Thee, Lord, my soul to keep;
If I should die before I wake,
I pray Thee, Lord, my soul to take."*

The first seed of divine truth was planted in my heart at that time. How well do I remember the heart stings and the dark cloud that came over our humble little country home the morning that mother left us. We all wept as though our hearts would break. How the cross words and unkind actions that I had given her haunted me night and day until her prayers were answered. And how I cried to mother's God for mercy; and my sins against mother and God were forever swept away by the blood of Christ.

Words can never describe my thankfulness for being able to say that I never saw my mother angry or out of patience. I often saw her in tears, weeping over my disobedience, and other sins of the family. I have often knelt by her grave and wept for joy while thanking God for her holy life and example. Often in revival meetings I have been melted to tears while relating her dying words and how her godly influence led to my salvation. The value and influence of her Christian life will never be known until we meet in heaven. -- Editor.

## 212 -- "I CAN SEE THROUGH -- I AM GOING NOW."

Who would not exclaim "Let me die the death of the righteous, and let my last end be like his," when they read such an account as this which we condense from a report by Rev. C. B. Jernigan, secretary of Texas Holiness Association, in the "Texas Holiness Advocate." We are well acquainted with Bro. Jernigan, who preached the funeral sermon of the one of whom he writes. -- Editor.

Brother Frank M. Major of Van Alstyne, Texas, was converted in 1888, in his sixteenth year, and was blessedly sanctified four years before his death at Elmont, Texas.

He was stricken with typhoid fever, November 6, 1900, of which he died fourteen days later, in the full triumph of the Christian faith. On being spoken to in the morning of the day before his death, he said: "I don't know just what has passed since I have been sick; it all seems to me like a fairy story." In a little while he was in an ecstasy of joy. His brother John coming in said: " Frank, we ought to thank God for his goodness to us." With a beam of glory upon his face he replied: "The best of all is to be one of His angels." Later he said to his brother, Judge R. Major: "Judge, it's wonderful to be free, isn't it? It's glorious to think of going to heaven." A little later when some flowers were brought in, he said: "They are so beautiful; a few more would be just like heaven."

On the following morning, long after the attending physicians had thought him in the throes of death, he said: "We are going to have a testimony meeting before I go. Light the lamp and get the books." On being asked if it was dark, he said yes. His wife asked him what song he wanted sung. He replied, "Any one, the Revival is full of them." Thinking his request a mental wandering, it was not complied with at once. A few moments later he said "Johnnie, sing ' There'll be no dark valley when Jesus comes." For days he had been able to talk only in short, broken sentences, but now to the surprise of all he joined in and sang bass with a full, strong voice, while a beam of heavenly glory rested on his face. Then he said, "There are plenty more." When they sang "'Tis so Sweet to Trust in Jesus," he sang the last stanza alone -- " I'm so glad I learned to trust him." Then he sang alone with wonderful appropriateness:

*"I will sing you a song of that beautiful land,*
*The far away home of the soul;*
*Where no storms ever beat on that glittering strand,*
*While the years of eternity roll."*

At the close he said: "Bless the Lord, I had rather have salvation than to own all the world; the world passeth away, but salvation is forever. I am so glad I'm sanctified; for four years I have been walking just where God wanted me to walk. My path has been strewn with flowers. I have had trials and difficulties, but God's grace was sufficient for me. It's all joy now. I like a faith good for a cloudy day, as well as a sunshiny day." Some one said "Frank, the Lord is blessing you now." He replied "He has always blessed me when I trusted Him." Then he said "If there are any here unsaved, let them come around the bed, for if we come unto the Lord He will in no wise cast us out, for whosoever will call upon the name of the Lord shall be saved." Then he sang:

*"I dreamed that the great judgment morning,*
*Had dawned and the trumpet had blown;*
*I dreamed that the nations had gathered*
*To Judgment before the white throne.*
*From the throne came a bright shining angel*
*And stood on the land and the sea,*
*And swore with his hand raised to heaven,*
*That time was no longer to be."*

One of the attending physicians seeing the power on him, said: " Frank, your work is not done; the Lord can use you yet. Don't you believe He is able to raise you up? He answered "Yes, if he is willing." "But," said the physician, "don't you think he is willing? The Bible says 'whatsoever you ask in my name believing ye shall receive." Frank replied "I look at it in this way: Sometimes God can get more glory out of a man's death than his life. Sometimes one prays for healing and God gives him the assurance before he gets the healing; another man just as good as him, may pray for the same but gets no assurance and can't claim the promise. If all could pray the prayer of faith no good man would ever die." A little later Judge Major said to him: " Frank, you will soon be with little John and Ethel and Pa. Tell them I'm coming." Smiling he nodded assent. A few moments later when his niece came in he took her by the hand and sung in a low, sweet voice:

*"Oh the soul thrilling rapture when I view his blessed face,*
*And the luster of his kindly beaming eye;*
*How my full heart will praise Him for His mercy, love and grace,*
*That prepares for me a mansion in the sky.*
*Oh the dear ones in glory, how they beckon me to come,*
*And the parting at the river I recall;*
*To the sweet vales of Eden they will sing my welcome home,*
*But I long to see my Savior first of all."*

A moment later he said, "I can see through. I am going now." Then, after a severe paroxysm, with the chill of death upon him, he said, "I am so tired. I have my stick and gown; I am going;" and he fell asleep in Jesus.

"O death where is thy sting? O grave where is thy victory?

## *213 -- "I'M COMING, MAMA."*

These were among the last words of a young girl seventeen years of age whose mother died when she was a babe. Her name was Susie Craig. Her home was in Muddlety, Nicholas County, West Virginia, and the facts were given us by her older sister, Mrs. Aggie Thomas of Erbacon, in the same state. For three years she had been an earnest, devoted Christian. After three weeks illness of typhoid fever, it was evident she was very near death. Her father was weeping in a room adjoining the one in which she was lying. She heard him and said, "Tell him not to cry -- tell them all not to shed a tear for me." Then after speaking of the band of angels all around her she added: "Yes, there's ma -- I'm coming ma," and then "O, Maggie," and thus greeting the friends from the other shore, she went to be with them and with her Saviour.

Her words, "O Maggie" were the more remarkable from the fact that Maggie was a cousin -- also an earnest Christian -- who had died only two days before, and of whose death the dying girl had not been informed.

## 214 -- "I LIKE YOU TOO."

Mrs. Fannie D. Bailey, of Kirksville, Mo., furnished us the following account of the illness and death of her little son, Willie Emmett, when six years and six months old.

His sickness was characterized by much patience and sweetness of spirit which could not fail to impress every beholder with an influence for God and heaven. On Sunday morning preceding his death, which occurred that night about midnight, we thought he was going -- as his whole appearance gave evidence that death was doing his final work. He requested us to send for one of the neighbor women and also for a minister and his wife with whom he was well acquainted. We complied with his request. Then he wished us to place many chairs in the room and send for his schoolmates and a "lot of people." We understood that he wished us to have a gospel service which we did, and while the singing and prayers were in progress he remained perfectly quiet as if comforted and calmed and satisfied.

When I asked him to whom I should give his pretty blocks, he said to give them to Jewell (his little cousin) and he then said, "You can give the rest of my things to whoever you want to." I said, " If the Lord takes you to heaven, darling, do you want Brother Thorson to preach your funeral?" He nodded yes, but after a little pause he said in tones that still ring in my soul, "I want you to."

About midnight while we were watching the little sufferer as he sat in his arm chair (he could not lie down as his disease was dropsy) he said, "I have to go." I said, "Where are you going, darling?" He answered, "Home." He would look all around the room with an upward gaze and then exclaimed, "See! see! they are coming." These we doubt not were the angelic messengers that were waiting to convey him to glory. He said, "Where's mama? " I sat in front of him and he said, "I like mama." He always used "like" for "love." He then pointed his forefinger toward Mr. Bailey, his step-father, and said, "I like you too." He then pointed towards Sister Ludden and repeated the same words; also to his Aunt Minda who sat near him he said, "I like you too," and pulled her down to kiss her. Then after a pause he lifted both hands high above his head and looking upwards he exclaimed, with angelic sweetness in his face and voice, "I like you too," then closed his eyes and fell asleep in Jesus.

## 215 -- "I KNOW THAT JESUS SAVES ME, AND THAT'S ENOUGH FOR ME."

These were the last words of little Maud Henderson, of Higdon, Arkansas, only seven years of age. Evangelist R. E. Smallwood, who preached the funeral sermon, writes us that during her last illness her parents bought for her a copy of our Children's Edition of "Touching Incidents and Remarkable Answers to

Prayer," and that it was through hearing it read that little Maud learned to pray and trust in Jesus, and was enabled to so gloriously triumph when death came to her. Six days before her death she said she was going to be with her" brother in heaven.

### 216 -- JOHN ARTHUR LYTH

" I shall soon be with Jesus. Perhaps I am too anxious. Can this be death? Why, it's better than living! Tell them I die happy in Jesus."

### 217 -- BISHOP PIERCE

"Rest, happiness and peace forever."

### 218 -- REV. JOHN WARBURTON

"O! What a blaze and a shout there will be when old John gets to heaven."

### 219 -- REV. PHILIP HECK

"Oh! how beautiful. The opening heavens around me shine."

### 220 -- MISS MARTHA MCCRACKIN

"How bright the room; how full of angels! "

### 221 -- BENJAMIN ABBOTT

"Glory to God, I see the heavens open before me."

### 222 -- REV. FRANCIS BRAZEE

"They sing! The angels Sing!"

### 223 -- REV. THOMAS H. STOCKTON

"I shall receive the crown of glory."

### 224 -- REV. ALFRED CROLL

"Is this dying? Is this dying? No, it is sweet living."

### 225 -- REV. WILLIAM STEPHENSON

"Do you see that bright light? Do you see those angels?"

### 226 -- JOHN BUNYAN

"We shall meet ere long to sing the new song, and remain happy forever in a world without end."

### 227 -- REV. SOLOMON BIGHAM

" I am sure of heaven, and will not have to wait long till I get there."

### 228 -- JACOB EIGHENINGER

"I see Jesus."

### 229 -- MOTHER MARGARET PRIOR

"Eternity rolls up before me like a sea of glory, and so near. Oh! that blessed company of redeemed sinners, and the glorious Jesus! What a Savior; and He is mine. Oh! what a speck of time is the longest life to prepare for that blessed world."

### 230 -- REV. P. CORL

"Oh, I see such a fullness in Christ as I never saw before. Tell the people I am trusting in a full salvation."

### 231 -- REV. DAVID S. MONTGOMERY

"I am on the border-land. All is well, all is well. Is this death? IF this be death, then it is pleasant to die."

### 232 -- SIR CICELY ORMES, MARTYR

Welcome, thou cross of Christ!" After the fire was kindled, she said, "My soul doth magnify the Lord, and my spirit doth rejoice in God my Savior."

### 233 -- THOMAS HUDSON, MARTYR

When the flames were rising about him, he slipped from under the chain which held his body to the stake, and, falling on his knees amidst the burning pile, his spirit wrestled with God. The martyr arose and exclaimed, "Now, I thank God, I am strong, and care not what man can do to me!"

### 234 -- GOVERNOR JOHN BROOKS, LL.D.

"O, what a ground of hope there is in that laying of an apostle, that God is in Christ, reconciling the guilty world to Himself; not imputing their trespasses unto them! In God I have placed my eternal all, and into His hands I commit my spirit!"

### 235 -- RICHARD BAXTER

"I have pain, there is no arguing against sense, but I have peace."

### 236 -- D. L. MOODY

"If this is death, there is no valley. This is glorious. I have been within the gates and I saw the children, Dwight and Irene" (his two grandchildren who had died). "Earth is receding. Heaven is approaching. God is calling me."

Made in the USA
Coppell, TX
04 April 2021